COMPUTER-ASSISTED PLANNING SYSTEMS

Management Concept, Application, and Implementation

JAMES B. BOULDEN, D.B.A.

Cofounder, On-Line Decisions, Inc.

McGraw-Hill Book Company

New York St. Louis San Francisco Auckland Düsseldorf Johannesburg
Kuala Lumpur London Mexico Montreal New Delhi Panama Paris
São Paulo Singapore Sydney Tokyo Toronto

Library of Congress Cataloging in Publication Data:

Boulden, James B, date.
  Computer-assisted planning systems.

  Bibliography: p.
  Includes index.
  1. Electronic data processing—Business.
  2. Electronic data processing—Management. I. Title.
  HF5548.2.B666   658'.05'4   75-14228
  ISBN 0-07-006657-4

1 2 3 4 5 6 7 8 9 0 BPBP 7 8 4 3 2 1 0 9 8 7 6 5

The editors for this book were W. Hodson Mogan, Douglas
J. Marshall, and Carolyn Nagy, the designer was Elliot
Epstein, and the production supervisor was Teresa F.
Leaden. It was set in Caledonia by University Graphics,
Inc.

It was printed and bound by The Book Press, Inc.

Contents

List of Illustrations

Preface

From a near-zero start a decade ago, the use of online computer-assisted planning systems has expanded rapidly throughout the industrial world. It is the unusual organization today that is not at least experimenting with the use of the computer to increase the speed and accuracy of management decisions as well as to eliminate the tedious and time-consuming activities associated with generating plans and reports.

The accelerating rate of change in the society is providing increasing pressure on management to incorporate the computer into the planning process. The implementation and use of these systems are, however, extremely difficult from the managerial, not the technical, viewpoint. Computer-assisted planning alters the power structure of the organization, changes patterns of communication, revolutionizes decision making, and makes new demands on the data base. Moreover, it restructures management roles and in general disturbs human relationships by threatening security and imposing new demands for cooperation. Traditional management theory and practices are no longer appropriate, and fragmented organizational perspectives must be abandoned. The focus of this book is, therefore, on the organizational, behavioral, and decision-making implications of computer-assisted planning rather than on the technical details of their implementation.

The book is divided into three sections: Concepts, Application, and Implementation. The presentation proceeds from the "why" of theory to the specifics of application and finally to the "how" of designing, implementing, and controlling the system. Readers should select from this smorgasbord according to their individual requirements and previous background. A major objective of the book is to provide information which will facilitate the interface between systems builder and user.

Operational systems and real-life organizational experiences are emphasized throughout the book, since this is a field where practice definitely leads theory. Wherever possible, principles or guidelines are supported by experimental evidence or original research; however, an uncomfortably large body of material remains that is pragmatic and supportable only in that it seems to work. The study of symbiotic relationships between management and computer is in its infancy.

My deep appreciation extends to the many who have contributed so much during the early years of computer-assisted planning. Gary Neale reviewed the entire manuscript and contributed generously from his experience. The consulting firm of On-Line Decisions, Inc., made available extensive case material. The love, support, and participation of Laureen Boulden have been indispensable, beginning with my early years in interactive computer-assisted planning and continuing through the preparation of this book.

CONCEPTS

Concepts

Part One is concerned with generating an awareness of the interdependency of systems, including those problems in integration which are somewhat unique and certainly critical to computer-based planning. The theory of the various feeding and using systems will be examined in some depth. The reader who has had limited experience with computer-based planning systems should work the exercise in the Appendix before reading any further than Chapter 2.

Chapter 1 focuses on the need for computer-based planning to cope with the accelerating size and complexity of the organizational environment. Fundamental to appreciating the problem is the concept of exponential growth. The future holds increasing problems of inflation, currency instability, raw materials availability, power, pollution, and social responsibility. Fortunately, a synergy of knowledge, information technology, and communication facility is currently becoming available to permit management to function effectively in this new world.

Chapter 2 is concerned with the systems perspective necessary to implement and operate computer-based planning systems. Planning models are briefly examined at the world, national, industry, and firm level, with comment as to their linkages and integration. The concept of an organization as a system is examined within the theoretical framework of Chester Barnard. A fragmented management perspective is just not adequate and will inevitably lead to underutilization or destruction of the computer-based planning system.

The basic theory of organizational purpose and objectives is reviewed in Chapter 3 with emphasis on its application to computer-based planning. The power of the interactive system is examined as applied to conflicting organizational goals. The human and technical constructs and conflicts of computer-based planning are examined in Chapters 4 and 5. Chapter 6 was the most difficult chapter in the book to write as the current state of planning theory and practice is just not appropriate when viewed in the context of computer-based planning systems. This problem should be resolved in the next decade as the result of current research in the area.

The Times Are Changing

Organizational survival demands a continual adaptation of goals and processes to the changing opportunities and constraints afforded by the environment. Planning is anticipatory decision making directed toward the design of a desired future; hence the difficulty of planning is a function of the rate and magnitude of change. The true significance of online computer-based planning must be considered in this context.

EXPONENTIAL GROWTH

The phenomenon of exponential growth is to be found in many aspects of today's society. The level of energy consumption for electric power generation in the United States, for example, is rising at an increasing rate. The growth was 7 percent per year for the period 1961 to 1965, 8.6 percent per year for 1965 to 1969, and 9.2 percent in 1970 (Figure 1-1) (1, p. 85).

Exponential growth can be better appreciated, perhaps, by thinking of the time it takes a quantity to double in size at a given growth rate:

Growth rate, percent per year	Doubling time in years
1	70
2	35
4	18
7	10
10	7

The impact of exponential growth is not apparent in the early years when the rate is applied to a small base. How-

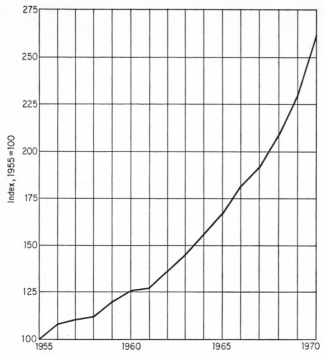

Figure 1-1. Increases in consumption of energy for electricity generation. Consumption of electricity has a high growth rate and is
increasing. (Adapted *from Earl Cook, "The Flow of Energy in
an Industrial Society," Copyright © September 1971 by Scientific American, Inc. All rights reserved.)*

ever, as in the instance of power, a modest problem can become a
crashing catastrophe in a very short time as the growth rate is applied
to a continually increasing base quantity.

Imagine continually depressing the accelerator of your automobile.
Certainly a crisis would be imminent. The world has long been de-
manding more and more energy. The power shortage came as no sur-
prise to the electric utilities which, for the last decade, have been major
customers for computer-based planning systems.

LIFE IN A PRESSURE COOKER

Exponential growth and its attendant problems are not confined to the
power industry. The world population has been growing exponentially
at a rate in excess of 2 percent per year, corresponding to a doubling
every thirty-three years. Not only is the population expanding at a
disturbing rate, but people are increasingly concentrated in urban

areas. The doubling time for city populations in less-developed regions of the world is fifteen years. This means that Calcutta, Singapore, Peking, Rio, and Manila will each double in size by 1990. Urbanization in the United States is illustrated in Figure 1-2.

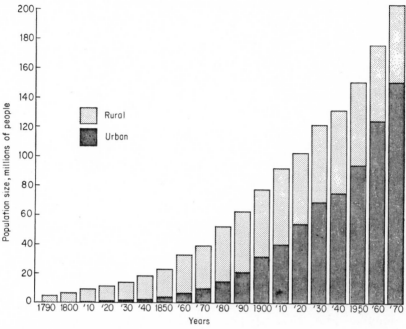

Figure 1-2. Urbanization of the United States. (From Population, Resources, Environment: Issues in Human Ecology, *2d ed.,* by *Paul R. Ehrlich and Anne H. Ehrlich. W. H. Freeman and Company. Copyright © 1972.)*

growth and urbanization must result in increased population density. Life begins to resemble a cooker with the molecules moving faster and faster and the pressure building. In India, population increased 12 million in the decade ending in 1921, 27 million in the decade ending in 1931, 37 million between 1931 and 1941, 44 million in the succeeding decade, and 78 million between 1951 and 1961 (2, p. 12).

Not only are there more people today, but they travel faster and have instant communication through television and telephone. In 1825, the speed of the first steam locomotive to provide passenger service was only 13 miles per hour. A more advanced steam locomotive in the 1880s increased this speed to 100 miles per hour. The airplane made it possible to pass the 400-mile-per-hour speed in 1938. This speed increased in order of magnitude to 4,000 miles per hour by the 1960s with the advent of rocket planes. Today space capsules circle the earth at 18,000 miles per hour (3, p. 26).

Split-second communication is constantly changing the needs and tastes of civilization. Mass consumer markets appear and disappear overnight. The traveler can no longer readily distinguish between Düsseldorf, Copenhagen, San Francisco, and London. Product life-span has shortened dramatically.

The world's resources are straining to meet the demands of this population expansion. Today, two-thirds of the world's population are hungry, despite increased agricultural production which has required the doubling of fertilizer consumption every ten years. For how many periods can this continue? The giant United States surplus grain stocks have been rapidly depleted.

World industrial production has been growing at a rate of 7 percent a year, with resulting exponential increases in carbon dioxide concentration in the air, depletion of oxygen content in the sea, and increased human consumption of lead and mercury.

Managers can no longer think simply of maximizing profits; they are also asked to protect the environment and conserve energy. Soon executives will have to face the nonavailability of many nonrenewable natural resources which are being depleted at an accelerating rate. New reserves will be found and old ones reactivated. However, the cost of recovery and hence raw materials prices will continue to increase. The efficiency of energy conversion is subject to thermodynamic limitations, so more and more investment is required to realize less and less improvement. Certainly raw materials will become prohibitively expensive for most applications long before the theoretical supply is exhausted.

Governments can no more *control* this inflation than they can *fix* the price of gold. It is a basic economic fact that prices will rise in the face of increasing demand and falling supply. How can management survive in this turbulent, uncertain environment?

A POTENTIAL FOR SYNERGY

Fortunately, knowledge and technology are also increasing exponentially. The manager has new concepts and more powerful tools with which to manage uncertainty and accommodate complexity.

Knowledge

One optimistic factor that appears on few balance sheets is the metaphysical constituent of wealth called knowledge, and this resource can only increase. Knowledge may be defined as "the sum of what is known; the body of truth, information and principles acquired by mankind" (4, p. 469). Knowledge may require considerable energy to acquire, but it is cumulative. Of great importance in the creative process is the fact that new knowledge interacts with existing knowledge in many permutations and combinations.

Knowledge is the fuel that is driving man's spiraling invasion of the universe. Europe, prior to 1500, was producing approximately 1,000 book ti⁻¹es per year. The rate had accelerated to 120,000 by the year 1950. The output of books on a global scale approached the incredible figure of 1,000 titles per day in the mid-1960s. The production of scientific journals today has a doubling period of fifteen years. Worldwide, scientific and technical literature amounts to 60 million pages a year. The rate of acquisition of knowledge continues to accelerate (3, p. 31).

Given this ever-increasing wealth of knowledge, how can it be accessed and messaged so that it is immediately available to humanity? This is the task of the computer.

Computers

The computer is now a fact of corporate and personal life, so perhaps it is no longer appropriate to marvel at the remarkable growth in technology and application of electronic data processing. In an otherwise depleting and contaminating world, the computer stands almost alone as continually providing more and more at less and less expenditure of time and energy (Figure 1-3). Only the computer operates at the speeds necessary to store and manipulate the vast information resources and apply them to the problems of accelerating change. The potential of the computer in processing time is theoretically limited only by the speed of light.

Communications

The past three decades have seen the advent of such developments as color television, long-distance dialing, tape recorders, cable television, tape recording, communication satellites, and multinational data telecommunication networks. A service industry based on person-to-person telephone calls and short telegraph messages has been converted into an international data pipeline.

THE SYNERGY OF COMPUTER-BASED PLANNING[1]

R. Buckminster Fuller notes that knowledge develops compound interest through synergy, which is a "one plus one equals three" phenome-

---

[1]The terms *computer-based*, *computer-assisted*, and *computer-augmented* are used interchangeably in this book.

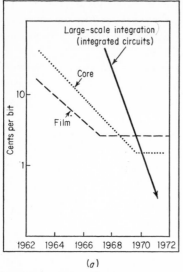 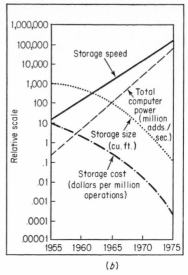

(a)   (b)

Figure 1-3. Computer performance characteristics: *(a)* computer storage costs; *(b)* computer performance. *(From John McHale, "The Changing Information Environment," in* Information Technology, *The Conference Board, New York, 1972.)*

non where the whole is greater than the sum of the parts. The synergetic potential of human knowledge and experience is being realized through the convergent interaction of knowledge with information technology and communications.

Online Computer-based Planning

Russell Ackoff states that "planning is the design of a desired future and of effective ways of bringing it about" (5, p. 1). Planning is "anticipatory decision-making" (5, p. 2). Harold Koontz notes that the core of planning is decision making that is "the actual selection from among alternatives to a course of action" (6, p. 135). Computer-based planning is, therefore, the integration and utilization of electronic data processing in the decision process.

An online computer-based planning system consists of a human operator accessing a computer through a remote terminal transmitting over a telecommunications network (Figure 1-4). A synergetic potential is achieved through using the judgment and intuitive logic of management, the memory and computational capacity of the computer, and the capability of the telecommunication network to eliminate time and distance constraints in the transmission of information. Other elements of the system include the resident housekeeping software, the models of the organization being simulated, and the data base.

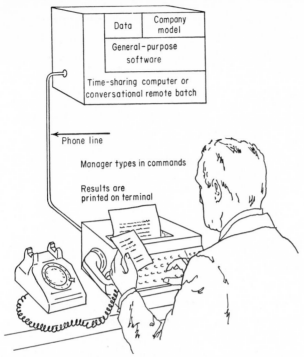

Figure 1-4. The online planning system. *(Courtesy of On-Line Decisions, Inc.)*

"Real-World" Illustrations (7)

It may be well to pause at this point to examine briefly a number of operating systems in diverse applications. A major oil company, for example, is using a computer-based system for long-range planning (Figure 1-5). The marketing model can be used either alone or in conjunction with the supply model to evaluate alternative courses of action, such as:

1. What is the effect of volumetric changes on the supply cost?

2. How do timing and levels of advertising and promotional expenditures affect profitability?

3. How sensitive are the divisional profits and returns on capital to variations in product mix, prices, and supply costs?

The supply model simulates the financial aspects of several refineries and a number of major transportation methods. For a given set of market conditions and volumes (coming from the marketing model), the supply

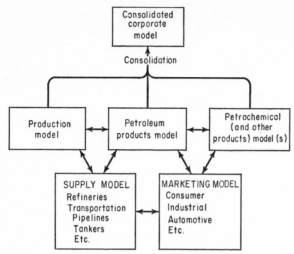

Figure 1-5. Long-range planning system for a major petroleum producer. *(Courtesy of On-Line Decisions, Inc.)*

model computes the supply costs, and by considering the refinery capacities and the yield requirements, identifies the future capital needs. The online executive support system integrates the various components of the long-range plan so that any change in one area, such as capacity, is reflected in all other areas.

A major consumer-products company has installed an online computer-based planning system for use in preparing the annual plan (Figure 1-6). The objective of this system is to provide an improved ability to answer such tactical questions as:

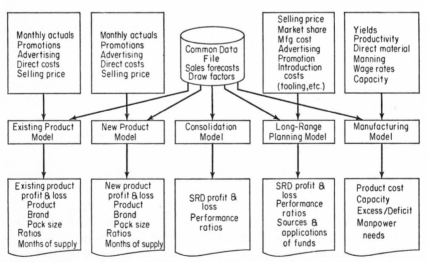

Figure 1-6. A consumer-products planning system. *(Courtesy of On-Line Decisions, Inc.)*

1. What if a particular product is promoted in March and April with 10 percent off invoice and a 5 percent cooperative advertising allowance, with a resultant 10 percent increase in sales? What is the effect of this promotion on trade inventory months-of-supply?

2. What if market share drops 3 points for the first three months of the year? What is the impact on the approved budget?

The time-consuming review and revision procedures that formerly occurred at various stages in the consolidation of the annual plans are now largely eliminated. Critical assumptions on price, volume, and cost can be altered in the final days of the development of the plan and computational errors can be eliminated.

An example of a system with plan update and performance analysis capability for a major steel company is illustrated in Figure 1-7. One immediate benefit of this application is that it relieves the financial

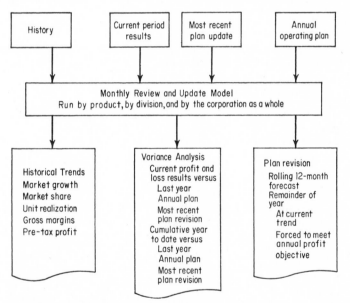

Figure 1-7. Current plan update and performance analysis for a large steel company. *(Courtesy of On-Line Decisions, Inc.)*

analysts from the routine, time-consuming drudgery of calculations and report generation so that they can spend their time studying trends and identifying relationships. The consolidation and analysis capability is critical at the corporate level where masses of operating data are continually being used to evaluate the quality of divisional performance and the achievability of current plans.

The system is used to close the gap between plan and performance by picking up the actual results to date, applying trends and seasonal adjustments, and forcing a fit with the planning objective so that the managers will know what must be done in the remaining periods to meet their objectives.

NEW TOOLS AND CONCEPTS

This human/machine interactive synergy has been achieved through a remarkable sequence of technological and managerial innovations over the past two decades.

The role of the computer in the organizational environment has been changing since the 1950s, when applications involved primarily routine, repetitive, clerical functions such as payroll and billing procedures. The use of the computer at that time was based on the cost justification of labor displacement and error elimination. This stage involved no significant change in organizational functions, only doing existing routine activities electronically.

The application of the computer extended in the late 1960s to the level of supervisory management. Operational functions were transformed, with emphasis on such activities as production scheduling and inventory control. Computer application was justified by improved operating performance and faster response time.

Middle- and policy-level management applications seem to be occurring concurrently in the 1970s. The computer-based planning system permits all levels of management to be involved in some aspect of the information-processing activity. The computer is no longer simply a useful but expendable tool; it is assuming a central, indispensable position in the decision processes of the organization. Certainly corporate success in the future, if not in the present, "will be determined by the effectiveness of computer application at all levels and in all areas of activity" (8, inside cover).

The practical realization of the human/computer synergy has required a number of significant technical and managerial innovations. Although the concept of computer-based planning is almost as old as the computer itself, the reality has been a long time coming.

The Corporate Model

Several attempts were made by operations research groups in the early 1960s to develop the corporate model, which was envisioned as a monolithic structure encompassing all organizational activities and capable of optimizing management decisions. Few of these efforts become operational because (1) the technical staff was divorced from management problems, (2) changing operations made the models obsolete before completion, and (3) conflicting goals made it difficult to define a precise measure of performance.

A Sun Oil team took a major step forward in 1965 when it broke with tradition and turned the emphasis from optimization to simulation and from probabilistic to deterministic models. Although less exciting to the mathematician, these models proved much more intelligible to management and capable of validation against actual operations.

Online Computing

A most important step forward occurred in 1967 when time-shared computing become commercially available in a quality that could be used for corporate planning. Suddenly the potential of remote terminals and a conversational relationship between management and computer became reality.

Time-shared computing provided multiple-user access to a large central computer, with payment only for the time actually used. The manager and staff were no longer dependent on the service schedule of the central computer. Such intermediaries as machine operators, keypunch operators, and programmers were eliminated. Leadership in the design and operation of the computer-based planning systems passed from the computer department and the operations research staff into the hands of the corporate planners and the controller.

Software

Concurrent with the technical developments of time-shared computing came impressive software innovations, including three major software developments relevant to computer-based planning: (1) standardized report generators; (2) English language systems; and (3) general-purpose software. The first movement was led by the banks as a fallout from their loan activities. Literally thousands of packaged planning programs were developed for firms of various industries and sizes. These systems have proven of considerable value to small firms with fairly standard reporting requirements.

The English language systems were developed on the premise that managers would develop their own corporate models if the programming was made simple enough. In fact, these software packages have proven very useful to financial analysts and other staff members in writing small programs for well-defined but limited applications, such as capital budgeting.

A third and most ambitious effort led to the development of general-purpose software for use by a wide variety of organizations in diverse industries. This software was conceived on the assumption that technical staff, not managers, write the programs for corporate simulation; the most efficient operation system is therefore necessary so that each user can superimpose a command structure unique to a particular organization. Capacity is provided in these systems for accommodating large networks of interrelated models, and flexibility is available for fast modification of inputs, logic, or output.

Communications

Interpretive data loaders were added to computer-based planning systems in the early 1970s to permit rapid, accurate input of information. Data transmission speeds tripled and improved in quality. Information storage and retrieval capabilities were greatly expanded. Communication networks became worldwide via satellite so that financial analysts in London could make a local telephone call to access their data base at the home office in Chicago. Terminals became silent and truly portable in briefcase size. Perhaps most important, the corporate model evolved into a totally integrated system encompassing the users, the computer, data sources, software, modeling networks, and the telecommunication network.

Management Theory

Management theory in the 1950s was concerned primarily with developing principles and cases which would serve as general guides for administration. This work was extended in the 1960s in recognition of the organization as a *system* of interdependent activities and forces. This systems perspective is indispensable to achieving the reality of computer-based planning.

Today, for the first time, there are no serious technological limitations to computer-based planning; the problem is management. Can executives utilize these systems to their potential? As further discussions will make evident, *computer-based planning alters the power structure, changes patterns of communication, revolutionizes decision making, makes new demands on the data base, changes management roles, and in general disturbs human relationships by threatening security and imposing new demands for cooperation.*

POTENTIAL BENEFITS

Computer-based planning systems are expensive and the possibility of failure is high. Truly, the potential benefits must be great to attract so many organizations to this new technology. Some of the advantages are specific and well documented, while others are less tangible but, in the long run, perhaps even more important. It seems appropriate at this early point in the discussion to review the potential benefits so as not to become discouraged as the problems become more apparent.

Shorter Planning Time

A leasing company reduced the time required to physically produce the budget report from three weeks to three days. The automated system provides the capability to generate an updated report in minutes rather than days.

Fast, Accurate Calculations

A food company ran the computer-based plan in parallel with the manual system for the first planning cycle. The manual plan calculated a multi-million-dollar cash deficit while the computerized plan reported a large cash surplus, given the same assumptions. Subsequent validation revealed twenty-eight arithmetic errors in the manual calculations. Long hours and intense time pressure almost inevitably result in numerous errors in a manual system.

Instant Answers to "What If?" Questions

What if interest rates rise from 5 percent to 10 percent? What is the impact on profits and cash flow? Every planner is familiar with the massive mechanical task resulting from such a simple management inquiry.

This one change will be reflected through many financial statements and will require thousands of calculations. The computer not only answers such an inquiry in an instant, but computes "sensitivity" to demonstrate the effect of changing one or more variables over a specified range as they impact various measures of performance.

Ability to Evaluate More Alternatives and Develop Contingency Plans

A steel company prepares three alternative plans based on the premises of no strike, a short strike, and a long strike. A food company prepares five alternative strategies relating to significantly different scenarios concerning market conditions. As events develop during the year, these firms quickly shift from one prepared strategy to another.

Broader Organization Perspective

The development and operation of a computer-based planning system force a systems perspective on the total organization. Suboptimization is reduced as all major management decisions are evaluated with reference to their impact on the total organization rather than on isolated units.

Improved Communications

A metals producer previously used five distinct sets of forecasts in the preparation of the same annual plan – staffs concerned with economics, marketing, production, corporate planning, and finance each developed their own assumptions. The computer-based planning system is, first of all, a communication system to which all elements of the organization are linked. Planning units are forced to adopt uniform definitions and assumptions. Objectives must be defined with precision.

Integration of Planning and Control

The annual plan must be consistent with the strategic plan. Moreover, the various functional areas are integrated. Marketing cannot plan to sell products which operations cannot produce. Operations cannot plan facilities commitments which finance cannot fund. Cash flow, capital budgeting, new-product development, acquisitions, and all other plans are integrated. Performance information flows back, is compared to plan; variances are analyzed and alternative corrective action is simulated.

Better Plans

Decision makers can defer critical assumptions until the last days of the plan rather than attempt to forecast the next year's markets in the preceding year. Managers are relieved of tedious housekeeping chores in preparation of the plan so that they direct their attentions to policy matters rather than to the mechanics of preparing the budget. Overall corporate objectives can be "exploded" into guidelines for operating groups so that only one iteration of the detailed budget is required. The trial-and-error approach is eliminated.

SUMMARY

The role of the computer in management continues to evolve as it assumes ever-greater importance in determining organizational capacity for survival and growth. The present-day online computer-based planning systems have been made possible by the implementation of symbolic models simulated on conversational computers, utilizing general-purpose software transmitting over extensive telecommunication networks.

Today, for the first time, there are no serious technological impediments to full implementation of computer-based planning. The success of these systems depends on the ability of management to rise to a new level of consciousness. Primary in this management evolution are the abandonment of fragmented thinking and the assumption of a systems perspective.

A Systems Perspective

Since the organizational environment is highly complex and in continual flux, managers have historically been forced into fragmented thinking. The result has been a continual faulty allocation of resources as the organization evolved from one crisis to the next.

Utilization of the computer in the planning process demands a new perspective. The manager in a computer-augmented environment must learn to think holistically if the potential of this new resource is to be realized. The properties of the organization are not derivable by merely summing up the parts; a gestalt perception of the total entity is necessary.

"A system is not something given in nature, but something defined by intelligence . . . coherence and pattern and purpose are, all three, acts of mental recognition rather than characteristics of physical things" (9, p. 242).

SYSTEMS CHARACTERISTICS

The term *system* may be defined as a regularly interacting or interdependent group of items forming a unified whole (4, p. 895). The systems concept applies equally well to the world environment within which the organization functions, to the organization itself, and to the individual personnel who constitute the organization.

A prime attribute of all systems is the interdependency of the component parts. Later discussions concerning the design, construction, and management of computer-based planning systems will relate to the following basic system characteristics as identified by Churchman. (10, p. 29):

1. The objectives of the total system; more specifically, the measures of performance

2. The fixed constraints on the system as imposed by its environment

3. The resources of the system

4. The components of the system, their activities, goals and measures of performance

5. The management of the system

Distinction should be made between the real and the stated objectives of the system. Corporations frequently publish socially attractive statements of their objectives which may have only incidental relation to the decisions criteria used in the organization. The true test is whether the system will knowingly sacrifice other goals to achieve the objective. Will management expend additional funds on sewage treatment to protect the environment, even at the expense of profits? Actions do speak louder than words.

The term *environment* is used by Churchman to refer to what lies "outside the system." The test for "outside" is that the organization can do relatively little concerning the characteristics or behavior of the environment. *All systems are parts of still larger systems,* and the dividing line between them is frequently not clear. System failures often result because managers mistakenly define part of their environment as a given factor and beyond their control. A major division may inadvisedly build a computer-based planning system without first examining the total corporate system of which it is a subset.

Resources are suggested as the third characteristic of systems. They consist of those things which can be changed by the system and used to its own advantage. This internal perspective of the system should cover both present and potential resources. As noted previously, knowledge is perhaps the most valuable resource of the firm, but is frequently omitted from formal resource inventories. Churchman comments that "resources are the general reservoir out of which the specific actions of the system can be shaped" (10, p. 39).

A fourth systems consideration concerns identification of those components which are truly related to the overall performance of the system. The basic elements of the computer-based planning system should follow the fundamental components of the organization rather than artificial lines of departmentalization. The organizational structure is continually in a state of flux which will render obsolete any system tailored to a particular form. The planning system of a European steel company, for example, was made obsolete overnight when the board determined to go from a centralized to a decentralized reporting structure.

Amazingly, planning systems are often designed without consideration of management itself as the fifth important characteristic of the system. Management is responsible for setting the goals, allocating the resources, and controlling the performance of the system. Management is very much a part of the system and receives feedback from all other elements of the system. A radical change in management can very significantly alter both the structure and functions of the planning system. The need for flexibility in the system is paramount.

SYSTEMS COMPLEXITY

Systems may be classified according to complexity as follows (11):

1. The *static structure* or level of frameworks, such as the astronomical universe or the atom.

2. The *simple dynamic system* or level of clockworks, including most of the theoretical structure of physics and chemistry.

3. The *cybernetic system* or level of the thermostat. The transmission and interpretation of information allow the system to move to the maintenance of a given equilibrium.

4. The *open system* or self-maintaining structure. This is the level at which life begins, as in the cell.

5. The *genetic-societal level* as typified by the plant and characterized by division of labor among cells.

6. The *animal level* as characterized by increased mobility, teleological behavior, and self-awareness.

7. The *human level* as characterized by self-consciousness. The ability to produce, absorb, and interpret symbols.

8. The *social system* as a human organization.

9. *Transcendental systems*—the level of inescapable unknowables; the ultimates and absolutes which also exhibit systematic structure and awareness.

The developers of computer-based planning systems are often engineers who attempt to apply the tools of their profession to human organizations without appreciating the vast increase in complexity. These technicians find it most difficult to understand the subsequent failure of their design.

At various points in future discussions, we will examine the hierarchy of systems beginning with the world we live in, the United States economy, industries, the firm, and finally the computer-based planning system with its human and technical subsystems. These systems are all interrelated and in various orders of complexity (Figure 2-1). Fortunately the same general principles apply to all systems. This book is specifically oriented toward planning systems at the level of the individual organization.

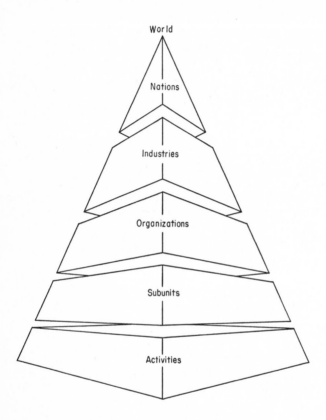

Figure 2-1. Interdependent systems.

THE WORLD SYSTEM

A controversial attempt has been made in recent years to develop a computer simulation model of the world system. A simplified model is shown in Figure 2-2. The driving variables are population, natural resources, capital, land, and pollution. Having established this basic structure, a useful simulation of the world can be accomplished by successive refinements in the model to accommodate more precise resource allocations, time functions, and feedback effects.

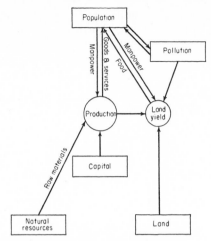

Figure 2-2. Simplified model of the world.

Feedback Loops

Feedback loops are of particular importance in all real-world systems. This is illustrated for the world model by capital investment in Figure 2-3. Much of the industrial output in each period is consumed, but a significant portion remains to further increase the capital stock. This

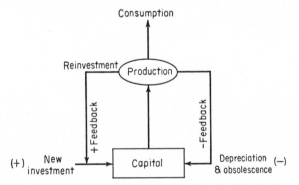

Figure 2-3. Capital investment feedback.

positive feedback is then available to produce still more output. Further, the investment rate increases as the income level of the society rises. The result is exponential growth, as discussed in Chapter 1, modified by the *negative feedback* of capital obsolescence. In other words, up to a point capital investment generates capital investment.

Other feedbacks may be observed, as in pollution, where the absorption time increases as pollution increases, thus tending further to increase pollution. Similarly, feedback is provided on population to recognize the limiting factors of crowding, food supply, pollution, and natural resources. The value of the computer simulation is that it allows us to examine these interrelationships under various assumptions over extended time periods.

Simulation Output

The basic behavior of one world model postulates that industrialization and population are eventually suppressed by declining natural resources. The behavior mode involves population overshoot and collapse. The industrial base ultimately fails, taking with it the agricultural and service systems. Living standards return to the levels of 1900.

Not surprisingly, there are many critics of the world model. However, the true value of computer simulation is thereby demonstrated in that attention is focused on the input assumptions and structural relationships. It is not enough to state that you feel the world model is overly pessimistic. You must specify precisely why you believe this to be true. Do you question the exponential growth in population? The capital investment generation rate?

Many a corporate policy meeting degenerates into an unproductive debate involving broad, unsupported statements of opinion concerning matters which have not been measured. A computer-based planning system provides a basis for testing alternative assumptions. Specific points of disagreement are quickly identified, and discussion can be directed toward them.

NATIONAL AND INDUSTRY LINKAGES

The world model is useful as a long-term conceptual guide to corporate policies; however, it remains to link global events to specific organizational plans. Inputs concerning wages, interest rates, inflation rates, and many other economic variables are critical to the planning process. As indicated by Figure 2-1, information concerning national systems must be translated into more specific industry forecasts, as required by the computer-based planning system at the organizational level.

In the past, this linkage was formally accomplished through digestion of general information published in written form by professional forecasting agencies. The organizational planner was forced to rely on the skills of a small group of economists whose premises were frequently not clearly stated. The corporate planner had no opportunity to explore alternative scenarios or systematically to bring his or her personal judgment to bear on the forecast. Such constraints are no longer a problem.

The organizational planner today has online, direct access not only to the forecasts of one or more agencies, but also frequently to the logic of the econometric models themselves so that the planner can produce personal forecasts. A large data base of national and industry economic series can be directly accessed and manipulated on line, using an impressive library of statistical and mathematical routines (Figure 2-4).

The planner can also, in some instances, manipulate online industry models, using the national forecasts as inputs and outputting directly to the organizational computer-based planning system. A computer-based forecasting model for the forest products industry is charted in Figure 2-5.

These models are used less for prediction than for forecasting. *Prediction* concerns an effort to foretell what is going to happen in the future. Econometric *forecasting*, in contrast, is of a conditional nature and suggests what will result *if* certain critical events occur. The planner has direct access to the industry and national planning systems so that organizational strategy can quickly be revised when significant events occur in the macrosystems of which the planner's organization is a part. The logic of the economic system is quantitatively defined so that complex interrelationships may be examined. Communication is established through international telecommunication networks so that centrally maintained econometric models, data bases, and mathematical tools can be shared by many planners in diverse organizations.

THE ORGANIZATION AS A SYSTEM

The formal organization was defined by Chester Barnard as "a system of consciously coordinated activities or forces of two or more persons" (12, p. 73). It follows from this definition that the general characteristics of systems, as previously described, are also those of organizations. As a consequence, the management perspective must be holistic, rather than fragmented.

A Communication Network

The perspective of an organization as a communication network greatly facilitates the development of useful simulation models. Managers are communication centers, receiving, processing, and transmitting information. Authority is defined by Barnard as the "character of a communication (order) in a formal organization by which it is accepted ... by a member of the organization" (12, p. 163). The organizational structure can be defined by examination of the input and output of management as nodes in the communication network.

Levels in the authority hierarchy represent points of consolidation for the computer-based planning system, i.e., consolidated reports are

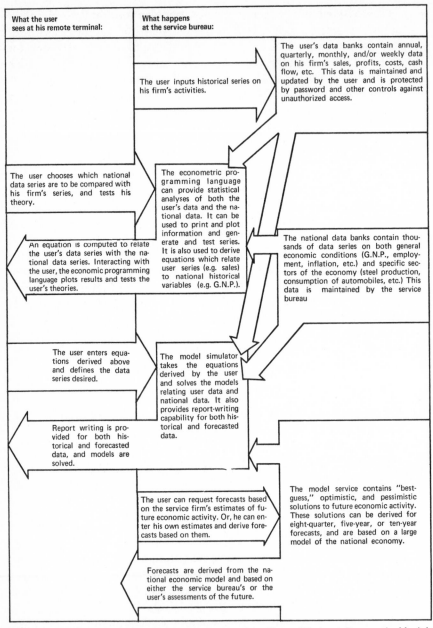

What the user sees at his remote terminal:

What happens at the service bureau:

The user inputs historical series on his firm's activities.

The user's data banks contain annual, quarterly, monthly, and/or weekly data on his firm's sales, profits, costs, cash flow, etc. This data is maintained and updated by the user and is protected by password and other controls against unauthorized access.

The user chooses which national data series are to be compared with his firm's series, and tests his theory.

The econometric programming language can provide statistical analyses of both the user's data and the national data. It can be used to print and plot information and generate and test series. It is also used to derive equations which relate user series (e.g. sales) to national historical variables (e.g. G.N.P.).

An equation is computed to relate the user's data series with the national data series. Interacting with the user, the economic programming language plots results and tests the user's theories.

The national data banks contain thousands of data series on both general economic conditions (G.N.P., employment, inflation, etc.) and specific sectors of the economy (steel production, consumption of automobiles, etc.) This data is maintained by the service bureau

The user enters equations derived above and defines the data series desired.

The model simulator takes the equations derived by the user and solves the models relating user data and national data. It also provides report-writing capability for both historical and forecasted data.

Report writing is provided for both historical and forecasted data, and models are solved.

The user can request forecasts based on the service firm's estimates of future economic activity. Or, he can enter his own estimates and derive forecasts based on them.

The model service contains "best-guess," optimistic, and pessimistic solutions to future economic activity. These solutions can be derived for eight-quarter, five-year, or ten-year forecasts, and are based on a large model of the national economy.

Forecasts are derived from the national economic model and based on either the service bureau's or the user's assessments of the future.

Figure 2-4. How an econometric modeling service works. *(From "Natural Economic Models Help Business to Focus on the Future,"* Computer Decisions, *October 1972.)*

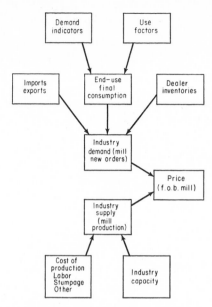

Figure 2-5. Online forest products simulation system. *(Courtesy of Data Resources, Inc.)*

generated for the department and the division. The number of levels in the authority hierarchy is determined basically by span of control limitations—the number of subordinates a manager can effectively supervise. The broader the span of control, the more decentralized the authority and the fewer the levels of supervision.

What determines the span of control? The number, frequency, and complexity of communications between the manager and his or her subordinates. A French consultant, V. A. Graicunas, established his immortality in management theory in 1933 with a paper demonstrating that the complexity of the communication pattern increases in much greater proportion to the increase in the number of subordinates (13).

According to one scenario suggested by Graicunas, a manager with five subordinates has 100 possible relationships, whereas the addition of a sixth more than doubles the relationships to 222. The number of all kinds of relationships will be represented by $n(2^n/2 + n - 1)$ where n equals the number of subordinates (Figure 2-6).

This analysis readily suggests that the installation of a computer-based planning system will have a very significant impact on authority relationships. The computer as an information-processing facility assumes certain functions of management and substantially alters span of control limitations. The locus of power shifts in the structure, with resulting tension and conflict.

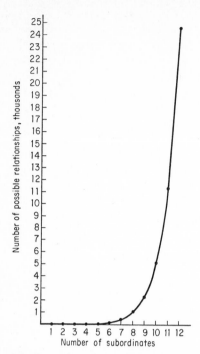

Figure 2-6. Span of control relationships.

CYBERNETICS VERSUS FEEDFORWARD CONTROL

Several times in the preceding models we have referred to feedback. The term *cybernetics* was adopted by Norbert Wiener in 1947 to refer to the process whereby the performance of a system is measured against its objectives and the difference is fed back against the objectives so that the system itself can be modified and brought back on course. The classic steps in establishing a feedback control system are, therefore:

1. Set the standard (objective).

2. Measure performance.

3. Compare performance with the standard to determine error.

4. Use the error to determine the control action to return the activity to standard.

The information feedback is termed *positive* if it tends to reinforce the original action, as in the instance of the capital reinvestment of the world model. The feedback is *negative* if it serves to oppose what the system is doing, as in the instance of obsolescence in the same capital model.

There are two big and interconnected problems, (1) time delay, and (2) sensitivity. Because of time delay, *error is inevitable in a feedback control system which is subject to input disturbances.* The amount of error is a direct function of the time delay required for (1) the process to occur, (2) performance to be measured, (3) information to be fed back, and (4) corrective action to be taken.

Sensitivity

Managers may attempt to reduce time delay by increasing sensitivity in the sense that they will initiate corrective action when a small deviation occurs rather than wait additional time to determine the nature and magnitude of the problem. Increased sensitivity, however, may result in a manager's taking unjustified action based on a random fluctuation in the system. The result may be that a major problem is created by the corrective action where none, in fact, existed. The manager is continually trading off the problems of time delay versus sensitivity. If an error in judgment is made, an unstable system may develop, with the error growing larger rather than fading out. What is to be done?

The answer to the dilemma is to eliminate or minimize time delay by initiating corrective action prior to the actual performance of the system. How can error in output be detected before it occurs? One possibility is monitoring the inputs to the system. Given well-defined relationships between systems input and output, the impact of a change in inputs can be predicted quite accurately.

The accuracy of many computer-based planning systems, for example, would allow prediction within one-half percent of the impact of a change in raw materials prices on the cost of the finished product. Banks do not wait for the operating results to come in before adjusting loan policies to reflect changes in the prime interest rates. The impact of interest fluctuations on profits can be predicted quite easily by financial institutions.

Koontz has labeled this concept "feedforward control" (14). This concept is quite simple, but very difficult to implement without a computer-based planning system. Using such a system, management can not only anticipate error, but can simulate alternative corrective measures before action is completed. This capability has been particularly important to a Midwest feed producer who must quickly adjust pricing to reflect continually changing commodity prices.

Feedforward in Cash Planning

A comparison of feedback and feedforward control systems is shown in Figure 2-7. Corrections of outputs are fed back into the process where a

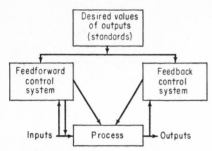

Figure 2-7. Comparison of feedback and feedforward control systems. In a feedback system, corrections of outputs are fed back into the process. In a feedforward system, undesired variations of inputs are fed into the input stream for correction or into the process before outputs occur. *(From Harold Koontz and Robert W. Bradspies, "Managing Through Feed-Forward Control,"* Business Horizons, *June 1972.)*

feedback system is used. In a feedforward system, however, the undesired input variations are detected prior to processing and corrections applied accordingly. Koontz provides the following useful illustration of feedforward control as applied to cash planning (14, p. 30).

Since cash forecasting lies at the base of cash planning and control, this widely used technique of control is one of the best for revealing the application of feedforward to management. The basic inputs and construction of a cash control system may be seen in Figure 2-8. As can be noted, a number of input variables account for a desired future cash level. This model, representing a fairly simplified prototype of reality, shows that if any of the input variables differ from those premised when the cash plan was made, the desired cash level for the future will be affected.

As can be seen, many of these variables can have either a negative or positive effect on cash flow and the desired cash level at a given time in the future. It is readily apparent that normal feedback techniques are not adequate and constant monitoring of the various input variables, with a feedforward of their influence on cash, is necessary for careful cash control. Of course, one way to avoid the problem of shortages is to have available a ready bank line of credit. But what is likely to happen in this case is that the enterprise will keep unnecessarily high balances of cash, with resultant avoidable interest costs or loss in investment income.

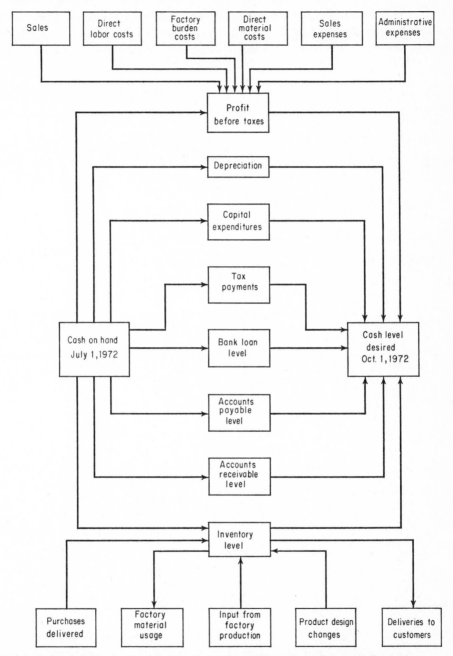

Figure 2-8. Input variables for a cash plan. *(From Harold Koontz and Robert W. Bradspies, "Managing Through Feed-Forward Control,"* Business Horizons, *June 1972.)*

It is also clear from cursory examination of this feedforward system that a mathematical model programmed to a computer can readily trace the influences of changes of input variables on cash flow and availability. Neither this nor careful monitoring of input variables should be very difficult to do in practice.

SYSTEMS INTEGRATION

It has been noted as a basic principle that all systems are parts of still larger systems. The success of a computer-based planning system is highly dependent upon integration with both feeding and using systems, as shown in Figure 2-9.

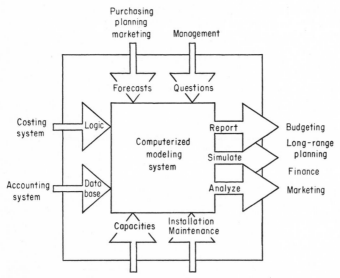

Figure 2-9. Systems integration.

1. The *costing system* provides the logical relationships used by the simulation models.

2. The *accounting system* provides the system with current, accurate data.

3. *Economics, purchasing, and marketing research* provide the input assumptions for the system.

4. *Manufacturing* and *distribution* provide information concerning physical capacities of the organization.

5. The *electronic data processing system* and *management science* operate the computer on which the system functions and perform the maintenance update on the software programs.

6. *Organization structure* defines the manner of consolidation for the system according to authority hierarchy and departmentalization.

7. *Management* asks the questions which are translated into the demands on the system.

8. *Reporting systems* determine the output specifications for the planning system.

Obviously, the opportunities for systems mismatch are large, since all these feeding and using systems are in continual flux. The planning system is worse than useless; it is dangerous if fed inaccurate data, foolish assumptions, or incorrect logic.

A new manager may ask different questions or request new reports. The style of leadership may be altered with resulting change in delegation of authority. A major acquisition or new-product line may occasion major alignment in the authority hierarchy and create new departments. The need for constant maintenance and upkeep on the system is apparent. Obsolescence is an ever-present threat.

Survival and usefulness of the computer-based planning system depend upon successful integration with *all*, not some, of the feeding and using systems. The ease with which the planning system can accommodate change in these supporting systems is a measure of its *flexibility*, the prime requirement.

SUMMARY

Computer-based planning systems cannot serve effectively in an organizational environment characterized by fragmented management perspectives. The planning system has no respect for artificial and politically motivated territories. System inputs must be received from diverse points in the organization and integrated into a unified whole. A change or malfunction in one part of the system will be reflected in many other parts. Time delays in information transmission or attempts at great accuracy will increase the instability of the system. Management must adopt a systems perspective since no organization exists in isolation from the environment from which it receives resource inputs and to which it outputs goods and services.

Value Systems

The formal organization has been previously defined as "a system of consciously coordinated activities or forces of two or more persons." Such a system cannot exist without a common purpose. Therefore, we are immediately concerned with the nature of the complex value system which forms one of the important bonds for coordinating organizational activities. The essence of planning is the identification of legitimate and achievable organizational objectives.

Unfortunately, objectives often seem "theoretical" or "self-evident." In fact, the converse is true. A useful computer-based planning system is technically not difficult to implement, given a clear statement of its purposes and function.

ORGANIZATIONAL PURPOSE

The purpose of the organization is its justification for existence as an entity in the environmental system. This purpose is to provide specific acts of service to satisfy the needs of the members of that society. Purpose, therefore, provides an external perspective.

In contrast to purpose, organizational activities are directed toward goals or objectives as viewed internally by the members of the organization. Organizational objectives are not necessarily the same as the external purpose, but the two must be compatible.

Needs of the Society

The first human organizations were formed to accomplish what one person could not do in isolation. A group of people could kill an elephant or build a bridge. Food and safety were the primary needs of the society. The economies of specialization of labor in meeting these materials needs subsequently led to the development of ever-larger and more complex organizations.

After the basic physiological needs of human beings were met in the industrial societies, organizations were asked also to satisfy the psychological needs of employees for recognition, self-respect, and self-realization. Today the responsibility of management is being further expanded to encompass a broad range of social goals. Minority representation in employment and pollution count in plant emissions are definable planning goals and/or constraints of more than academic interest. If the simulations of the world model are correct, the future growth of humankind may be in new dimensions. Organizational objectives cannot remain fixed when the needs of society are continually evolving.

Models of Social Responsibility

The range of alternative models relating to the organic relationship of the firm to its environment, "corporate ecology," is illustrated in Figure 3-1. This matrix suggests the relationship of policy to goals and to beneficiaries and the appropriate conceptual model for each.

The Austere Model. This is the traditional model used implicitly by corporate managers in the decision-making process. The responsibility of corpo-

A Types of Policy	B Dimensions	C Primary Goal	D Primary Beneficiary	E Expectational Level	F Model
Financial	Internal	1. Profit realization	1. Stockholders	OBLIGATORY	1. Austere
Industrial		2. Resource utilization	2. Employees		2. Household
Market		3. Sales volume	3. Customers		3. Vendor
Social	External	4. Survival	4. Firm as entity	VOLUNTARY	4. Investment
		5. Health and welfare	5. Public at large		5. Civic
		6. Education and the arts	6. Cultural community		6. Artistic

Figure 3-1. Corporate ecology. (*From* Corporate Social Responsibilities by *Clarence C. Walton.* © 1967 by Wadsworth Publishing Company, Inc., Belmont, Calif. 94002. Reprinted by permission of the publisher.)

rate managers is to pursue the interests of stockholders, and this means to make a profit. Business should stick to the economic function and leave welfare and social objectives to other agencies.

The Household Model. The first obligation of the organization is toward the employees. Guaranteed annual income, respect for human needs, and stable employment are obligations equal to or above profits for stockholders.

The Vendor Model. A major obligation of the corporate management is toward the rights, interests, and tastes of the consumer. Automobile safety, pure food, qualified service, and truth in advertising have come about only as a result of legislation. The vendor model is primarily coercive.

The Investment Model. Enlightened self-interest by corporate management and emphasis on survival and long-term profits are paramount, rather than short-run opportunism. The firm pursues its own interests by supporting those aspects of the society which are protective of the corporate interest, for example, by making donations to higher education from whence future managers will come.

The Civic Model. Corporations must observe the responsibilities of citizenship. Organizations have a franchise from the political system which, in turn, protects the industrial system of which the corporation is a part. A positive and voluntary commitment is required of management to support such political goals as balance of payments and full employment. Managers must assume the systems perspective and recognize the relationship of the organization to the community and the hidden costs assumed by the latter.

The Artistic Model. The corporation has a higher role to meet than fulfillment of material and physical needs of the society. Creative managers should not restrict their talents to any one narrow sector of the society, but rather, serve in the development of a higher civilization and culture. Even the immediate self-interest of the corporation must at times be sacrificed. The traditional separation of business, government, and spiritual responsibilities is no longer valid.

Priorities

Maximization of profits as an organizational objective is obviously a great oversimplification. Organizations find it increasingly necessary to observe not just one purpose, but a constellation of diverse and sometimes conflicting ones. " . . . management by objectives is concerned with the search for the one right objective. This search is not only likely to be as unproductive as the quest for the philosopher's stone; it is certain to do harm and to misdirect" (16, p. 62).

The value models previously described suggest both long- and short-term obligations to shareholders, employees, the community, and the government. Given that the organization cannot be all things to all parties at the same time, it remains to define the priorities. In many instances, these priorities become constraints on the planning process as simulated on the computer.

THE NATURE OF OBJECTIVES

Common purpose has been identified as an indispensable characteristic of every organization. Objectives provide the measure of effectiveness for management performance from which are derived the specifications for computer-based planning systems.

Common Purposes

Every organization has a common purpose to which all parts of the system contribute either directly or indirectly. *Each system is characterized by a certain integrity.* Every organization exists because of some human need. The problem of management is to clearly define that need in order to establish the correct systems viewpoint.

The starting point in systems analysis is the identification of the central objective from which are derived subobjectives. The design of a computer-based planning system starts with the management decision process, not the flow of activities within the structure. The organizational objective provides the measure of performance for the system.

What are the objectives of your organization? A most difficult question to answer. Maximization of profits is an embarrassingly inadequate statement in today's complex environment. What profit in what time period? What of social costs, such as the effects of pollution and conservation of resources? The manager is faced with a constellation of sometimes conflicting objectives requiring trade-offs for the various alternative courses of action.

Efficiency and Effectiveness

Barnard proposed that organizational performance be measured in terms of effectiveness and efficiency. Effectiveness refers to the degree to which the organizational objectives are achieved. Efficiency refers to the consumption of resources relative to output.

For most organizations, the measure of effectiveness is the objective of the system. If a computer-based planning system is to be used, the measures of effectiveness must be precisely defined and quantified. The computer cannot accept ambiguous statements of purpose. A new discipline in precise thinking is imposed on management. *The effectiveness of the systems design increases with the precision with which the objectives can be defined.*

Managers normally measure efficiency of operations in terms of costs incurred. "Efficiency expert" was the turn-of-the-century label for an adviser retained to reduce the consumption of resources as measured by time, money, and/or human energy.

Unfortunately, the efficiency approach to management is usually directed toward the component parts of the system. It reflects fragmented thinking. The result is that a cost reduction in one part of the organization may actually increase the total cost of the system. A classic example is a reduction in maintenance staff which improves the efficiency of that group while greatly increasing the downtime of the production line. A broad mandate for across-the-board reduction in costs, as is often found in government, can be a dangerous command.

THE HIERARCHY OF OBJECTIVES

Strategic goals are made meaningful to every member of the organization by a hierarchy of objectives, as shown in Figure 3-2. Financial

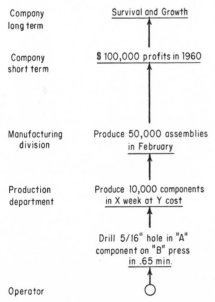

Figure 3-2. Hierarchy of objectives.

budgets, for example, present a specific quantitative goal in monetary terms for each element of the organization.

Each organizational objective, such as earnings per share, is accompanied by a complex of derivative objectives needed to implement it. Major goals are reduced to subgoals. Here we encounter the problem of *suboptimization.* The controller may be so effective in holding the line on costs that goods remain unsold on distributor shelves because of inadequate promotion. Suboptimization refers to the maximizing of a lower-order objective to the detriment of general systems goals.

It is a common characteristic of the value system that individual contributors to the system attempt to do the best job possible in their own specific areas. In fact, what else can they do? It is provable that suboptimization is unavoidable; the best we can do is try to minimize it by integrating the subgoals. Only the computer can handle a problem of this complexity.

Means versus Ends

The hierarchy of objectives is a means-end chain. The achievement of each lower-order objective becomes the means of fulfilling the more general objectives. Unfortunately, the focus of decision making in the organization often becomes concerned with the means to be used rather than the ends to be achieved.

This strong tendency for managers to overemphasize the means relative to the ends is represented by the cult of efficiency. Attention is directed to maintaining a smoothly running organization with most efficient conversion of inputs into output. Techniques of organization and control are stressed while goals are taken for granted. The objective is obvious? Not so.

The objective provides the measure of effectiveness of the system; if it is not appropriate, the actions in the system will be ineffective. Thus, classic management theory proposes the *principle of the objective:* The organizational objectives must be clearly stated before any course of action is undertaken.

OBJECTIVES AND MOTIVATION

Objectives in and of themselves have the unique property of stimulating activities. Individuals will not contribute to a system unless they can identify themselves with some objective of their cooperation. A formal cooperative system does not arise out of a vague feeling or desire to associate with others, but rather, it must have some specific object of action.

There is no reason to assume that objectives and motives are identical. To quote again from Barnard, "Individual motive is necessarily an internal, personal, subjective thing; common purpose is necessarily an external, impersonal, objective thing, even though the individual interpretation of it is subjective" (12, p. 89).

Managers must continually reconcile the differences between organization purposes and individual motives by stressing the concept of *harmony of objectives*. As the organization grows, new executive positions are created which provide opportunities for employee advancement, thus satisfying individual needs for recognition and economic reward.

Later, cases will demonstrate how management incentives are directly tied to achievement of planning goals. This relationship provides the driving force that makes the computer-based planning system meaningful.

Establishing Objectives

Our discussion to this point is not controversial. Who can argue, in principle, against the necessity of setting objectives? The question is, how? By top-down or bottom-up management? By centralization or decentralization of authority? By control or motivation?

Top-down Planning. The goals of the organization must be consistent with market conditions, legal restrictions, money markets, competition, and all other aspects of the environment, including investor expectations. How can the district manager be expected to recognize the impact of changing interest rates on corporate policy? Further, can the line manager take the necessary time from daily operations to formulate well-conceived goals for the next year, much less the next five years?

Can operating managers be expected to set realistic goals for themselves, or will they take the safe way out? If organizational goals are generated by summing objectives specified by the line units, the result is often poorly integrated and unrealistic at an aggregate level.

Bottom-up Planning. Conversely, management theory has long taught that bottom-up or participative management is desirable. Line managers will not be motivated to achieve objectives set by others. Each manager must feel identification with organizational goals and internalize them as personal objectives; this can only be achieved through participation.

Then we have the matter of familiarity with operations. How can a staff planner be expected to know that a major account in a specific territory is facing a threat which may cut the performance of that district in half? Only the responsible manager is aware of the specific variables affecting performance of that organizational unit.

Illustration. The Wells Fargo Bank and Potlatch Corporation cases in this book present a very interesting contrast in philosophy for establishing objectives. The bank uses a top-down approach because (1) the operational units are quite similar; (2) corporate staff has demonstrated superior skill in forecasting overall results; and (3) it is much more efficient.

Potlatch has moved in the opposite direction into the bottom-up approach, with planning decentralized to the various operating units which are quite diverse in their character and which serve unique markets. The function of corporate planning in this company is basically the generation of common assumptions concerning the economy and the industry as well as coordination and consolidation of the operating plans.

Several of the senior executives at the bank have testified that top-down planning would be "impossible" without the computer. It would simply not be feasible to "explode" corporate goals into the detail required for the multitude of operating units. Massive allocation problems are involved. Similarly, although perhaps less critically, the computer is very important at Potlatch as a means of consolidating plans from the operating units and subsequently applying corporate overheads.

System Implications

Leadership style is an important consideration in developing a computer-based planning system. A system which is to be operated by diverse line groups will have logic reflecting the operating functions of those units and will be oriented to the types of detail questions they will ask. Corporate-level logic in such a decentralized system will be that of simple report generation with provision for aggregations and overhead allocations, but limited "what if?" interrogation.

Conversely, centralized planning requires extensive mechanistic forecasting capabilities and complex logic for "exploding" organizational objectives into plans for the operating units. Interrogation capability to ask "what if?" questions will be limited.

Actually, many firms use a parallel but independent planning effort involving both top-down and bottom-up perspectives. In such instances, computer-based planning has elements of both centralized and decentralized systems as described earlier, with provisions made for comparing and reconciling objectives into a final integrated plan.

MANAGEMENT BY OBJECTIVES

According to this concept, every manager should have clearly stated objectives concerning his or her specific performance in the system. All such objectives are derived from the overall objectives of the organization and should spell out the contributions expected from each area of the firm. These objectives should also indicate important contributions to and from other units relating to achievement of each manager's own objectives. Managerial performance is measured against achievement of objectives, and appropriate incentives are directly related thereto.

Iteration to Objectives and Parametric Analysis

The traditional precomputer approach to management by objectives was the repeated trial-and-error allocation of resources in an attempt to achieve a combination which might permit the achievement of the objective. Alternative pricing and production schemes would be tested against goals until a satisfactory and achievable plan was developed.

As every manager knows who has suffered through a budgeting cycle, this manual exercise can be a very frustrating experience. Laborious plans are constructed only to be later rejected because, upon consideration, it is apparent that they are not consistent (for example, marketing is selling more than production can manufacture) or that the aggregate performance falls short of the objective.

Iteration to objectives refers to use of the computer to search for specific input or performance values which will result in achievement of the general objective. The manager specifies a desired value for any performance measure, such as earnings per share or share of the market, and the computer determines the value of a specified variable which will permit the achievement of the desired objective, all other variables remaining constant.

A very useful application of this tool is, for example, in determining pricing strategy to achieve a desired profit margin under new cost conditions. These calculations are not feasible without the computer, since many of the cost or demand functions are curvilinear or discontinuous. Labor overtime rates, plant capacities, elasticity of demand, and many other complex relationships must be computed.

An immediate objection to iteration to objectives is that in reality all other variables do not remain fixed. However, this problem is handled by the manager who interacts with the computer by alternatively "playing" with pertinent variables. In fact, it is not possible for a manager conceptually to follow a simulation wherein more than a few variables are manipulated at any one time.

Multiple parameter analysis is a related and most useful technique: The computer is used to manipulate a number of variables within feasibility limits by specified increments with instructions to the computer to report only those combinations which will produce a specified constellation of objectives. For example, the computer is told, "Manipulate price between value *a* and value *b* and materials cost between value *x* and value *y*, and report those combinations producing a profit not less than *z* at a volume not exceeding *c* capacity." Thousands of alternative plans will be computed within seconds and feasible strategies reported with which the manager can then be concerned.

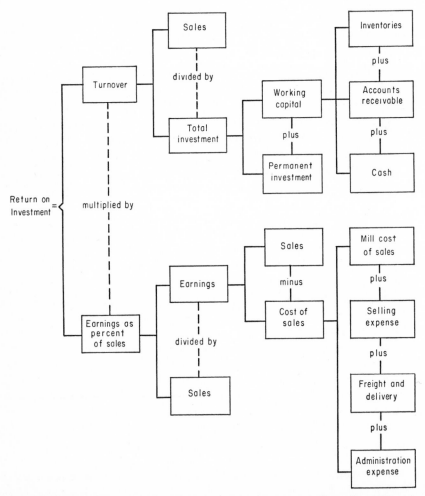

Figure 3-3. The relationship of factors affecting return on investment. (*From Harold Koontz and Cyril O'Donnell,* Principles of Management, *5th ed., McGraw-Hill Book Company, New York, 1972.*)

FINANCIAL OBJECTIVES

One can make an excellent case for the statement that "all business decisions are financial" in that they affect the profit of the firm in some way. Similarly, all computer-based planning systems are financially oriented. Certainly, capacities and material flows are often computed; however, the primary expression of planning is normally in financial terms.

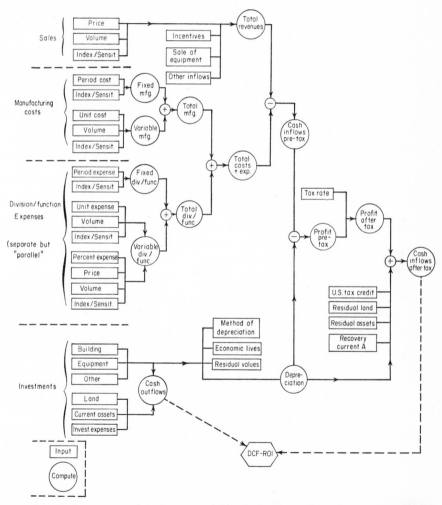

Figure 3-4. General flowchart of CIBA-GEIGY model. (*From Michael C. Luecke, "Computer Models: 'Black Box' or Management-Oriented?"* Management Adviser, *January–February 1973.*)

Return on Investment

Possibly the earliest and best-known financial model is the return-on-investment formula shown in Figure 3-3. This framework may be viewed basically as a profit and loss statement and a balance sheet laid on their sides and *integrated*.

The great advantage of this basic model is that it acknowledges the interrelationships between capital and profits. The managers' attention is directed to the general corporate objective of *return on objective* rather than to the suboptimization of lower-order objectives, such as sales maximization or cost minimization. Rate of return is a common measure which can be used to compare alternative investment proposals as well as performance of various operating units.

The computer model brings such a framework alive, as shown in Figure 3-4. The manager can inquire as to what profit margin will be necessary to achieve a specified rate of return on a contemplated investment or what increase in sales volume will be necessary to offset an anticipated rise in the cost of sales. The overall organizational goals are "exploded" by the model into a multitude of objectives for various levels and functional units in the hierarchy. Complex interrelationships are computed routinely. Computer graphics can be used to chart performance under alternative input assumptions, as in Figure 3-5.

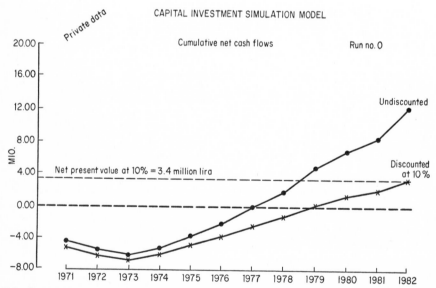

Figure 3-5. Computer graphics for sensitivity run.

SUMMARY

The design and application of a computer-based planning system begin with an explicit statement of organizational goals and priorities. The fact that these objectives are always complex, sometimes conflicting, and often difficult to quantify means that managers must have the flexibility to enter subjective judgments into the system. Outputs from the computer-based system are very useful in evaluating trade-offs between competing ends with respect to allocation of organization resources.

The Human System

Management may be defined as the process of accomplishing results through the efforts of other people. This means that managers must not only plan and control, but also organize and motivate, large numbers of human beings. Any discussion of computer-based planning is strictly academic unless it acknowledges the total dependence of these systems upon human effort in their design, implementation, and application.

We have previously examined the applicability of the systems concept to the world we live in and to the formal organizations within it. Let us now take one step further and build a model of human behavior. Such a model will be valuable in understanding the major reasons for failure of computer-based planning systems and will suggest appropriate concepts and practices for improving their acceptance.

A MODEL OF HUMAN BEHAVIOR

Although human beings are exceedingly complex organisms, a very simple model can be constructed for predicting behavior. This model is based on the assumptions that all human behavior is directed toward goal satisfaction and that motivation to action is provided by physiological and psychological needs. Achievement of the goal satisfies the needs and action ceases.

This closed-loop system is illustrated by the activity of eating. The body needs nourishment; a feeling of hunger provides the stimulus; and the human seeks food. Consumption of food fills the stomach, stopping the stimulus and eliminating the food search. Successful achievement of the objective eliminates the tension.

The objective of the following discussion is to predict how individuals will behave with respect to the computer-based planning system. One can make human behavior understandable by focusing on the needs of the individual, the goals sought, and the stimulus to which he or she reacts.

Human Needs

Human needs may be classified as (1) primary or physiological needs, and (2) secondary needs derived from interaction with the environment. The primary needs of the individual for preservation, survival, and perpetuation are generally not difficult to satisfy in an advanced society. The more complex secondary needs are social in character and exist in a rather definite order of importance. As the more basic needs are satisfied, other needs at different levels increase in importance. The following levels of need priority have been suggested by A. H. Maslow (17).

1. *Basic physiological needs:* These are the primary needs of survival and life—food, water, air, and warmth.

2. *Safety:* Safety from external danger is quite basic. People are concerned not only with safety from pain, injury, and other physical discomforts, but also with economic and social security.

3. *Love, affection, and social activity:* We all desire some degree of interaction with other people and acceptance by them.

4. *Esteem and self-respect:* Every individual to some extent needs to feel important and to believe that he or she is making a worthy contribution and is respected by others. It is particularly difficult for the individual to maintain a personal identity in a large corporation with tens of thousands of employees.

5. *Self-realization and accomplishment:* This is the need of individuals to achieve their optimum purpose in life, to utilize their abilities to the highest degree possible.

Great strides have been taken over the last 100 years toward satisfying the most basic needs for survival and safety. However, many trends in modern society have acted to increase the feeling of insecurity. Not the least of these trends is the rapid change in the environment, as discussed in Chapter 1.

The computer is still seen by many managers as a threat to their security in much the same manner that workers a half-century earlier perceived automation as eliminating their jobs although the actual result was a mass upgrading in skills. The individual today is highly dependent on many associates in the organization, a situation that further increases her or his insecurity. A computer-based planning system serves to heighten this awareness of interdependence.

The Adjustment Process

The dependent relationship between the organization and the individual is a two-way affair. Not only must the individual make an adjustment to the demands of the organization, but the organization must also make an adjustment to the demands of the individual. The behavior of the individual is the result of the combination of, and interaction between, his or her original nature and unique experience and the environment.

People can be affected only by those environmental factors which they actually experience. Our behavioral model has a closed loop, called the learning process, consisting of behavior, measuring and evaluating, recording the results, and modifying the behavior based on past experience. The individual is continually receiving information, acting on the environment, and modifying personal behavior.

The way in which the individual responds to pressures is greatly influenced by previous experiences. This fact helps us to understand *attitude*, which may be defined as a predisposition to act in a specific manner toward a person, object, or situation. The attitude of an individual toward computers and quantitative techniques generally will have a major impact on that person's specific reaction to a computer-based planning system. We know that attitudes, unfortunately, are highly resistant to change. In fact, often an individual's attitudes cannot be changed unless the attitude of the group is also altered. Group acceptance, then, is a prerequisite to acceptance by the individual.

Perception

Social behavior is largely determined by the manner in which individuals perceive themselves in the environment in which they function. The nature of this perception is primarily a learned response to both internal and external stimuli; a response learned mainly through social experiences. People see what they want to see.

People behave in accordance with the way in which they perceive their environment, not necessarily according to the way it actually is. This tendency often leads to strong resistance to change as a result of past learning which has built up emotional barriers to accurate perception. People are selective in their perceptions which are closely related to their attitudes. Thus, an appeal to reason may be quite ineffective as a means of selling the computer-based planning system.

Frustration

Frustration is an emotional state resulting from the inability of the individual to achieve desired goals. Such a situation arises when the person's behavior is not effective in reaching the goals to remove the irritation. When thus frustrated, the individual will assume various behavioral patterns in an attempt to remove the obstacle to goal achievement.

Frustration is a feeling, not a fact, and the type of behavior which results from it is largely determined by the individual's own self-image. Conflict is entirely a psychological phenomenon reflecting the individual's perception of the situation. There is no conflict in the situation per se, only in the way it is perceived.

Frequently, frustration is a result of management's setting unrealistic goals beyond the individual's ability to attain them. In other instances, frustration arises from conflict between goals. The personality of the manager is threatened by conflicts involving intense personal needs and critical goals.

Managers or staff members threatened by a computer-based system may react by changing their perception of the situation. In less desirable instances, they may react by attacking the system. They may also adjust by ignoring it in the hope that "it will go away." Or, using another adjustment mechanism, individuals may compensate by directing their energies with new intensity in other directions or by substituting one goal for another. *Frustration is inherent in the interaction of human beings and is aggravated by any change in the customary modes of living.*

THE GROUP

A predictive model of human behavior must consider the individual as a member of the group. People behave differently as members of a group and as isolated individuals. The person in a group situation is something different and apart from the individual in the solitary situation.

A group may be defined as two or more persons in frequent reciprocal communication. All groups are manifestations of the interdependency of people in a specialized society. The first characteristic of a group is common purpose. A second characteristic is availability of communication. Significantly, the computer threatens the group structure by altering the communication network.

Groups are increasingly specialized in modern society. Moreover, status differentials are inevitable. "Status anxiety" may be a strong motivating force in one manager's failure to cooperate in a computer-based system directed by another manager. Research has well documented that *conflict results when those of lower status originate the action to be taken by those of higher status in the organization.* The young operations research technician who originates demands on a senior manager can anticipate trouble.

Personal status is an important determinant of the way in which an individual will behave and the way in which others will respond. Generally, the person tends to identify with the group that will award the highest status. The management scientist will identify with his or her profession, which may promise applause for its members. The mathematical complexity or the originality of the planning system may, therefore, be of more importance to its sponsor than its usefulness to management.

Roles and Responsibilities

Social role may be defined as the culturally defined pattern of behavior expected of an individual in a specific social position. Along with status, roles are an important determinant of the way in which people behave toward one another. Roles tend to standardize behavior both through the selection process in which certain personality types are assigned specific roles and through modification of the behavior of the person to the requirements of the role.

The increasing specialization of labor results in roles becoming more rigid and tightly defined. Roles are called positions in the formal organization. These roles are interdependent, so one person's failure properly to fulfill a specified role will interfere with the performance of other people in the organization. Roles are extremely important in the organization, as they permit a higher order of consistency in behavior.

SOCIETY AND CULTURE

Our model of human behavior is completed by considering the impact of the society and the culture on the behavior, as well as the attitudes and sense of values, of the individual. The term *culture* refers to the patterns and products of learned behavior, such as attitudes and values, which are shared broadly by members of the society.

The individual learns to behave and to experience emotions as prescribed by the culture. Social acceptance is very important. Rapid change in the society results in tensions because the behavior patterns which were socially acceptable yesterday are no longer approved today. Managers and staff are threatened by obsolete knowledge, behavior, and emotional problems.

PEOPLE IN THE PLANNING SYSTEM

Let us begin with a statement of fact: Most computer-based planning system failures are of human, not technical, origin. Operator training, technical documentation, efficient programs, error-free transmission, accurate logic, and the many other aspects of the technical system are relatively unimportant when compared with the human problems encountered in computer-based planning.

This discussion may be related to the previous concepts presented in connection with systems integration in Chapter 2. Figure 4-1 illustrates

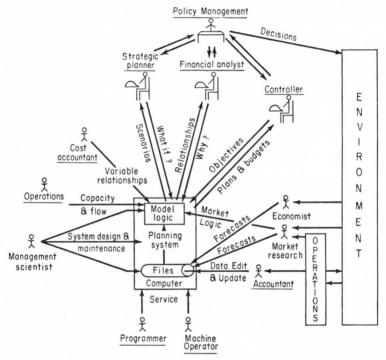

Figure 4-1. The human system.

the human system as related to the computer-based planning system. The first systems characteristic we must consider is that the participants are tied together by the flow of information, just as certainly as are the workers in an automobile assembly line linked by the flow of materials. Any significant delay or break in the information flow will destroy the usefulness of the planning system. An interruption in materials flow on the production line is readily apparent, while delays or distortions of inputs to the computer-based planning system may go undetected and the system may continue to function with erroneous outputs. This is very dangerous.

Organizational Conflict

Let us look at the major participants in computer-based planning to appreciate more fully the magnitude of the human problem. Consider that these various positions involve different organizational perspectives and emphases on limited functional objectives. Experience, education, language, and personalities differ broadly among the individuals who fill these roles. Conflict is built into the organization structure; communication is difficult because of fragmented perspectives.

The *director of planning* has a long-term strategic perspective. Planning may be emphasized instead of control, flexibility rather than accuracy, broad scope more than precision, and centralization more than decentralization. Primary concern will be given to rate of growth in corporate profits. Orientation is to the external environment.

The *controller* often has an accounting background which may carry over into a concern for accuracy of numbers and the preparation of detailed reports. Thinking may be in terms of "how come" that results do not conform to plan. Emphasis may be directed to the objective of reducing costs in the immediate planning period.

The *vice president of finance* is primarily concerned with the flow of funds in the enterprise. Allocation of financial resources is determined by return on investment or similar measures of performance. Cost of money is a major concern.

The *director of marketing* may think qualitatively as well as quantitatively regarding markets and products. Volume of sales is an important measure of performance. Concern is more with personal exposure in the field than report preparation. Orientation is external to the firm.

The *vice president of manufacturing* is concerned with production costs and capacity, and in this connection he or she must focus on the details and immediacy of operations. Sources of supply are a major concern.

The primary concern of the *management scientist* is the technical excellence of the computer-based planning system. Involvement is often more in the construction rather than in the usage phase of the project, and specialized terminology is used. The orientation of this individual is first of all to his or her profession rather than to the organization.

The chief concern of the *manager of computing* is with the massive commercial data processing activities of the organization. The computer-based planning system requirements are specialized; they may constitute a distraction from normal operations and may be assigned secondary priority to them.

Reorganization

Now let us compound the human problem by considering what happens when a shake-up occurs in top management. A new officer often starts with the basic assumption that whatever the predecessor did was probably defective and, in any event, can be improved on. Further, any questionable items must be written off at the start of the new administration so as to avoid future charges or criticism. The computer-based planning system is in serious jeopardy.

GAINING ACCEPTANCE

The previous review of behavioral theory suggests that managers and staff will accept the computer-based planning system to the extent that they are capable of distinguishing and anticipating the ability of the system to satisfy their needs. This is a problem of education and experience.

Primacy of experience is critical; it is very important that the first exposure of a manager to computer-based planning be a favorable one. The initial installation must be successful; a failure may require a decade to erase. To assure this success, it is best to start where management attitudes are the most favorable. An enthusiastic management can make even a poor system work; but a skeptical management will destroy the best system. Choose the division or function that is favorable from the behavioral standpoint, even if this is not the best application. Never force a system on management.

Training programs do not seem too effective in communicating the advantages of computer-based planning. Skeptical managers are sold by seeing successful applications to which they can relate. One good application in the organization will lead other managers to become enthusiastic. Unfortunately, the original user of the computer-based planning system often attempts to create a "fiefdom" by holding the system and its application highly secretive, thus restricting its expanded use in the organization.

The classic rule for gaining acceptance is *participation*. User involvement is important in the development of computer-based planning systems not only to gain acceptance but also to validate the system. Experienced managers can observe a computer simulation and immediately put their fingers on an error in the logic. An up-through-the-ranks steel executive, for example, sat through a systems presentation and soon spotted a major error in the complex logic of the production model. Surprisingly, instead of losing confidence in the system, the executive became a believer and supporter.

If participation is clearly helpful, why, then, is it so often ignored? The answer lies in the basic psychology of computer-based planning. A system frequently comes into existence because some very ambitious, bright individual becomes its champion. The system is perceived by this person as a means to gain recognition and promotion within the organization. Career and reputation are laid on the line and the concept and execution of the system are aggressively promoted. The champion is both the best friend and worst enemy of the computer-based planning system.

Unfortunately, such system sponsors are often destroyed by their own egos. The system becomes *their* system and they reject any assistance or participation by other managers in the organization. Consider the director of long-range planning of a European paper company who built the total system without once referencing to real data. On proceeding to validation, the accounting department flatly refused to cooperate, with the result that the system now sits on a shelf. Many companies have had this same experience, with really tragic results for both the individual and the company involved.

Let us again recognize the importance of time. It seems to take at least four years under even the best conditions for a computer-based planning system to become *firmly* established throughout an organization. The system may become operational the first year, but many individuals in the organization will not be convinced until they have seen it operate successfully through several planning cycles. Efforts to accelerate this acceptance by autocratic methods seem to create more obstacles than they eliminate. *An evolutionary process of phased expansion with demonstrated tangible benefits at each stage is the best, in fact the only, way to proceed.*

The Technical System

The technical problem in computer-based planning is primarily that of gathering available resources into a single integrated system of compatible elements to achieve the desired objective. A total system will include the operator, the modeling network, the data base, computer and terminals, programs, and the telecommunication network. The following discussion will focus at the conceptual level, since the specific details of each element will vary with the application.

It is strongly recommended that those readers with limited previous exposure to computer modeling pause at this point to work the executive exercise in the Appendix. A few minutes spent in reviewing fundamentals by completing that exercise will make the following sections much more meaningful.

THE SYSTEM

The general organization of an online computer-based planning system is shown in Figure 5-1. The operator uses a remote terminal to interface with the computer through a telecommunication network. The data base and model logic are contained in the permanent storage of the computer. An input code identifies the user and the organization to be simulated and calls up appropriate models and data into the working area of the computer. A simulation is run and the results are stored in temporary files for later analysis and comparison. Selective reports are outputted on command through the terminal. The general-purpose operating software does the housekeeping for the system and facilitates human-machine communications.

The operator continually modifies assumptions and

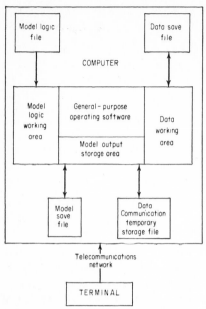

Figure 5-1. Computer-based planning system (simplified). *(Courtesy of On-Line Decisions, Inc.)*

accepts or rejects solutions. One may begin with a general problem in a full-scale simulation and then focus on a particular aspect of that problem, which may subsequently be magnified still further to look at particular relationships within that defined area (Figure 5-2). Of course, the sequence may also be reversed.

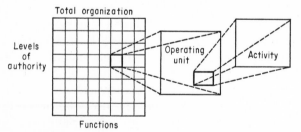

Figure 5-2. Progressive definition.

The online coupling of the complementary capabilities of human and machine as applied to the planning function has been studied by Aiko N. Hormann. His research indicates that the human performs

the imaginative and innovative mental functions, which in turn depend on his capabilities for making plausible inferences in the face of incomplete information, for recognizing patterns and relationships and inventing categories, and for taking differing points of view and restructuring the original problem.

Remarkably ill-defined as these functions might seem, they contain and depend on subprocesses that can be clearly specified for the machine. These include generating combinations of conditions and attributes from assigned relations and conditional features, keeping track of detailed changes and evaluating and classifying them with differing sets of criteria, extracting pieces of data from diverse files of stored information and rearranging these with a specific set of inference rules, and making detailed calculations on data. In these subprocesses, man is the specifier of rules and criteria which he can change in different contexts and at different levels of abstraction, and the formulator of relevant questions in the light of new findings and insights gained with the aid of the machine.

The machine can be increasingly helpful when man is able to *(a)* guide the machine's processes for selective exploration of the problem situation rapidly at varying levels of detail to gain insights and test new ideas and hunches as they come to him; *(b)* instruct the machine to summarize results in various ways and display them for visual inspection in a variety of formats; *(c)* request machine as assistance in choosing and using certain decision-aiding tools and techniques or in devising new aids to suit his unique needs and situations; *(d)* delegate more and more detailed functions to the machine, as these become identified as useful and delineable, so that his own efforts can be directed toward strategic-level decisions and creative ideas; *(e)* ask the machine to remind him with a checklist at an important decision point regarding crucial issues or factors that could not have been known at the outset; and *(f)* give rules for handling a certain set of subprocesses semiautomatically, receiving notices only when something wrong or unusual is detected [18, pp. 72–73].

Hormann proceeds to point out that the machine has particular value in problems which are unbounded in that they have unexpected "ripple effects" in other areas, in problems which are never really solved permanently because the environment is continually changing, and in those problems of high complexity which have many interrelated variables interacting in involved patterns of relationship. The extra effort and cost of establishing the human-machine system are justified when decisions are of high importance in their consequences, cannot be changed once made, have very significant effects over the long run, are made repeatedly, or must quickly adapt to rapidly changing conditions.

User Profile

The characteristics of the online user are summarized in Table 5-1. Very few line managers ever touch a computer terminal; the image of the executive interacting directly with the computer is just not true.

TABLE 5-1 Online User Characteristics from Statistical Studies

Timing and Pacing

1. More often than not, the time-sharing user will employ a terminal only once a day, and not every day; this rule is subject, however, to numerous exceptions for individual users and between different users.

2. The typical user spends between half an hour to an hour at his console at each session; this rule is also subject to great intra- and inter-subject variability.

3. Approximately 10 percent of the typical user's total working time is spent in man-computer communication at his console, whereas 90 percent of his working time is spent away from the console.

4. His median input rate is at the general order of one request every half-minute, whereas his average input is rougly one per minute at the terminal.

5. Half of the time he will insert a new command some 10 seconds after he has received a complete output from the computer; only on comparatively rare occasions will he wait as long as a minute before making a new request after receiving an output.

6. The ratio of human time to central processor time is at the general order of magnitude of 50:1; that is, approximately 50 seconds of elapsed human time is associated with one second of computer operating time on the user's program.

System Effectiveness

7. Users with tasks requiring relatively small computations become increasingly uncomfortable as computer response time to their requests extends beyond ten seconds, and as irregularity and uncertainty of computer response time increases. Users with problems requiring much computation tolerate longer intervals, up to as much as 10 minutes for the largest jobs.

8. As system load rises with increasing numbers of users, system response time increases, and, at high-load levels, both central system effectiveness and user performance tend to deteriorate.

Individual Differences

9. The computer is generally more verbose than the human; each line of human input tends to be accompanied, roughly speaking, by about two lines of computer output. New users tend to be more verbose; more terse responses occur with increasing experience.

10. Programmers seem to use, on the average, larger object programs and more computer time than non-programmers.

11. As the central system matures, and as users become more experienced, there is a tendency for object programs to grow in size and complexity, and for experienced users to require more computing time and a larger share of system capacity. Experienced users are more adept in exploring central system resources.

Source: H. Sackman and R. Citrenbaum, ed., *Online Planning towards Creative Problem Solving,* Prentice-Hall, Inc., Englewood Cliffs, N.J., 1972, p. 26, Table 1-3.

Faced with this reality, an effort is normally made to train analysts or management scientists in the operation of the system so that they may act in a service capacity to the managers asking the questions. Most frequently, the analyst reports to the corporate controller or to the director of planning, and all inquiries are processed through this facility.

THE MODELING NETWORK

Management really does not have the power to decide whether computer models will be used in a modern organization of any significant size. Analysts and planners will just not use manual methods when they know there is a better and more pleasant way to do their jobs. The only question is whether these models will be compatible and integrated into one officially sanctioned system, or, alternatively, will be written in various languages with differing file structures, and input/output formats, and operational on different computers.

A European paper company, for example, has been debating the development of a computer-based planning system for the past four years. During that period, various functional groups within the organization have developed no less than six separate planning systems, all quite incompatible.

Many large organizations which have ignored policy questions relating to computer-based planning now find themselves with a large library of special models. Each model requires its own data base, documentation, and manual conversion of inputs from other systems. The problem is compounded daily as new models are built in different languages and customized to particular computers.

It is most helpful to think in terms of modeling networks rather than of a corporate model, since a computer-based planning system almost invariably consists of more than one model. A general guide is to start with a few models and break them apart into subdivisions as the system grows. This is simple to accomplish if the builder is operating in a good software environment.

Modeling networks are not connected like pieces of pipe with outputs of one model directly inputting to another model. Rather, all models receive inputs from, and provide outputs to, common data files. This structure provides a great flexibility for diverse applications. Further, the system will normally have alternative modes so that the models can be run in several predefined sequences. It may be desired at one time, for example, to drive the system from marketing inputs, whereas at another time production may be the driving force.

Computer models consist of algebraic equations or algorithms (called *logic*) representing the accounting practices and operational interrelationships of the organization. This logic tells the computer the calculation procedure. Simulation involves the manipulation of this symbolic logic, utilizing values supplied by the data base. It is most important that the logic of the models not contain data values, since a change in the latter will require the reprogramming of the former. Also, as previously discussed, it is frequently desired to use one model to simulate a number of similar organizations, as in the instance of bank branches, but to use different data values for each installation. The data accomplish the customization of the model.

A good modeling policy is to *start with a simple model and add complexity as required.* The graveyard is full of conceptually beautiful models that no one could run. The limitations do not lie with the computer, but with the inability of the planner to understand what is happening in the system during the simulation. A blind simulation is of no value; the operator must comprehend the implications of what is happening so that erroneous conclusions will be recognized and further inquiries formulated toward the solution of the problem. Complexity is easy to add as required if the basic model is sound.

Should models be simulation[1] or optimizing? The answer is, both. Mathematical techniques for computing the "best" solution may be applied to models in the system, such as production capacity, where the problem structure is clearly defined. However, strategic planning or management-control systems as entities are almost always built for simulation.

What about deterministic as opposed to stochastic[2] models? Undoubtedly the quantification of uncertainty will become more common in the future to reflect real-world conditions more accurately; however, the use of probabilistic models is limited today because of the difficulty in (1) defining the frequency distribution, (2) operating a large random-number generator on a time-share system, (3) validating the models, and (4) communicating the results to management. Probably the major application of probabilistic models at the present time is in capital budgeting, where risk analysis has achieved broad acceptance. Almost all organizational planning models built today are deterministic in nature. The beautiful advantage of these models is that they can be proven to the reluctant manager with pencil and paper if necessary. After the model is established, uncertainty can later be added.

---

[1]A simulation is a model of some situation in which the elements of the situation are represented by arithmetic and logical processes that can be executed on a computer to predict the dynamic properties of the situation (19, p. 8).

[2]Deterministic models use values of the variables as assigned by the planner. Stochastic models involve properties which vary randomly.

DATA BASE

Let us pause to distinguish wisdom from knowledge from information from data. Wisdom refers to wise judgment resulting from an understanding of the situation. Knowledge refers to the condition of apprehending truth or fact. Information is the communication of knowledge. Data are the unstructured, uninformed facts.

Information can, therefore, be considered as selected data which reduce ignorance or uncertainty in a decision. It is useful to think of information as anything that causes adjustment in the assignment of probability. The information contained in a message is a measure of the difference in the knowledge of the planner before and after the message is received. The amount of information required by a decision maker is proportional to the uncertainty surrounding the situation.

Information can also be thought of as evaluated data. Data refer to materials that have not been evaluated by specific planners in a particular situation. Information, in contrast, is material that has been evaluated with respect to the user and to the time and place that it is going to be used. Material that is information for one manager may lack any value to another manager.

It is readily apparent that planners may suffer from a surplus of data while having insufficient information. Experiments indicate that generally managers do not know what information they need, so that it is difficult to set up appropriate filters. Fortunately, the very process of model building to solve management problems in a specific organizational context results in the evaluation of data. *The logic of the models explicitly defines the data base.* The equation

$$\text{Sales} = \text{price} \times \text{volume}$$

tells us we must have values for price and volume to compute sales.

The design and application of strategic planning and management-control systems demand a different perspective from that exercised in the operating-control system where data are derivative from transactions. Data requirements in computer-based planning are derivative top down from the managerial problems to which they will be applied. The design of the data base for such systems begins with a review of the top-management inquiry pattern and the construction of symbolic models. Certain variables in the model logic are computed from other variables, but ultimately the computations demand specific inputs. The meaning and precise form of these inputs are established by the model logic.

A frequent management concern is that the development of computer-based systems for strategic planning and management control should be deferred until the data base is computerized. Let us establish with emphasis that the elusive concept of a management information system (MIS) is largely irrelevant to computer-assisted planning systems and is thus not a condition for their accomplishment. The management information system is concerned with gathering transaction data for the operating-control system. The development of such a data collection system is a matter of many work-years and the expenditure of perhaps a million dollars. In contrast, the computerization of the data base for computer-based planning is frequently accomplished with only a few months of effort. In point of fact, the data collection system for most computer-based planning systems is manual, not computerized.

The relative magnitude of the two data bases is illustrated by the familiar data pyramid shown in Figure 5-3. At the base of the pyramid

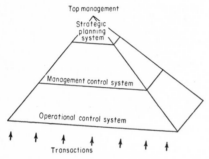

Figure 5-3. Data pyramid.

are the operating data, consisting of individual transactions numbering many billions of characters. At the middle of the pyramid is the management-control system, with a data base in the range of a few millions of characters. Finally, at the pinnacle of the pyramid is the strategic planning system, with storage requirements of a few hundred thousand. It is very rare that this total data base is computerized with the data edited and consolidated for the management-control system and subsequently further edited for input to the strategic planning system.

A major consideration encountered in the data-base design is that of defining the basis of classification. Will the users wish to call up the data by customer, geographic unit, product line, processes, or other groupings? What is the relative priority of these alternative classifications?

A great advantage of the computer is that it can use one data base to accumulate information by any *preestablished* criteria. This capability is in contrast to manual planning systems which normally require the same information to appear in various forms for different applications.

Redundant data greatly increase the problems of maintenance and update. A computer-based planning system should result in a major reduction in the size of the data base for this reason and also for the reason that the system itself is capable of generating many data values from related information.

The coding of data reflects the structure of the data base and should be graphically summarized in matrices for convenient reference by users of the system. The user who wishes to interrogate the system concerning the profit impact of a cost change of a particular raw material needs an efficient indexing system to determine the necessary coding for that variable.

The coding of the data base is also important as related to systems security. Most large companies use an elaborate system of internal security involving periodic issuance of codes to the various individuals or groups using the computer-based planning system. The division manager can look at anything pertaining to the divisional level of aggregation, whereas a brand manager can access only that information pertaining to a specific product. Scrambling codes are often provided as a protection against outsiders' accessing the company data base.

Additional security is provided so that only one authorized person, usually an accountant, can change the permanent values in the data base. Users can temporarily alter these values for purposes of simulating their areas of interest and can store the results in their own files if desired. However, the authorized values in the computer-based system should remain constant until changed by management decree. Any user can automatically index back to these values at any time upon giving the appropriate system command.

Perhaps the most perplexing problem relative to the data base is the matter of detail. How much data should be inputted? The answer relates to the basic philosophy of the system, to who will be using it for what applications, and to how the system concept may change. One thing to keep in mind is that the more detailed the data, the more flexibility the system has. Classifications can later be altered quite easily if information is available at a basic level of detail. This is important, since the concept of the system often changes considerably over years of usage. If the data were not detailed enough in the beginning, it may be necessary to scrap the entire data base and start over. One can always go from district to regional to national data, but not the reverse. Similarly, monthly data can be aggregated by quarters or years, but the reverse is not feasible. Since the volume of data increases exponentially as the level of detail becomes greater, the decision concerning this trade-off is a critical one requiring experienced judgment.

THE COMPUTER CONFIGURATION

It is a temptation at this point to enter into a discussion of the strengths and weaknesses of specific computer configurations as related to the requirements of computer-based planning. However, details of this nature are certain to be obsolete by the time these words are published. Therefore, let us continue to focus on concept and perspective. Recognize that the computer should be comparable in size to an IBM 360-50 or larger and that a major consideration is speed in file access. The requirements of a computer system for online planning are itemized in Table 5-2.

The first computer question is usually time-share versus batch operation. It is evident from our previous discussions that this also is not an either/or question, but rather, we desire the advantages of both modes of operation. A conversational capability is important when:

1. Data input and output requirements are relatively small.

2. A turnaround time of seconds or minutes is desired between input and output.

3. Direct user-machine interface is important.

4. The value of processed output has a high economic worth.

Just how important is this conversational capability in the planning function? Indispensable! The user normally does not ask the right question the first time around; he or she must engage in continual iterations to identify critical elements in the problem, determine their interrelationships, and formulate an acceptable course of action. This human-machine conversation may involve 20 or 100 inquiries, each conditioned by the preceding computer response. Even the best batch turnaround time is prohibitively slow.

It seems that speed of response is very critical in this symbiotic relationship between human and computer, as evidenced by the great improvements realized when the terminal speeds increased from 10 to 30 characters per second. The train of thought is lost by the operator if for some reason the service from the system is interrupted for a few seconds. In fact, experienced operators cannot tolerate the time required for prompting and prefer to operate in *express mode* with suppression of messages.

Time sharing is more expensive per computation than batch operation. An organization of approximately 300 million dollars in sales can expect a time-share computer bill for the planning system in the order of several thousand dollars per month, of which half will be for storage.

TABLE 5-2   Requirements of an On-line, Time-shared Computer System (24, p. 68)

Simplicity—The manager must understand the logic exercised by the computer and be able to verify the calculations when desired.

Secrecy—Confidential data and analyses must be protected. Data such as corporate profit plans and merger analyses are highly proprietary.

Conversational—The manager must be able to interact directly with the computer in his own language. An extensive program must be available to guide the manager in asking meaningful questions with reasonable protection against operating errors.

Fast response—The answer to one question normally suggests another question. The manager must be able to establish a meaningful dialogue with the computing system to facilitate the creative process of problem solving.

Management control—The decision process must be under the control of the manager, not the computer. A manager should be able to change assumptions, alter logic, and specify exact output desired without resorting to reprogramming.

Accessibility—The system should be accessible from the manager's office or from any other point within his sphere of operation, so that problems may be explored from a conference environment or during business trips.

Data availability—Current as well as historical and projected operating information must be available through the system. Accounting, financial, statistical, and mathematical tools should be readily available for analyzing and transforming data.

Flexibility—The system must have the flexibility to explore a wide range of problems encountered by the manager. The system should be available for use by a number of staff and operating personnel with diverse interests without reprogramming.

Economy—The manager needs a system which will give results now and at a reasonable cost. He does not have two years to develop a system which may or may not function. Cost should be dependent on time usage of the system.

GENERAL-PURPOSE OPERATING SOFTWARE

The construction of a corporate model in 1965 required almost 300 man-months of effort. A comparably sized and much more powerful system, built in 1972, involved thirty man-months of effort. This order of magnitude reduction was accomplished primarily by the elimination of custom programming. The answer lay, not in a new simulation language, but in the concept of an "unstructured environment" whereby users in effect built their own languages for the specific application. The concept and structure of this general-purpose operating software are described in the following paragraphs.

The general-purpose operating software accomplishes the housekeeping functions of the computer-based planning system, including user interaction, computation, and report generation, as detailed in Figure 5-4. The conversational portion of the software establishes user communication with the computer, while the computational portion manipulates the data, utilizing a broad range of tools for making quanti-

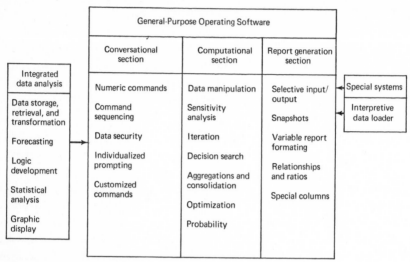

Figure 5-4. Software concept.

tative analyses and handling time relationships. The report-generation portion of the program is capable of producing selective outputs in formats specified by management. A schematic drawing of the system provided by one vendor is shown in Figure 5-5.

The housekeeping software must have the capability to access external files, thus avoiding restriction on the size of the models as well as permitting linkage to an external data base and other modeling systems. Further, the system should encompass a data analysis facility for developing the model logic, forecasting the arrays, and outputting graphic display and statistical analysis.

The system should be fairly machine-independent and capable of running in various modes, including batch, remote job entry, or time sharing, according to the tasks to be performed and the facilities available.

A number of significant advancements in the software have been made in recent years, including *user modes, command* files, and expanded tools for decision analysis. A user-mode subsystem provides a programming language for the automation of small tasks, e.g., custom-written routines for loading or displaying the contents of a particular file, desk-calculation type procedures, and similar tasks.

A command-files facility provides a convenient way of cataloging

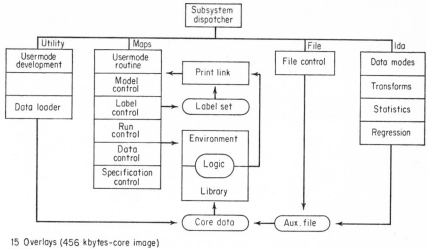

15 Overlays (456 kbytes-core image)
150 Subprograms in library
116 Basic commands

Figure 5-5. General-purpose operative system. *(Courtesy of On-Line Decisions, Inc.)*

frequently repeated series of commands, enabling the entire sequence to be called up by one instruction. In order to provide a framework for this facility, the *input stream* concept is used to handle an ordered sequence of messages containing input for the system. This tool is employed to standardize such procedures as investment analysis.

Using the capabilities of the user modes and the command files in combination, the modeler can construct an English language system customized to specific requirements. Further, this system will tutor unskilled users and lead them through a complex systems run. Not only is this system unique to each company, but it runs very efficiently on the computer in contrast to generalized English language systems.

Interpretive data loaders are being installed in most modern computer-based planning systems to assure rapid, accurate updating of the files. These loaders allow offline loading of data by untrained personnel. The data loader performs the diagnostics to check the data for errors, permits online editing, and then loads the corrected data into the proper files. It is significant that much of the data received from operating sources contains extensive arithmetical or mechanical errors. Research indicates that approximately one out of three systems has an interpretive data loader and that the usage on such systems is almost double the usage on systems without this feature.

In those instances where a computerized data base is available, file editors are written to assemble information in the proper form and load it into the planning system on command. This capability is particularly important for in-house installations.

Should the organization develop the housekeeping software internally or purchase it from an outside vendor? The answer again is to do both. Custom COBOL programs for batch report generation of operating-control budgets are simple and should be written internally. The time-share modeling environment, in contrast, will require software costing in the order of a million dollars and several calendar years to develop. This expenditure in time and money is difficult for any one organization to justify when compared with the cost of systems available from specialists in this field.

What about English language systems as compared with modeling in FORTRAN or PL1? Highly interpretive languages are prohibitively expensive for large planning systems. A factor of 10 increase in running cost is not unusual for a planning system running on highly interpretive software. Certainly this will change when APL or a similar language is hardwired into the computer by the manufacturer. At the present time, however, the user can create a customized command structure as desired in an unstructured modeling environment.

TELECOMMUNICATIONS

All the previous discussions assume relatively error-free data transmissions between the remote terminal and the computer. These terminals may be located in geographically diverse locations, thus necessitating the availability of an extensive telecommunication network. The sophistication of a modern data communication network is indicated in the following discussion.

The time-share network may be in the nature of a star with all traffic routed through a central location, or, alternatively, a central control may be used to distribute the load among diverse computer installations. Dedicated cables or a communication satellite may be used to transmit data between continents. Several networks are available which link major cities in the United States, Canada, and Western Europe. The user in London may access a data base in Chicago by dialing a local number. A portable terminal can then be carried to Paris to continue planning activities, with the French subsidiary using the same network.

The telecommunication network notes the user identification and makes a suitable adjustment for speed and special terminal features. Sophisticated algorithms are used to detect errors resulting from noise on the long-distance lines. Provision is made to accommodate power failure with automatic startup. Alternate routing is provided to improve reliability. The user receives messages in the instance of trouble and thereby is informed as to the condition of the system.

Backup computers are provided and automatically accessed as the need arises. Response time is improved by monitoring the load on each computer and rerouting inquiries to balance the level of usage. International networks have the advantage of operating in a number of time zones, a condition that serves to distribute the load and assure higher computer utilization throughout the operating period. Data files are protected from unauthorized access by extensive security measures and from loss on equipment shutdown by frequently updated backup files.

SUMMARY

The various technical components of computer-based planning must be mutually compatible and integrated into a functioning system. The design specifications for the system are derived from the management-decision requirements. The logic of the computer models is tailored to the objectives and to the operators who are to use the system. The models, in turn, define the data base, although in some instances data may serve as a constraint on the total system.

It has been established that computer-based planning systems develop over time through an evolutionary process of programmed extensions. Thus it is of great importance that the ultimate expansion be visualized at the outset, at least in general terms, so that the technical system does not later become a serious constraint. Flexibility is the key measure, since the technical system will change continually to reflect the rapid improvements being made in the state of the art and to accommodate the ongoing evolution of the organization it represents.

Computers in the Planning Process

The very essence of planning is the phenomenon of time as defined subjectively by the occurrence of events. The future exists only as a projection of the present. The purpose of planning is to anticipate the future and, in some sense, to fashion it according to the requirements for organizational survival and growth.

Unfortunately, planning theory is not at present sufficiently rigorous for effective application in the computer-based environment. Conceptual weaknesses which are not apparent from a general review of the literature become critical in system design and implementation. Upon precise examination, the terminology of planning becomes a semantic swamp and the concepts appear as generalizations of limited utility.

The computer-based system as a planning tool has a very significant, but as yet poorly understood, impact on the planning structure and process and even on the organization itself. The following discussion will attempt a speculative review of the computer in the context of planning theory and practice. It is hoped that these concepts will be greatly improved through theoretical and applied research over the next decade.

THE PLANNING FUNCTION

Planning is primary to the other managerial functions of organizing, motivating, and controlling. Classical management theory delineates six logical steps in planning:

1. *Define objectives.*

2. *Establish premises* concerning the values of key variables as they will exist in the future period.

3. *Identify alternative courses of action which will achieve the objective* under the assumed planning environment.

4. *Evaluate alternative courses of action* relative to risk and efficiency.

5. *Select from among alternatives.* Make a decision.

6. *Formulate derivative plans.* Explode the organizational plan into derivative programs for the components.

The computer is valuable in accomplishing each step in planning. First, the computer helps in establishing objectives which are achievable under the assumed conditions. We have previously described the role of the computer in both bottom-up and top-down approaches to setting objectives.

Second, the computer is extremely useful in identifying which variables are critical to achieving the objective. Every manager must deal with an incomprehensible number of variables from which those having the greatest impact on the organization must be selected. The executive exercise in the Appendix illustrates the use of sensitivity analysis to determine the relative impact of changing inputs as they affect performance of the organization.

The computer is, perhaps, most valuable as a tool for evaluating alternative courses of action through the activity of simulation. The computer permits management to examine not one or three alternatives, but as many as may be desired. Not only will the computer simulate the outcome of many strategies, but it will also assist the manager in evaluating the results of these alternatives against specified decision criteria. Once the manager has made a decision, the computer can explode the plan into derivative plans.

Time Relationships

Since time is the essence of planning, the capacity of a computer-based system to manipulate complex time relationships is indispensable. Every plan must designate not only *what* action is to take place, but *when* such action will occur.

Inventories are a time function of production and shipments. Production capacity is a time function of capital investment. Cash receipts are a time function of sales, which in turn are partially a time function of promotional expenditures. Staffing is determined by past recruitment effort.

The computer must scan both previous and future periods to establish the state of the organization at a given time period n, as well as to determine what actions are necessary in that period to satisfy the decision logic built into the system. It must handle such questions as "Will capacity be sufficient to meet sales in period n plus t?" If not, "How much additional investment is necessary in period n?" "Can such investment be accommodated from internally generated funds?" If not, "How much should be borrowed on what terms within stated borrowing restrictions and guidelines?" "What will be the impact of such borrowing and investment on earnings in the intervening periods between n and n plus t?"

Such questions are difficult to handle without the computer. Manual methods require simplified time assumptions, such as a sixty-day collection period of receivables, which ignore the fact that receivables are a function of sales in several previous periods and that the collection period normally varies seasonally.

Without the computer, the cash planner cannot play with the sensitivity of cash flows to collection effort or time discounts. The computer must frequently compute the full set of financial statements five, ten, twenty times as it scans various values and relationships and relates them to the requirements set forth by management.

DECISION MAKING

At the heart of planning lies the decision, the selection from among alternatives. A very useful concept of decision making is that of the *strategic factors* as described by Chester Barnard:

The analysis required for decision is in effect a search for the "strategic factors." . . . The limiting (strategic) factor is the one whose control, in the right form, at the right place and time, will establish a new system or set of conditions which meets the purpose. . . . It goes perhaps without further saying that the process of decision is one of successive approximations—constant refinement of purpose, closer and closer discriminations of fact—in which the march of time is essential [12, pp. 202–203].

Barnard, some thirty years prior to online computing, thus beautifully described the simulation process utilizing a computer-based planning system.

A plan normally consists of a number of interdependent decisions. Each decision is conditioned by both preceding and succeeding decisions. Each decision imposes constraints on the stream of succeeding decisions with which it must be compatible as measured by achievement of organizational objectives. The computer-based planning system facilitates the analysis of decision patterns by automatically accomplishing time and functional linkages.

Policies and Programs

A policy is a general guide to decision making and, as such, is often incorporated into the logic of the simulation models. Such guidelines may relate to utilization of various financial sources, employment practices, pricing strategies, or other areas of organizational activity. Unless overridden by the planner, these logic statements assure a consistency in decisions made through successive time periods and in various functional sectors of the firm.

A planning program is a complex of decisions to achieve a specific objective, such as the expansion of production capacity. Alternative planning programs can be stored on the computer and called up on command as the need arises. Thus, after pursuing a particular line of analysis, the planner can place the resulting program on file for later retrieval and comparison or integration with other planning programs. This capability is particularly important when fast reaction time is required, as in the reevaluation of plans in light of recent market actions by competitors or significant changes in the availability or cost of materials.

Online Decision Making

One of the few really vigorous attempts to document the impact of interactive computing on the decision process was the in-depth experiment conducted by Professor Michael Scott Morton. One company utilizing an interactive planning system was observed over a period of time (20).

The problem represented was that faced by the market planning manager (MPM) in setting specific production targets for the various products for which he was responsible. "He was pressured . . . on the one side by the sales people who wanted to have ample supplies of all products everywhere, and on the other side by the production divisions who were responsible for inventories and wished to keep these as low as possible as well as minimize their production costs" (20, p. 45). The market planning manager had to evaluate expected demand, merchandising plans, available inventory, and production availability. The decision-making cycle before and after introduction of the online computer-based system is shown in Figures 6-1 and 6-2.

Morton found the result of utilizing a conversational computer-based planning system was that "the length of time spent actually working on a problem in order to arrive at a solution was reduced from six days to half a day." The length of time between starting and finishing the problem-solving process was reduced from twenty-two days to one day. The more general conclusions of his study were as follows:

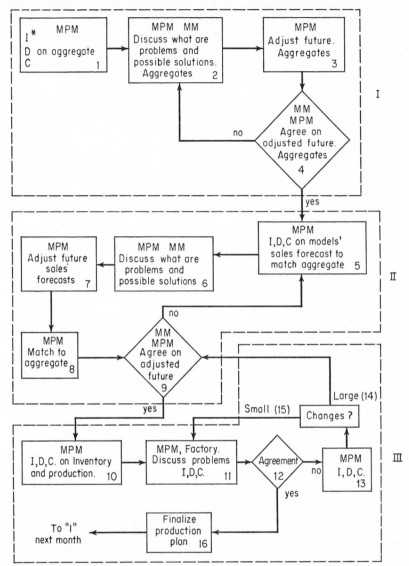

*I, D, C = Intelligence, Design, Choice.

Figure 6-1. Manual process—decision-making cycle. *(From Michael S. Scott Morton, Management Decision Systems, Division of Research, Graduate School of Business Administration Harvard University, Boston, 1971.)*

Nontechnical managers engaged in solving complex problems found that the man/machine combination is a highly convenient, powerful adjunct to their decision process. It provided them with flexible access to a large data-base, but more significantly it allowed them to explore the future. They had the ability to look forward and test strategies easily and simply.

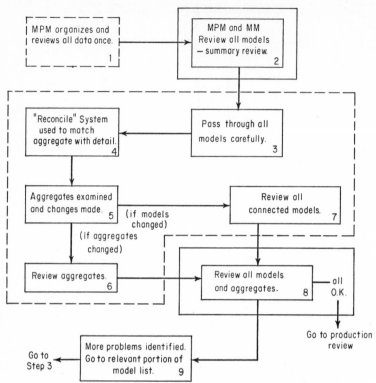

Figure 6-2. Computer-based process—decision-making cycle. *(From Michael S. Scott Morton,* Management Decision Systems, *Division of Research, Graduate School of Business Administration, Harvard University, Boston, 1971.)*

As a result of these features, the decision process changed considerably. Time was reduced sharply, which not only released managerial talent for other problems, but also induced more vigorous, logical problem solving. The reduction in elapsed time led to management's greater familiarity with the problems' complexities, and . . . , the reduction in response time led management to explore a wider set of solution strategies.

In addition to the time effect there was a change in the problem-finding and problem-solving processes. Problem finding was characterized by the ease with which a problem could be viewed from various directions. This at least offered the possibility of more effective work in finding relevant problems. Problem-solving was enhanced by the access to computational power, the ability to specify the required action easily and simply as it was required, and the resulting creation of several viable solutions.

Communication between the managers was changed considerably with the use of the system. Less effort was required to make one's point clear and less time was spent on discussing misunderstood issues. Communication was simple, and there was some indication that it led to a greater sense of commitment to the fulfillment of the plan that was finally selected [20, p. 17].

Problem Characteristics

Morton's study suggests that certain classes of problems are more suitable than others for application of online computer-based planning. The problem which he investigated had:

1. A significant profit impact on the organization

2. A large data base

3. Data requiring more manipulation than could be done conveniently in manual fashion

4. Several dimensions, so that no one criterion could be used to identify a good solution

5. Multidimensional factors in that a number of functional skills were required for the solution

6. Complexity so that casual relationships were difficult and managerial judgment was required

7. A rapidly changing environment

To this list of characteristics might be added *repetition*. Decisions which are made repetitively are particularly amenable to online simulation.

PLANNING STRUCTURE AND PROCESS

The classic concept of planning structure and process is illustrated in Figure 6-3. The foundations of all planning activities are the fundamental socioeconomic purposes of the organization, the values of top managers, and the external environment. Of these basics, the value structure of management is perhaps the most difficult to quantify. Frequent subjective, judgmental inputs are required so that the computer-based planning systems must be interactive to permit management intervention.

A strategic plan is formulated to guide the fundamental development of the enterprise. Normally such plans extend over long time periods; consequently, the terms *strategic planning* and *long-range planning* are used somewhat interchangeably. Technically, a strategic decision

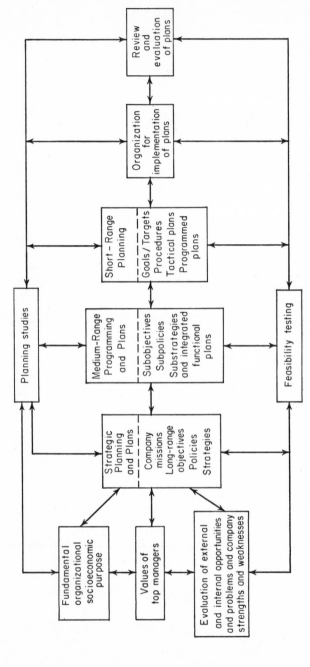

Figure 6-3. A structure and process of business planning. *(From George Steiner,* Top Management Planning, *Copyright 1969 by The Macmillan Company, New York.)*

may be identified by its critical impact on the future evolution of the organization.

Strategic plans, normally with a five-year time horizon, provide the general guidelines for the operating plan of the management-control system, which is much more detailed and specific over the next fiscal year (21). Once approved, the annual operating plan becomes a control device against which performance is measured. Information is drawn from the accounting system for this analysis, and management control becomes concerned with possible ways of reacting to internal and external system disturbances. As operations proceed, reforecasts are made and the annual plan is updated and extended.

Operating control, a third major category of planning activity, is concerned with very specific individual transactions. Although the annual operating plan may specify general inventory levels, the operating-control system will indicate which parts will be ordered in what quantities in which specific time periods. The concept of computer-based planning systems as discussed in this book is not directly applicable at the level of operating control.

Contrasting System Requirements (22)

A computer-based system for strategic planning requires a much higher order of flexibility than one used for management control, since the latter activity involves planning within rather well-defined guidelines. This flexibility in the strategic planning system is accomplished at the expense of detail and precision.

The strategic planning activity is irregular and imprecisely defined in contrast to management control, which follows a present rhythm regarding pattern and time. Outputs from the operational planning system are extensive and standardized in contrast with the much simpler and individually tailored responses of the strategic planning system.

Strategic planning requires information concerning the external environment which can be accommodated with a high order of imprecision. Unique data may be assembled to meet the needs of a specific planning exercise. In fact, a computer model relevant to a particular strategic problem may be built, used, and discarded within a time span of a few months.

The annual operations plan for use in management control is developed on large computer-based systems encompassing many integrated planning models. Input data for the management control system reflect internal operations and must be relatively accurate and consistent between time periods. Functional relationships are precisely defined in the system.

Because of these divergent planning characteristics, it is very difficult for one computer-based system to meet all requirements. Human/machine interaction may be critical at one level of planning while economy and capacity in massive data processing and report generation may be much more important at another level. All systems should be compatible, but not necessarily integrated.

Impact of the Computer on the Planning Process

Electronic data processing is often considered as simply another tool which can be superimposed on existing planning processes and structure. This is a dangerous assumption which limits the utility of the system and ignores the feedback impact of computer-based planning on the organization being simulated. Although only poorly understood at this time, it is apparent that significant changes do occur in organization structure, power relationships, information flow, reaction time, and human relationships. Computer-based planning systems permit a convergence of objectives that was previously not feasible. Moreover, they transcend artificial divisions of authority and responsibility.

Traditional organizational planning assumes a seriality of planning activities oriented to functional departmentalization. This fragmented sequential process is a most inefficient way of planning when compared with the holistic perspective of the computer-based system which permits concurrent and cooperative planning activities involving managers at various levels and functions in the organization.

Effective planning using a computer-based system requires consistent assumptions from all elements of the organization. Outputs from one segment of the organization become inputs for another segment. Time flows are integrated. Consistency between plans is assured by the logic of the system.

Formal planning cycles as used in manual effort are replaced by a continuous planning activity using the computer-based planning system. Reforecasting and updates are made frequently. More planning alternatives are considered and evaluated as to their relative impact on a base case. Often several planning strategies are prepared. The traditional concept of "a corporate plan" appears to be rapidly passing from the scene.

Information flow in an online computer-based environment is shown in Figure 6-4. Data describing transactions and events from internal operations and the external environment are stored in the computer. This massive information base is the foundation of the accounting system and the operating-control system. Data requirements are also supplied from this base in accordance with inquiries from the strategic planning and management-control systems. File editors process the data so that they are in the proper form for the planning models.

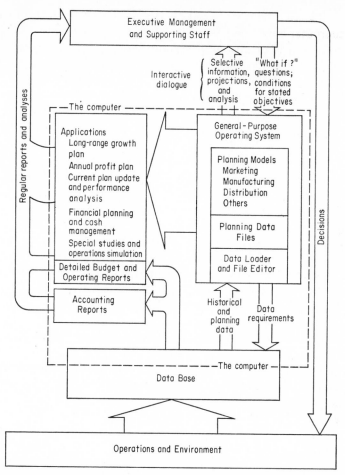

Figure 6-4. On-line executive support system. *(From James B. Boulden and Ephraim R. McLean, "On-Line Executive Support Systems," unpublished manuscript, 1974.)*

Management addresses the system through "what if?" questions directed to planners and analysts operating remote terminals. The general-purpose operating software accomplishes the housekeeping in the system to permit human-machine interaction. The output of the system is in the form of various reports and projections.

THE MANAGEMENT OF UNCERTAINTY

The indeterminacy of future events lies at the crux of the planning problem. Commitments based on assumptions concerning tomorrow must be made today. Such premises must be precisely defined and quantified if a computer-based planning system is to be used.

The logic of the planning models define the interrelationships between variables; however, the utility of the systems output is determined by the validity of the input assumptions. The computer-based system is only a tool, and it does not guarantee good plans. In fact, there is some evidence that the computer has the effect of magnifying the performance differential among planners of varying skills.

Alternative Scenarios and Probability Theory

Since all input assumptions carry an element of uncertainty, a measure of the likelihood of occurrence is an important element in every decision. It is necessary to state, however, that relatively few firms use formal probabilistic models in either strategic planning or managerial control at a corporate level. This is not to say that they should not, or will not, in future periods, but that they do not now. We can note those industries characterized by heavy capital investment where capital budgeting in particular uses risk analysis; however, these tools are seldom used for organizational policy simulations.

Rather than define probability distributions for critical forecast inputs, strategic planners normally construct several scenarios. Each scenario is a synopsis of a future environment, usually built around a few very critical assumptions. The union will strike or it will not strike. If it strikes, the duration will be short, medium, or long. Major competitors will take this or that basic course of action.

A scenario will be composed of a constellation of mutually consistent assumptions. For example, a power shortage over the next decade will result in a number of quite predictable events which in total will constitute the strategic planning environment. Senior management will examine the alternative scenarios as developed by the staff and weighted most likely to least likely, or most favorable to worst possible, which is, of course, a rough form of quantifying uncertainty.

Strategic plans are developed for not one future, but several very divergent futures. This is possible because the computer-based planning system permits preparation of five plans almost as easily as one. The most likely future profile is adopted as a basis for the annual plan; however, the environment is continually monitored to identify major deviances which would suggest a shift to alternative strategies. Management desires to avoid piecemeal opportunistic actions and achieve dynamic stability through planned growth.

Forecasting

A few critical predictions lie at the foundation of every plan, and these assumptions most frequently concern the level of activity to be anticipated in the organization. Although mechanical computer forecasts standing alone often have only limited value, the construction of mathematical models to produce these forecasts is of great benefit in defining the structure or logic of the external and internal relationships. It is one thing intuitively to forecast a 10 percent increase in sales; it is quite another thing to support this judgment with a detailed analysis of the underlying logic.

The process by which the elements of a sales forecast are brought together in a computer-based system is illustrated in Figure 6-5. Information is drawn from the environment, historical records, and market channels. This information is assembled and processed using a variety of techniques, such as time-series analysis, correlation, intuitive judgment, and market surveys. Several different forecasts may be developed using various forecasting tools that reflect both the top-down and bottom-up approaches. The results are compared and analyzed for submittal to executive decision.

The computer is useful in determining the sensitivity of performance to various environmental and operating assumptions. Those inputs determined to be critical may justify further research to improve their reliability. Because the assumptions are defined, they can be monitored and new forecasts prepared as the future becomes more visible. Planning is a continuous process involving redefinition of purposes and refinement of forecasts. Although the computer cannot eliminate uncertainty, it does permit plans to be rapidly changed. The planner using a computer is no longer frozen into a given posture.

APPLICATIONS

As noted previously, most systems are financially oriented and the outputs are primarily in monetary units. Further, systems are generally applied to more than one problem area; therefore, systems classifications must be considered only as indications of the primary users of the system.

The scope of computer-based planning applications is rather impressive, as shown in Figure 6-6. The budgeting/annual profit plan is currently the most popular application. Long-range planning is the second. Financing, operations, pricing, and cash management are less common applications which are rapidly increasingly in significance.

The most important manner in ·which the systems are used is in asking "what if?" questions. Analysis is second in frequency of application, report generation third, and forecasting fourth. Control applications involving comparison of actuals with plan seem to be of very minor importance.

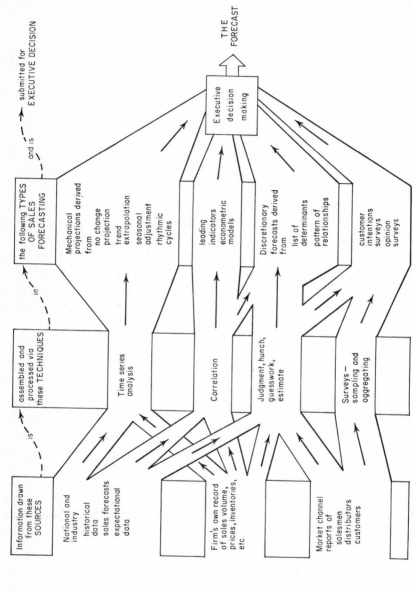

Figure 6-5. Elements of forecasting. *(From James B. Boulden, "Fitting the Sales Forecast to Your Firm," Business Horizons, Winter 1958.)*

TOP MANAGEMENT STRATEGIC PLANNING		
Finance	**Marketing**	**Other**
Annual plan	Sales forecasts	Mergers & Acquisitions
Budgets	Pricing	New ventures
Performance analysis	Brand strategy	Labor negotiations
Cash management	Marginal revenue analysis	Facilities planning
Resource allocation	Promotional strategy	Capacity utilization
Financing	Commission structure	Production planning
Capital budgeting	Manpower allocation	Transportation
Inventory plan	Geographic strategy	Distribution plans
Long-range plan	Transfer pricing	Service programs
Overhead allocations	New product strategy	Routing
Cost analysis		
Tax planning		

Figure 6-6. System applications. *(Courtesy of On-Line Decisions, Inc.)*

A Planning Application of Inland Steel (23)

As pictured in Figure 6-7, the online computer-based planning system at Inland Steel is focused on the production processes at the steel division. Each model deals with a basic process in the sequence from raw materials to finished products. The models simulate various costs incurred in:

1. Conversion of ores to molten iron

2. Conversion of molten iron to steel ingots

3. Processing of ingots

4. Finishing the steel to various end products

The end results of the system are the cash flow statement, the balance sheet, and the profit and loss statements for the steel division and for the corporation. The corporate model provides for the consolidation of a corporate-level income statement and balance sheet. These models have provided Inland's operators and managers with a clear and concise framework for communication with one another, as well as a new basis for evaluating operating and policy questions.

The Inland financial models were installed in the fourth quarter of 1969, too late for use in the 1970 annual profit plan. However, the models were used to test alternative strategies, changes in key variables, parameters, and assumptions on a test basis by the corporate

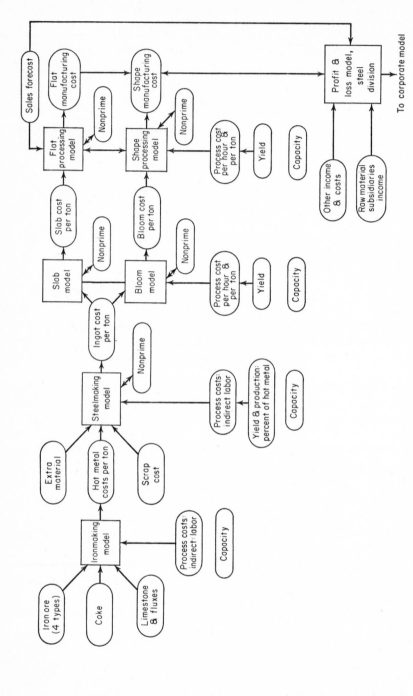

Figure 6-7. Inland Steel model. *(Courtesy of Inland Steel Company and On-Line Decisions, Inc.)*

planning staffs during the first half of 1970 as part of a training and experimentation program.

The first live test of the models was in the preparation of the 1971 profit plan and the related five-year profit and cash projection. For the first time, alternate strategies and assumptions were used during the planning process and during the executive review of the total corporate formal plan.

In approaching the profit-planning cycle for 1971, the company management was faced with unusual uncertainties. This situation led to the use of the model to simulate four major alternative sets of conditions. All four were based on a basic premise that a strike in the automotive industry was a near-certainty during the fourth quarter of 1970, and that if the strike should occur it would have a significant impact on fourth-quarter shipments of the Inland Steel Company. However, the sales forecast for 1971 indicated a very strong sales demand for the first seven months of that planning period, ending with the August 1 deadline date for negotiations with the steelworkers union.

The first assumption was that the sales forecast for 1971 would follow a normal seasonal dispersion of shipments, much like what would happen in any normal year, with no impact from customers' hedge buying steel inventories in anticipation of a possible strike. This gave a base-condition type of planning forecast.

The second assumption was made that the historic pattern of pre-strike hedge buying would occur in the first seven months of 1971, as it has in all similar periods in the postwar period, and that there would be no strike, since agreement would be reached late on July 31. In this condition, sales demand would decline sharply in August, September, and October, with some recovery in the later months of the fourth quarter of 1971.

The third assumption involved the previous basic premise but assumed a thirty-day strike in the industry, with resumption of production in shipments after thirty days.

The fourth assumption assumed a ninety-day strike, with the same prestrike hedge-buying sales pattern occurring as stated in the basic premise.

The financial model was used to simulate these four primary assumptions, all based on the initial premise that there would be an auto strike in the fourth quarter of 1970. Management selected assumption number 2, which was a prestrike buildup of inventories, but no strike occurring in the industry. This forecast was used as the basis for the formal profit plan for 1971, but the other options were maintained in the profit-planning manual as alternate strategies in the event conditions should change as the August 1 strike deadline approached.

A major decision was made in September 1970 by top management to build semifinished and finished inventories to the largest level in the company's history to capitalize on the strong demand forecast for the first half of 1971. The reason for this was that if the forecast was correct and if inventories were not accumulated, the mills would not be able to produce the steel fast enough to meet the customer delivery requirements, and there would be loss of sales revenue. This plan was followed, the excess inventory was liquidated on schedule by June 1, 1971, and the company achieved an all-time record industry market share of 6.8 percent instead of the normal rate of 4.8 percent to 5.2 percent.

SUMMARY

The historical approach to computer-based planning has been to computerize the existing manual systems and procedures. Experience over the past decade indicates that this simplistic approach sharply limits the potential contribution of the computer. Both research and field experience reveal that the human-machine synergy of a computer-based planning system changes the fundamental decision processes of the organization itself.

The computer is useful in every step of the planning process. It automatically manipulates complex time relationships and facilitates the search for strategic factors. It also shortens the time required to arrive at solutions, broadens the scope of the search activity, and reduces unproductive communication. Complex, repetitive, or important decisions involving access to a large data base are particularly appropriate for simulation.

The precise design of the computer-based planning system depends upon its focus as to strategic planning, management control, or operational control. Different purposes and characteristics of these various applications require divergent and sometimes conflicting systems characteristics. A single system cannot, at the present stage of the art, be all things to all people in the organization.

APPLICATION

Application

The reader should be attentive to both what is said and what is *not* said in the following cases. The subject of computer-based planning is a highly sensitive one in most organizations, so it is not possible to tell the entire story in print for any system. The organizations represented in Part Two were very cooperative in relating their experiences. Still, each case is only partially complete, and some extrapolation, based on the conceptual material presented in Part One, is necessary.

The cases were selected to represent various industries, sizes, design styles, problems, and management orientation. Most systems are used for several planning applications so that the general functional categorization represents only primary emphasis. These are all highly successful systems with proven track records. In most instances, detailed use data on the system are available and demonstrate the acceptance by management in real-world applications.

The strategic, financial, and budgeting applications are best defined. Marketing and operations applications are in less widespread use and still in rapid evolution. Chapter 13 on multinational planning systems should be approached with caution, as the state of the art in this area of application is primitive.

7

Strategic Planning / Potlatch Corporation

Strategic planning has been previously defined as concerned with those decisions which establish or change the basic character or direction of the organization. The Potlatch Corporation has been selected for study because (1) the strategic planning process is highly structured and well documented; (2) the firm has been a pioneer in online, real-time planning systems; (3) the system has survived a major decentralization in the planning function; and (4) indices of actual usage of the system since inception are available.

ORIENTATION

Potlatch Corporation is a large, integrated forest products company employing some 11,000 people in 44 plants with 36 sales offices spread throughout the United States. Earnings for 1973 were $33,979,000 on sales of $442,467,000.

One of the major markets for Potlatch products is in new housing construction, and this fact results in a pronounced cyclical sales performance. This market is characterized as a free auction, so that wide price fluctuations occur with resulting variations in profit margins. During recent years, the corporation has been successfully pursuing an objective of obtaining a more advantageous market balance and a consistent pattern of growth.

A planning concern of Potlatch management is the continuing decline in sales of timber from public lands by the United States Forest Service. Corporate strategy is, therefore, concerned with "assuring a growing profit by better management of company forests and conversion of the harvest to optimum value end uses within the competitive business environment."

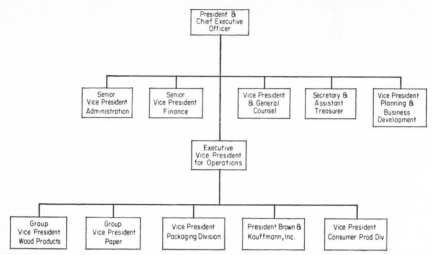

Figure 7-1. Potlatch Corporation organization chart. *(Courtesy of Potlatch Corporation.)*

The 1973 Report to Shareholders, presented at the annual meeting, contained the following statement by the chief executive concerning the company's organization (Figure 7-1, organization chart):

Relative to our longer term objectives, we have reorganized the operating structure of the company into six divisions. Each of these divisions is a distinct business defined by the markets it serves rather than by its function. The activities of four of these divisions are coordinated by two group vice presidents. These two groups, plus the other two divisions, represent Potlatch's four areas of major interest: Wood products, paper, packaging and consumer products. Within the various divisions are many smaller business building blocks doing business within their own markets and competitive environments. The organization of the corporation along these market-oriented lines facilitates the management of the individual businesses in their drive to be competitive and responsive to the market place.

The conversational computer-based planning system was built in 1969 by the director of planning, who reported to the vice president of financial analysis and planning. This director has since moved to the position of assistant general manager of a major division of the company, and the Planning Department has evolved to Planning and Business Development, headed by a vice president reporting directly to the chief executive of the company. The function of the corporate planning department has changed from consolidating the operating plans to establishing an overall corporate strategy and coordinating the preparation of the divisional plans in support of that strategy. The strategic plan provides the premises for the annual budget, which is administered by the Controllers Department.

THE PLANNING PROCESS

The chief executive at Potlatch is very strongly oriented toward planning, as indicated by his comments at the 1973 annual stockholders' meeting:

To assure systematic business analysis, all of our divisions are now on five-year planning cycles. Each analyzes its own capabilities, competitive situations, plus current and future market trends. Reviews for the purpose of revision and updating are held annually to plan new tactics against a backdrop of five-year objectives. The combination of divisional plans creates a corporate operational plan which also must be analyzed and evaluated against an even larger business scene: The national economy combined with the socio-political climate. Through this procedure of evaluation and re-evaluation from bottom to top and back again, we feel that we can reduce the impact of cycles which have so often plagued the various businesses in which we operate.

The 1973 planning cycle is illustrated in Figure 7-2. The premises for the five-year plan are published by the operating committee as a part of a comprehensive planning document. These premises are derived from the corporate philosophy as discussed in Chapter 5. This public state-

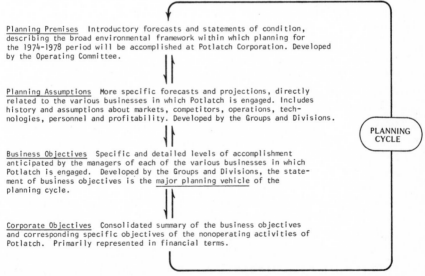

Figure 7-2. Potlatch Corporation 1973 planning cycle. *(Courtesy of Potlatch Corporation.)*

ment of philosophy defines the purposes of the company as well as its organizational values and priorities. The philosophy clearly states the goals and standards.

As a part of the planning premises, the corporate Planning and Business Development Department provides national economic forecasts of such key planning variables as new housing starts. It also provides premises in the following areas:

Employee relations—rate of increase in wages, salaries, and benefits by geographic area

Purchasing—availability as well as costs of certain materials and capital equipment

Transportation—costs by regions and by mode

Forecasts concerning specific markets, competitors, operations, technologies, personnel, and profitability are developed at the division and group levels. A major element in the planning cycle is the statement of business objectives as anticipated by the managers of each of the various businesses. A consolidated summary of these specific levels of accomplishment, as represented in financial terms, constitutes the corporate objectives.

The planning workbook contains a schedule of timing and responsibilities (Table 7-1). Although the operating divisions are not required to use the computer-based planning system, the complexity of the planning procedure is such that compliance with these schedules would be almost impossible without use of the computer.

The Planning and Business Development Department is concerned with filling the planning gap between the overall company business strategy and the performance which is projected by the operating divisions. Allocation of resources and the development of new business opportunities are stressed. The coordination of the strategic planning effort remains the responsibility of this department, which accomplishes the final corporate consolidations. Planning and Development maintains the computer-based planning system and trains the divisional staffs in its use; however, the data base and models of operating units are built and maintained by the divisions.

ONLINE, REAL-TIME PLANNING

The specific details of the Potlatch computer-based planning system are, of course, confidential. It is possible, however, to describe a model which closely approximates the actual models and therefore can be related to the actual Potlatch system (24, pp. 67–83).

TABLE 7-1. Potlatch Corporation: 1974 Planning Cycle Chronology

Proposed date or period	Activity	Planning & Business Development Dept.	Group/Division officers	Operating committee
September	Develop proposed procedures and premises for 1974 planning cycle	X	—	X
to	Discuss proposed 1974 planning cycle procedures and 1974 premises in Operating Committee	X	—	X
November 1973	Develop final procedures and premises for 1974 planning cycle	X	—	X
	Send final procedures and premises to Groups/Divisions	—	X	X
November 1973 to February 1974	Develop 1975–1979 planning assumptions and strategies	—	X	—
December 3, 1973	Advise Operating Committee of definitions of Lines of Business	—	X	X
February 23, 1974	Submit 1975–1979 planning assumptions and strategies for Operating Committee review	—	X	—
March 11–15	1974 assumptions and strategies meeting	—	X	X
March 22	Return reviewed 1975–1979 planning assumptions to Group/Division officers	X	—	—
April 26	Submit 1975–1979 business objectives for Operating Committee review	—	X	—
April/May	Consolidation of business and functional objectives for Operating Committee review	X	—	X
May 20–24	1974 planning meeting and companywide review of 1975–1979 objectives	—	X	X
June	Revise and review 1975–1979 business and corporate objectives	—	X	X
July	Review final 1975–1979 consolidated objectives with Executive Committee	—	—	X
August	Review final 1975–1979 consolidated objectives with Board of Directors	—	—	X
September	Develop procedures for 1975 planning cycle	X	—	X

Courtesy of Potlatch Corporation.

Pattern of Operations

The physical flow of materials for a plywood operation is shown in Figure 7-3. Company-owned logs, together with purchased logs (if required), are processed in the veneer manufacturing phase. The procedure involves cutting a thin sheet of veneer from the surface of the log (peeling) and drying it to a specified moisture content. By-products of

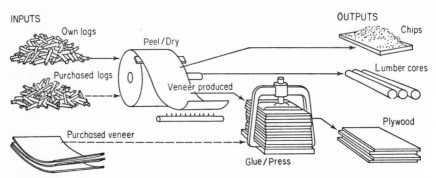

Figure 7-3. Plywood operation. (Harvard Business Review, *July–August 1970.*)

the peel/dry process are green lumber cores and chips, which are sold at transfer prices to other divisions of the company. Plywood is then glued and pressed with veneer produced in the previous operation or (if required) purchased.

Although this description of the process is simplified, it serves as an adequate basis for our discussion. The capacity of the glue/press operation in relation to the available company-produced veneer determines the amount of purchased veneer required. Similarly, the capacity of the peel/dry operation in relation to desired veneer output determines the amount of purchased logs required.

Showing Profit and Loss

The plywood model deals with profits and losses from plywood operations. The construction of the model is based on the simple algebraic relationships of sales and various costs. These relationships are based on a set of parameters which define the important factors in the model. Table 7-2 shows a list of the parameters for the plywood model, identified by parameter number. At the end of the parameter list are V-arrays, which involve important input data concerning prices and production.

Each line on the profit and loss statement then is computed according to a formula using the pertinent parameters. These formulas, or algebraic relationships, are shown in Table 7-3. Each numbered line (from .01 to 31.00) defines a corresponding line in the profit and loss statement. Following line 14.00, net profit before tax, is a list of computed ratios and other items of data of particular interest to management.

TABLE 7-2. Data in Plywood Case (24, p. 73)

Parameters (written as P1, P2, and so forth)

Parameter number	Description
1	Labor growth rate
2	Operating supplies growth rate
3	Raw materials growth rate
4	Initial pressing capacity (millions of square feet per month)
5	Month number (1–72) of pressing capacity increase
6	Increase in P4 as a fraction of P4
7	Initial veneer capacity (millions of square feet per month)
8	Month number (1–72) of veneer capacity increase
9	Increase in P7 as a fraction of P7
10	Price of own logs (dollars per log MBF*)
11	Price of forest service logs (dollars per log MBF)
12	Fraction of logs from own supply
13	Discounts and allowances for plywood as a fraction of sales
14	Selling commission for plywood as a fraction of sales
15	Freight-out for plywood (dollars per MBF)
16	Yield MSF veneer per log MBF
17	Yield MSF ⅜-inch plywood per MSF* veneer
18	Yield MBF lumber per MSF veneer produced
19	Yield chip units per MSF veneer produced
20	Operating supplies (dollars per MSF veneer produced)
21	Operating supplies (dollars per MSF plywood produced)
22	Labor hours per MSF veneer produced
23	Labor hours per MSF plywood produced
24	Labor cost (dollars per hour)
25	Sales eliminations of chips and lumber (percent as decimal)
26	Cost eliminations of own logs (percent as decimal)

V-arrays (written as V1, V2, and so forth)

Array number	Description
1	Desired plywood sales-production (millions of square feet per month)
2	Plywood prices (dollars per MSF)
3	Lumber transfer price (dollars per MBF)
4	Chip transfer price (dollars per unit)
5	Veneer purchase price (dollars per MSF)
6	Fixed costs ($1,000 per year)
7	Selling expenses ($1,000 per year)
8	General and administrative expenses ($1,000 per year)
9	Other expenses ($1,000 per year)

*Read: MBF = thousands of board feet; MSF = thousands of square feet.

TABLE 7-3. Plywood Model (24, p. 74)

Preliminary calculations	
Desired plywood production	DPP = V1
Pressing capacity	PC = P4 if time P5
	P4 × (1 + P6) if time P5
Actual plywood production	APP = Min (DPP, PC)
Required veneer	RV = APP/P17
Veneer capacity	VC = P7 if time P8
	P7 × (1 + P9) if time P8
Veneer produced	VP = Min (RV, VC)
Purchas d veneer	PV = RV − VP
Required logs	RL = VP/P16
Lumber produced	FLP = VP/P18
Chips produced	CP = VP/P19
Own logs	FOL = P12 × RL
Forest service logs	FSL = RL − FOL

Line number	Description	Logic
.01	Plywood sales	APP × V2
.02	Chips sales	V4 × CP
.03	Lumber sales	V3 × FLP
.04	Sales eliminations	− (.02 + .03) × P25
1.00	Total sales	.01 + .02 + .03 + .04
1.01	Discounts and allowances (plywood)	(.01) × P13
1.02	Commissions on plywood	(.01) × P14
1.03	Freight-out for plywood	APP × P15
2.00	Total allowances	1.01 + 1.02 + 1.03
3.00	Net sales	1.00 − 2.00
3.01	Raw materials	[P10 × P12 × RL + P11 × (1 − P12) × RL] × GROWTH (P2,0)
3.02	Veneer purchase	PV × V5
3.03	Operating supplies, manufacturing overhead	[VP × P20 + APP × P21] × GROWTH (P2,0)
3.04	Labor	[VP × P22 + APP × P23] × P24 × GROWTH (P1,0)

TABLE 7-3. *(Continued)*

Line number Description		Logic
3.05	Raw material cost eliminations	$-P12 \times VP \times GROWTH$ $(P3,0) \times P26 \times P10/P16$
7.00	Total direct expenses	$3.01 + 3.02 + \ldots + 3.05$
8.00	Gross profit	$3.00 - 7.00$
9.00	Fixed costs	V6
10.00	Selling expenses	V7
11.00	General and administrative expenses	V8
12.00	Other expenses	V9
13.00	Total indirect expenses	$9.00 + 10.00 + 11.00 + 12.00$
14.00	Net profit before tax	$8.00 - 13.00$
22.00	Gross profit/net sales	$8.00/3.00$
23.00	Indirect expenses/net sales	$13.00/3.00$
24.00	Net profit/net sales	$14.00/3.00$
25.00	Plywood production (million square feet)	APP
26.00	Veneer production (million square feet)	VP
27.00	Lumber production (million board feet)	FLP
28.00	Chip productions (units)	CP
29.00	Percent of new veneer capacity needed	$[RV - VC]/VC$
30.00	Percent of new pressing capacity needed	$[DPP - PC]/PC$
31.00	Labor (1,000 man-hours)	$VP \times P22 + APP \times P23$

These extra lines can be varied at will to provide other computed measures if desired.

The great flexibility built into the model is related to the parameter list. The value of any parameter can be changed at will and the simulated effects of the change determined very quickly.

Asking Questions

An example of the profit and loss report for the plywood model is shown in the upper part of Figure 7-4. The report is for 1969 by quarters, based on actual data for quarters 3 and 4. Following the profit and loss report, the teletype has printed "P-L MODE =," asking whether any further manipulation of the profit and loss statement is desired. Let us see what happened to produce certain numbers in the exhibit:

The analyst responded in this instance by typing "7/." This number

YEAR 69

LINE ITEMS	QR1	QR2	QR3	QR4	YRT
SALES PLY	35800.0	37950.0	31200.0	33600.0	138550.0
SALES CHIPS	1350.0	1953.0	1827.0	1921.5	7051.5
SALES LUMBER	843.8	1260.0	1181.3	1260.0	4545.0
SALES ELIM					
TOTAL SALES	37993.8	41163.0	34208.3	36781.5	150146.5
D&A PLYWOOD	716.0	759.0	624.0	672.0	2771.0
COM PLY	2148.0	2277.0	1872.0	2016.0	8313.0
FREIGHT PLY	242.2	267.7	306.0	306.0	1122.0
TOT COM	3106.2	3303.7	2802.0	2994.0	12206.0
NET SALES	34887.5	37859.3	31406.3	33787.5	137940.5
RAW MATERIAL	4824.2	6831.2	6914.9	6999.7	25570.0
VENEER PURCH	8375.2	5694.4	9034.8	9252.4	32356.5
OP SUPPLIES	2860.8	3504.6	3844.5	3891.6	14101.2
LABOR	6544.8	8840.6	9181.2	9293.8	33860.4
COST ELIMIN					
COST OF SALE	22605.0	24870.2	28975.4	29437.6	105888.1
GROSS PROFIT	12282.5	12989.0	2430.9	4349.9	32052.4
FIXED COSTS	1250.0	1250.0	1250.0	1250.0	5000.0
SELLING EXP	750.0	750.0	750.0	750.0	3000.0
G&A EXPENSE	750.0	750.0	750.0	750.0	3000.0
OTHER EXPENSE	-125.0	-125.0	-125.0	-125.0	-500.00
TOT IND EXP	2875.0	2875.0	2875.0	2875.0	11500.0
NET PROFIT	9407.5	10114.0	-444.1	1474.9	20552.4
GP/NS	.35	.34	-.08	.13	.23
TIE/NS	.08	.08	-.09	.09	.08
NP/NS	.27	.27	-.01	.04	.15

P-L MODE = 7/

ITERATION

DESIRED YEARLY PROFIT = 0/

TOT SALES	PROFIT	FRAC I
150146.50	20552.36	1.0000
120117.20	14141.89	.8000
53870.76	.00	.3588

Figure 7-4. Example of a profit and loss report. (Harvard Business Review, *July–August 1970.*)

called for an iteration on a desired profit level, and the diagonal called for the execution of the command. The program responded by printing "ITERATION" and "DESIRED YEARLY PROFIT = ." At this point the analyst responded by inserting the desired profit figure. "0" was inserted to indicate a request for a calculation of sales required for break-even or zero profit.

The teletype then printed out the sales, profit, and fraction of sales to forecasted total sales for three levels of sales volume, including the break-even level. As we see in Figure 7-4, break-even takes place at yearly sales of $53,870.76, or 36 percent of the forecasted sales level.

The conversational language mentioned earlier is illustrated by the program's direct questions and the analyst's equally direct and simple answers.

Anticipating Effects

Now suppose that the manager wants to assess the impact of a labor cost increase on net profit. For example, the analyst could vary the value of

```
P-L MODE = 8/
PARAMETER SENSITIVITY
P#/MIN/MAX/INCREMENT/ = 24/5/6/.25/

        YEAR 69                    P/L

    P24 = 5.000

    LINE ITEMS                 YRT
    NET PROFIT                 20552.4

    P24 = 5.250

    LINE ITEMS                 YRT
    NET PROFIT                 18859.3

    P24 = 5.500

    LINE ITEMS                 YRT
    NET PROFIT                 17166.3

    P24 = 5.750

    LINE ITEMS                 YRT
    NET PROFIT                 15473.3

    P24 = 6.000

    LINE ITEMS                 YRT
    NET PROFIT                 13781.0
```

Figure 7-5. Effect of varying labor cost. (Harvard Business Review, *July–August 1970.*)

the parameter for labor cost per hour, denoted by the symbol "P24" in Figure 7-5. Parameter sensitivity is called for by specifying "P-L MODE =8/." The program responds by asking which parameter is to be varied, the range of variation, and the steps in which it is to be varied. The analyst types the parameter number, the minimum and maximum values of the parameter, and the increment of step size of the variation.

If the analyst wishes to see a plot of the sensitivity of net profit to labor cost, this can be called for from the standard programs available, as is shown in Figure 7-6. Note that over the range of the labor costs

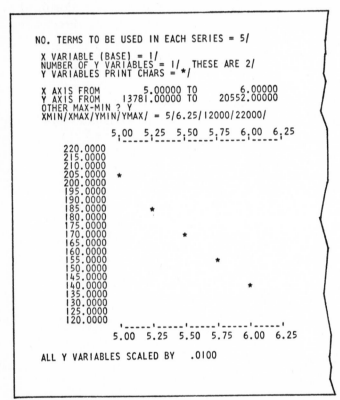

Figure 7-6. Sensitivity of net profit to labor cost. (Harvard Business Review, *July–August 1970.*)

stated, there is a nearly linear relation to net profit. Above the plot in Figure 7-6 are further examples of the conversational language employed. The statements on the left are questions asked by the program; to the right are the analyst's responses—in most instances simple numerical answers, such as the identification of the scales in the plot and their ranges.

Varied Potentials

Let us pause for a moment to reflect on the general nature of the input/
output structure represented by the plywood model. The upper half of
Figure 7-7 summarizes the nature of the input/output relationships for a
divisional type of operation such as that in the plywood model. A

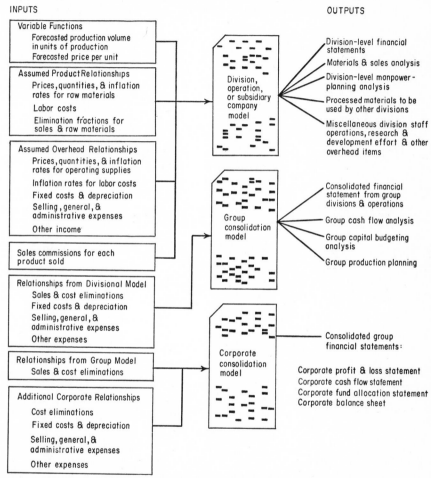

INPUTS

Variable Functions
  Forecasted production volume
  in units of production
  Forecasted price per unit

Assumed Product Relationships
  Prices, quantities, & inflation
  rates for raw materials
  Labor costs
  Elimination fractions for
  sales & raw materials

Assumed Overhead Relationships
  Prices, quantities, & inflation
  rates for operating supplies
  Inflation rates for labor costs
  Fixed costs & depreciation
  Selling, general, &
  administrative expenses
  Other income

Sales commissions for each
product sold

Relationships from Divisional Model
  Sales & cost eliminations
  Fixed costs & depreciation
  Selling, general, &
  administrative expenses
  Other expenses

Relationships from Group Model
  Sales & cost eliminations

Additional Corporate Relationships
  Cost eliminations
  Fixed costs & depreciation
  Selling, general, &
  administrative expenses
  Other expenses

Division, operation, or subsidiary company model

Group consolidation model

Corporate consolidation model

OUTPUTS

Division-level financial statements
Materials & sales analysis
Division-level manpower-planning analysis
Processed materials to be used by other divisions
Miscellaneous division staff operations, research & development effort & other overhead items

Consolidated financial statement from group divisions & operations
Group cash flow analysis
Group capital budgeting analysis
Group production planning

Consolidated group financial statements:

Corporate profit & loss statement
Corporate cash flow statement
Corporate fund allocation statement
Corporate balance sheet

Figure 7-7. Input-output relationships. (Harvard Business Review, *July–August 1970.*)

number of such models may be consolidated to form group models with
the general input/output relationship shown in the middle section of
the figure; or the process of consolidation can be carried still further so
that a model of the whole corporation is formed, as in the lower part of
the figure.

What top executives are likely to be most interested in, of course, are the group and corporate models. Yet, by using the kind of structure illustrated by the plywood model as a basic building block, together with the successive layers of aggregation indicated in Figure 7-7 management can ask for the effects of proposed changes in prices, costs, equipment, financing, and so on, at any level; it can estimate the net effects on the total corporation quickly and accurately.

The revenue and cost flows involved in the input/output relationships appear in Figure 7-8 in generalized form for a large, integrated

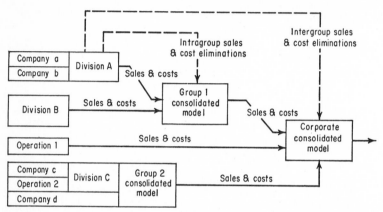

Figure 7-8. Flows of sales and costs. (Harvard Business Review, *July–August 1970.*)

corporate operation where a complex of subsidiary companies and divisions is consolidated in group models and a corporate model. The flows of revenues and costs take into account sales among groups and divisions, as the dashed lines indicate.

Financial Flows at Potlatch

The company developed twenty-two models to describe its various operations, groups, and subsidiaries. The plywood model previously discussed is a good example of the type of models used by Potlatch (although actually the company's models are more sophisticated and involve more relationships). By interrelating these models, management can obtain a model for the whole corporation and thus see the end result of changes made at the operational or group levels.

Management decided to express its corporate financial planning in a real-time computer system because of the difficulties of assessing the interactions of interplant buying and selling and of changing product mixes. Furthermore, Potlatch management witnessed a continuous flow of proposals for change and improvement of operations at all levels. In the past, the assessment of the financial effects of many of these changes had involved long time lags. The new interactive system, however, greatly reduces the time and effort needed to evaluate alternate plans because the logic of the twenty-two models takes into account the complex financial flows between divisions and groups.

SYSTEM PERFORMANCE

The pioneering nature of the interactive planning system at Potlatch provides an unusual opportunity to observe changes in the state of the art since 1969, when it first became operational. Technically, we may observe that the noisy 10-character-per-second (cps) teletype terminal has been replaced by a 30-cps noiseless 28-pound portable thermoprinter. Computer response time and quality of transmissions have greatly improved. The communication network on which Potlatch is operational is now available to all facilities and is international in scope.

The software has evolved from semistructured financial statements to an open modeling environment permitting total freedom of definition. User commands and sequences of financial manipulations can now be defined uniquely to Potlatch and in the terminology of that organization.

The system in 1974 has 30 models, 3,000 lines of logic, and 4,000 data elements. The planning horizon is seven years by quarters. It was originally intended that members of the planning staff would take computer terminals to the divisions where they would assist in preparing plans on site, using data supplied by those organizations. With the reorganization, the divisions assumed this responsibility so that some of the plans were constructed by hand. The macro computer model was used by corporate planning to consolidate these plans.

One by one the divisions have recruited talent to operate the computer-based system, models have been modified in accordance with the reorganization, and training programs have been held and terminals located in the field. As a result the 1974 planning cycle was the first at Potlatch to utilize a totally integrated online planning capability.

Patterns of Usage

Inspection of the monthly index of connect hours in Figure 7-9 reveals wide fluctuations.[1] Much of this variation is seasonal, ranging from a low of approximately .57 in the summer to a peak of 1.6 in the fall, with rather intensive usage early in the year.

There is no clearly defined time trend in terminal connect hours, as some periods of very high usage are related to intense model usage. It is interesting to observe that the average usage for the first quarter of 1973 was the same as in the corresponding period in 1970.

[1]Month one refers to the first month operational after system development and shakedown. Index base 1 is the average monthly usage during the first quarter.

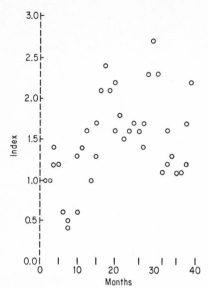

Figure 7-9. Potlatch terminal connect hours index. *(Courtesy of Potlatch Corporation and On-Line Decisions, Inc.)*

The efficiency of computer utilization as measured by central processing units (CPU) per connect hour has remained relatively constant over the past five years at around 200 seconds per hour connect. The trend in data storage is well defined, Figure 7-10 showing a correlation to time of around .9. Data storage at Potlatch has increased at an annual

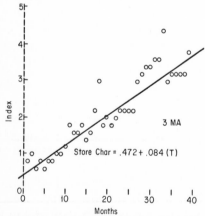

Figure 7-10. Potlatch index of data storage (three-month moving average). *(Courtesy of Potlatch Corporation and On-Line Decisions, Inc.)*

rate of 95 percent (not compounded) over the four-year period of the study. Presumably, this startling growth in data base is at least partially the result of decentralizing the system to the divisions.

Economics

Computer costs on an outside times-share vendor have risen rapidly at Potlatch over the past four years (Figure 7-11). This increase was not

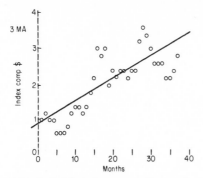

Figure 7-11. Potlatch index computer cost. *(Courtesy of Potlatch Corporation and On-Line Decisions, Inc.)*

due to connect charges, which have remained relatively constant, but mostly is the result of the soaring data storage. Vendors' prices have remained approximately constant during this period. CPU charges are a relatively unimportant 15 percent, while storage is approaching 70 percent of the total bill.

MANAGEMENT COMMENTARY

It is useful to supplement the formal description of the planning system and process with commentary from the personnel primarily involved. Unfortunately, the division personnel do not yet have sufficient experience with the computer-based system to add their comments, so we must turn to the corporate staff.

Vice President, Planning and Business Development

"Potlatch Corporation is staffed very lean with the result that we have little competition between the division and the corporation in performing the planning function. We all have more than we can take care of.

"The computer-based planning system has made possible the handling of an enormous amount of data and an almost-infinite capability to play "What if?" A potential problem is that managers tend to become quantitatively oriented. The computer may give them a false sense of security. Qualitative factors are often more important in interpretation of performance and in determining planning strategies. Formerly, we would sweat to get a number, and now the computer can do a sensitivity in seconds. It is too easy to get numbers; judgment is required as to what is a good assumption.

"Potlatch has many options. The function of this department is to determine conceptually what the company should be and to coordinate the operating groups's development of the five-year plans. The planning gap is our primary concern along with management of the growth trend.

"We have a series of profit opportunities and are concerned with timing them to obtain a pattern of more stable growth in the highly cyclical markets in which we function. We use the computer to do sensitivity analysis of the timing of capital expenditures to prevent earnings distortion such as would be caused by several major installations coming online at one time.

"We could not look at many alternatives without the computer, which allows us to play with volume and prices. The computer is invaluable for sensitivity analysis to identify and simulate changes in such key variables as product mix, raw materials costs, and capital overruns. We also use the computer to iterate to objectives as a prescreen. Starting with the market, we work back from return-on-investment objectives to determine resource requirements and feasibility.

"The chief executive of Potlatch has a commitment to planning and gives freely of his time. Plans are living, dynamic documents that require involvement of operating managers from the divisions. A fair plan with field support is better than the best plan without such commitment."

Former Director of Corporate Planning

"I've consistently been surprised at the flexibility of the computer models under a variety of planning philosophies during the last five years. The models were conceived during a period of extremely centralized strategic planning, a period when the corporate staff was seldom given an opportunity even to discuss alternative futures with the downstream line organization. The models were intended to solve the purely mechanical problems of number generation across a variety of businesses, accounting methodologies, and geographic differences.

"The models were implemented during a period of progressively increasing planning decentralization. The corporate staff was then responsible for communicating a planning philosophy and an expression of headquarters needs to the line organization. The models served a facilitating role as a device through which both groups could communicate and identify their own areas of concern. During this same period, online simulation was used extensively at the corporate level in acquisition and major project analyses. I believe it helped us to avoid some substantial exposures by encouraging more rigorous and careful analysis than had prior practices.

"The planning function has now been successfully decentralized, with an appropriate emphasis placed on the qualitative aspects of the strategies of Potlatch's businesses. The models now serve, where they are used, as a time-saving device to permit managers to concentrate on the nature of their underlying assumptions without getting bogged down in the quantitative implications of strategic alternatives and sensitivities. They also provide a convenient data base for senior management to use in their qualitative deliberations.

Planner Responsible for the Computer-based Planning System

"As a result of internal transfers and promotions, I am the only one left of six men formerly associated with this system. The change from centralization to decentralization has had a great impact on the planning function. The system would never have survived without modularity and flexibility.

"The stand-alone corporate macro model has been the one most used. This is the third full planning cycle and each time the system works better. For the first time, all our divisions have terminals and use the system. Division consolidation and product-line planning is in the division; we pull the corporate plan together and coordinate the effort. The divisions keep their own data bases and build their own models now. We are using young people from the business schools who take right to it. Recruiting qualified people has been our biggest problem.

"We use five years' history, the current year, and five years' future data. The strategic plan covers the past two years and five years quarterly into the future.

"The president has requested that he never be shown raw computer output, so we do not use the computer system for generation of the final corporate reports."

CONCLUSION

Of first importance in this study is the fact that planning generally, and the computer-based planning system specifically, receive strong support from senior management. Certainly the system would not have survived through the major organizational changes without this endorsement. An important aspect of the Potlatch philosophy with respect to planning is that human factors should take preference over technical considerations. As quoted earlier, "A fair plan with field support is better than the best plan without such commitment."

It is interesting to note the observation of the vice president of planning and business development that there is a tendency for the qualitative aspects of planning to be sacrificed for the quantitative because numbers come so easily in a computer-based planning system. This qualitative concern will be echoed several times in succeeding cases. Quantitative outputs of the computer may give a false sense of security to management. Conversely, this case suggests that the use of the computer-based system encouraged rigorous and careful analysis that helped the firm to avoid substantial exposures.

The impact and rationale of planning decentralization of Potlatch should be compared to the centralization experience of Wells Fargo in a later case. In neither case could the computer-based planning system have survived without modularity and flexibility in the basic architecture.

The use of a computer-based strategic planning system to design a future is nicely illustrated by its application to timing capital expenditures to prevent earnings distortion. Filling the planning gap between desired and projected earnings is of primary concern in the strategic planning exercise.

This case beautifully illustrates the *integrated* approach to strategic planning. The profit centers are analyzed both individually and in total. The strategic planning perspective is holistic in that the parts are analyzed in the context of the overall organization to assure that the individual growth plans are in coordination with the long-range plans of the total corporation. Long-range capital allocation among the operating units is accomplished with a perspective of the alternatives available.

After four years, Potlatch is just reaching the point of full implementation of the computer-based planning system. It may be argued that the installation was premature, since it was somewhat in advance of the widespread understanding by operating management of its concept and function.

It is also apparent, however, that this exercise has resulted in an extremely well-conceived and formalized strategic planning process at Potlatch. Objectives and planning premises are clearly defined and communicated to all operating groups. The data base is complete. During the interim of the reorganization, the macro model has been most useful in analyzing acquisitions and performing consolidations from manually prepared divisional inputs. Strategic planning questions could be simulated at the corporate level. Divisional models have been recast and debugged. Key variables have been identified.

The diverse operations of Potlatch are now truly integrated by a nationwide computer-based planning system. Trained personnel and computer terminals are available in each division, with conversational capability to interact with their respective data bases and organizational models. Plans can be rapidly consolidated at corporate headquarters to determine the impact of divisional activities on aggregate performance. The full payoff from this effort is yet to be determined, but it should become apparent in the next planning period.

8

Mergers and Acquisitions

The major concern in strategic planning is filling the planning gap between projected performance of present lines of business and the growth goals established by management. The gap can be filled through internal actions, such as new-product developments and penetration of new markets, or by acquisition of external operations. Mergers and acquisitions constitute a major application of computer-based planning systems because of the complexity and importance of the decisions as well as the time urgency frequently involved in these transactions.

Merger negotiations, as reflected in this model, are essentially opportunistic in nature and involve a strategic encounter of emotional and economic forces requiring an integration of conflicting interests (25, pp. 3–10). The language of the model is that of the securities market, although the economic confrontation occurs in a highly charged emotional environment. The management objective of increased stock price and its prerequisite, growth in earnings per share, is very much the focus of most strategic planning today.

THE EMOTIONAL ENVIRONMENT

The economic model that follows must be modified to reflect the psychological environment within which the negotiations are conducted; a major consideration is the element of "power" as reflected in control. The president of the selling company is very conscious of relinquishing managerial control as well as ownership, and henceforth will have to subordinate personal objectives and ethics to the management interests of the acquiring company. Self-interest becomes a prime consideration under these conditions. The top-management group of the acquiring company is similarly concerned with control, since the acquisition represents a further dilution of their equity position.

THE BUYER, AN ECONOMIC MODEL

The objective of corporate mergers has been traditionally visualized as establishing a synergism—full utilization of physical facilities, acquisition of new lines to distribute through existing marketing channels, increased technical know-how, stronger financial position, geographic expansion, and so on. In many instances this may be the case, but more frequently, acquisitions reflect the immediate objective of increase in stock price. Acquisitions, in turn, often depend upon achieving a premium market price for the corporate stock, the medium of exchange by which most major acquisition programs have been accomplished:

Premium market price ⟶ acquisitions ⟶ growth

Acquisitions are, then, a means of achieving the corporate objective of growth (which happens to correspond to the executive objectives of recognition, challenge, and compensation). The objective of the corporate shareholders is also satisfied by the company's achieving a premium market price, since this is the only way they can benefit from the growth of the firm; dividends are rarely distributed by a true growth company. *The immediate objective of most corporate acquisitions is to effect a maximum immediate increase in the market value of the corporate stock. The stock price is determined by (1) the price/earnings ratio and (2) the earnings per share.*

The Price/Earnings Ratio (P/E)

The feasibility of any stock acquisition program depends primarily upon the maintenance of a price/earnings ratio that will allow the buyer to offer a premium to the seller and still realize an increase in earnings per share through the acquisition. Acceptance of this reality is fundamental to understanding the problems of corporate acquisitions. The price/earnings ratio is subjectively determined by the investors' estimate of the market appreciation potential of the company stock and is closely related to the anticipated growth potential of the industry. This anticipation is primarily psychological and subject to sharp fluctuations that are largely beyond the control of the company. Unfortunately, the acquisition that increases current earnings per share the most (where there is the greatest differential in price/earnings ratios) may result in a reduction in investors' confidence.

Earnings per Share

As mentioned previously, the market price of the company stock is determined by both the price/earnings ratio and the earnings per share. The effect of an acquisition on earnings per share appears to be easily calculated:

Combined earnings per share after merger (E/S)

$$= \frac{\text{present earnings } (Eb) + \text{acquired earnings } (E_s)}{\text{stock outstanding before merger } (S_b) + \text{stock to be issued } (S_i)}$$

Should the negotiator use verifiable historical earnings or anticipated future earnings? The latter appear more significant since management is concerned with the effect of the acquisition on immediate or future earnings; however, the buyer must also evaluate the effect of the acquisition on consolidated historical growth trends in sales, earnings, and earnings per share.

The economic buyer will attempt to maximize the market price of the stock by minimizing the number of shares outstanding and maximizing earnings available to common stock as well as maximizing the growth potential of the firm and the investigators' confidence in that potential (see Figure 8-1).

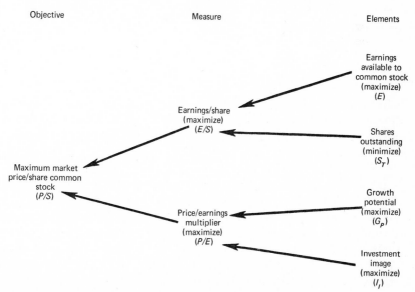

Figure 8-1. Summary of buyer's program. (*From James B. Boulden, "Merger Negotiations: A Decision Mode," Business Horizons, February 1969.*)

THE SELLER: AN ECONOMIC MODEL

The economic objective of the seller is to maximize the total realizable value received in exchange for equity interests. The total value actually realized by the seller depends partly upon the form of the transaction — cash, debentures, common stock, deferred compensations, and the like. Cash is immediate and certain in sum; however, the seller often prefers an exchange of stock, so as to postpone the payment of income taxes. The time factor now becomes critical —the total value is realizable when? The stock market is notorious for sharp fluctuations in value, with the result that the restrictions on the sale of the stock often become a limiting factor in estimating value.

Aside from legal restrictions, there is also the practical question of the stability of the market to absorb the stock. If dollar volume traded is light relative to the stockholdings of the selling shareholders, the result will be a sharp fall in the price of the stock when any effort is made to "unload." Generally, the sellers will have a higher gain potential to the extent they (1) take stock instead of cash; (2) emphasize long-term rather than short-term gain; (3) choose capital appreciation rather than ordinary income from dividends; (4) take speculative instead of guaranteed stock; and (5) negotiate a price contingent on future performance rather than a flat sum. Each of these speculative alternatives requires a sacrifice of security and a potential loss in equity.

USE OF THE MODEL IN NEGOTIATIONS

The first and primary point of negotiation in every merger is mutual acceptance of a value for the exchange. Extensive economy in time and expense is effected by negotiating the economic basis for exchange before entering into financial, legal, and accounting audits. These tools should be used to confirm the assumptions, but the economic feasibility must be established first, at least within a relatively narrow negotiating framework.

The buyer focuses on earnings per share, attempting to maximize this figure by minimizing the number of shares issued. The seller, conversely, is attempting to maximize market value by maximizing the number of shares received. The solution is complicated by fluctuations in market price of the common stock through the period of negotiations. Another problem arises in translation, since the seller is thinking in terms of the price per share received for the seller's stock, while the negotiations are in the form of total number of shares and the price of the buyer's stock.

A first step in negotiations is to establish feasibility and define the negotiating range. The buyer normally cannot issue a number of shares that will dilute projected earnings per share for future periods; conversely, the seller will not accept a price for the stock that is less than the current value on the market.

The manager, or more often, a financial analyst, inputs data on the buyer's current earnings and stock price. These data remain stored in computer memory through the screening of a number of merger prospects. The information is updated regularly as the number of outstanding shares increases, the market price varies, or earnings change. The computer program contains various constraints, such as ensuring that

```
SELLER PARAMETERS
1      3225.000  = PRESENT DIVIDEND  ($THOUSANDS OR $THOUSANDS/SHARE)
2        63.500  = COMMON STOCK PRICE ($/SHARE)
3          0.    = ASKING PRICE  ($THOUSANDS OR $THOUSANDS/SHARE)
4      2691.000  = OUTSTANDING COMMON SHARES (THOUSANDS)
5      9300.000  = EARNINGS AFTER TAX ($THOUSANDS OR $THOUSANDS/SHARE)
6         0.025  = NET WORTH ($THOUSANDS OR $THOUSANDS/SHARE)
7    190000.000  = TOTAL SALES ($THOUSANDS)
MERGE MODE =?

3
BUYER PARAMETERS
1        33.000  = COMMON STOCK PRICE ($/SHARE)
2         2.418  = TOTAL AFTER TAX EARNINGS ($MILLIONS)
3         2.418  = TOTAL OUTSTANDING COMMON SHARES (MILLIONS)
4         1.500  = PREMIUM IN E/S ON COMMON OFFERED OVER PRESENT BUYER'S E/S (FRACTION)
5         0.250  = PREMIUM PAID OVER CURRENT SELLER'S MARKET PRICE (FRACTION)
6         0.    = PREMIUM ON SELLER'S DIVIDEND OVER THAT PRESENTLY PAID (FRACTIONAL)
7         0.050  = DIVIDEND CARRIED ON PREFERRED (FRACTION)
8         2.000  = # COMMON SHARES/PREFERRED SHARE UPON CONVERSION
9        15.000  = NET WORTH ($MILLIONS)
10       80.000  = TOTAL SALES ($MILLIONS)
11      100.000  = PRICE OF PREFERRED STOCK ($/SHARE)
MERGE MODE =?

7
NOT FEASIBLE PP TOO LARGE
249. =STOP
251. +READY          START(0)
ENTER SELLER NAME
GENERAL SIGNAL
MERGE MODE =?
8
   GENERAL SIGN COMMON $ 63.50/SHARE      BUYER COMMON $ 33.00/SHARE
       4518124.94   SHARES COMMON STOCK     VALUE ($1000)=149098.12
        645000.00   SHARES PREFERRED STOCK VALUE ($1000)= 64500.00
     213598124.00   PURCHASE PRICE
             79.37  EQUIV. PRICE SELLERS STOCK
EPSA= 2.05   EPSB=  1.60   TESTAB= 2.50
```

	BUYER	SELLER	COMBINED 1	COMBINED 2
SALES ($1000)	80000.00	190000.00	270000.00	270000.00
PROFITS ($1000)	2418.00	9300.00	8493.00	11718.00
COMMON SHARES (1000)	2418.15	4518.12	6936.27	8226.27
EARNINGS/SHARE	1.00	1.60	1.22	1.42
EQUITY / SHARE	6.20	11.58	11.86	10.00

249. =STOP

Figure 8-2. Merger screening by computer. *(From James B. Boulden, "Merger Negotiations: A Decision Mode,"* Business Horizons, *February 1969.)*

the acquisition will not dilute earnings per share before or after conversion of preferred stock, and that the acquisition will not threaten management control of the combined companies. The seller's basic data are then typed into the terminal. An input and output are shown in Figure 8-2.

The computer output indicates whether a merger is economically feasible and the terms for a transaction that will meet the seller's requirements and maximize the buyer's earnings per share after the merger. If the transaction is not feasible, the program will so indicate along with the basis for the decision. The manager may elect to waive this constraint, and the program will again compute the basis of a feasible transaction.

As mentioned previously, the feasibility of a merger depends upon maintenance of a positive differential between the price per earnings multiples of the buyer and seller, and these are continually changing. Therefore, the analyst will want to explore the effect of a change in the market price of the stock and may ask the program to compute the effect of this change in price upon some factor such as the equivalent value received by the seller, the number of shares exchanged remaining constant. Figure 8-3 is an example of such an output.

STOCK PRICE	PURCHASE PRICE	SELLERS PRICE/SH
$ 30.00	$ 60000.00	$ 150.00
$ 32.00	$ 64000.00	$ 160.00
$ 34.00	$ 68000.00	$ 170.00
$ 36.00	$ 72000.00	$ 180.00
$ 38.00	$ 76000.00	$ 190.00
$ 40.00	$ 80000.00	$ 200.00

Figure 8-3. Stock price iteration. *(From James B. Boulden, "Merger Negotiations: A Decision Mode,"* Business Horizons, *February 1969.)*

Elaborate computer models are commercially available for the processing of historical data on the buyer and the seller, with a comprehensive output of financial statements past and future. These programs require more extensive data and projections than are normally available at the initial stage in negotiations. Hence, they are more useful after the general terms of the transaction have been established and a preliminary agreement has been reached. At that point, an expanded computer simulation can be very valuable in exploring alternative forms of structuring the transaction (see Table 8-1). Because of the complexity of these negotiations and the existence of diverse and sometimes nonquantifiable objectives, it has generally not been feasible to use optimizing techniques in this analysis.

FINANCIAL ANALYSIS APPLICATION

In one case, the acquisition involved a manufacturer of equipment for natural-resource exploration. Part of that equipment was leased and some sold outright, both activities involving different but unknown profit margins. Domestic markets for the products were declining while export markets were growing. Profitability forecasting was further clouded by the existence of (1) large seasonal and cyclical sales patterns, (2) changes in accounting practices, (3) reorganization, and (4) dirty accounting data.

It was believed that certain properties could be sold off after the merger and remaining production facilities consolidated with those of the acquiring company, which transaction would generate significant cash. Time was of the essence in negotiating the deal.

The historical data for the proposed acquisition were loaded into the storage files of a time-shared computer and subsequently messaged, using statistical routines to eliminate the "noise" occasioned by poor accounting practices. Distorted data series were then broken out and recombined with other series to obtain consistency of reporting and accounting. Seasonal and cyclical fluctuations were eliminated to identify trends in physical volume of sales and leases.

Multiple correlation was used to relate costs to sales and leases and hence to derive profit margins for each area of activity. Margins and volumes were then forecasted mechanistically and compared with the estimates supplied by the seller. Adjustment was made for the differential performance among various major product lines in domestic and international markets.

The divestment of facilities was simulated and the resultant profit and cash flow forecasts were combined with the profit simulations of the acquiring company. Alternative simulation runs were made under best and worst assumptions as they impacted return on investment and earnings per share.

It was apparent at this point that the acquisition had been dressed up for sale and that the purchase price was not justified. The basic analysis and graphic outputs were presented to the seller, who then agreed to a major reduction in asking price. The time required for this total experience was one month, of which two weeks were spent by the accountants in gathering the data and entering them into the computer. The merger was consummated.

A MULTINATIONAL MERGER

In another case, the merger involved two giant multinational companies. A consulting firm was retained to investigate the operations and

TABLE 8-1. Acquisition Analysis

Corporation price	$54.00	Ratio 0.5926	Corporation common dividend	$1.0000
Company price	$32.00		Dividend to company	$0.8000

Per share of company

	Dividend	Market value
0.4706 Shares corporation common	$0.4706	$25.41
0.1220 Shares corporation convertible preferred	$0.3294	$ 6.59
0.5926 Total	$0.8000	$32.00

Dividend on convertible preferred is $2.7000   Return on conversion price 5.00 percent
Number of new common shares is 229647   Number of new convertible preferred shares is 59538
Conversion ratio = 1.00 share corporation common for 1.00 share convertible preferred
488000 shares of common stock at $32.00 per share = $15616000.00 total value

Acquisition projection

Year	1961	1962	1963	1964	1965	1966	1967	1968	1969	1974
Corporation earnings per share	$ 1.27	1.53	1.81	2.24	2.44	2.63	3.00	3.28	3.56	3.85
Corporation operating earnings	25000	29000	34000	42000	47000	51000	57200	62700	68200	73700
New company earnings	157	175	195	217	241	268	295	325	358	394
Combined earnings	25157	29175	34195	42217	47241	51268	57495	63025	68558	74094
New preferred dividends	161	161	161	161	161	161	161	161	161	161
Net to common	24996	29014	34034	42056	47080	51107	57334	62864	68397	73933
Corporation shares outstanding	16084	16248	16288	16632	17070	17480	17480	17480	17480	17480
New common shares	230	230	230	230	230	230	230	230	230	230

Total common shares	16314	16478	16518	16862	17300	17710	17710	17710	17710	17710
Combined earnings per share	$ 1.53	1.76	2.06	2.49	2.72	2.89	3.24	3.55	3.86	4.17
Earnings increment/decrement	0.26	0.23	0.25	0.25	0.28	0.26	0.24	0.27	0.30	0.32
Conversion of convertible preferred										
New common shares	16314	16478	16518	16862	17300	17710	17710	17710	17710	17710
Converted shares	60	60	60	60	60	60	60	60	60	60
Total	16373	16537	16577	16921	17359	17769	17769	17769	17769	17769
Combined earnings per share	$ 1.54	1.76	2.06	2.49	2.72	2.89	3.24	3.55	3.86	4.17
Earnings increment/decrement	0.27	0.23	0.25	0.25	0.28	0.26	0.24	0.27	0.30	0.32

Source: James B. Boulden and Elwood S. Buffa, "The Strategy of Interdependent Decisions," California Management Review, vol. I, no. 4, Summer 1959.

recommend the basis for a securities exchange. The models were built in Europe and stored via satellite on computer files in Cleveland, Ohio.

The consultants used the models in Chicago to analyze the transaction. Further attention was given in depth to the various major subsidiaries of the buyer and the seller which were dispersed throughout Europe and the United States. Consultants boarded airplanes with portable terminals in hand for on-the-spot conferences with line executives.

Local telephone calls in various cities provided access to the common data base and the merger models, so that it was not necessary to shift data or accounting staff from one location to another. Various alternatives were simulated, including divestiture or consolidation of common operations between the two companies. Assumptions and forecasts were made specific through use of the computer-based system.

Again, as in the first example, time was critical and the computer most useful. Because of the availability of commercial time-share services with multinational telecommunication networks as well as general-purpose software, the consultants were able to build a complete, customized computer-based planning system for this specific problem within a few months.

SUMMARY

Acquisitions are one means of achieving the corporate objective of growth. The successful acquisition program often depends upon a premium market price resulting from increased earnings and maintenance of a high price/earnings ratio, both of which can be enhanced by good acquisitions. The result is, therefore, that a successful acquisition program becomes a self-generative process. Stock acquisitions become increasingly acceptable as a large positive differential is established between the price/earnings ratios of buyer and seller.

A successful acquisition program depends upon satisfying the seller's objective of maximum total realizable value, a deceptively simple statement. Assistance from the best legal and accounting minds, as well as flexibility and sensitivity on the part of the buyer, is required to satisfy the often-conflicting requirements of owners and managers.

The basic economic model, as developed in this chapter, is well suited to computer simulation. A simple screening model has been found useful in reviewing merger candidates and establishing feasibility of various acquisition alternatives. More elaborate models are useful at a later point in negotiations to explore the detailed financial effect of the transaction.

Because of the complexity of merger negotiations and the existence of diverse and sometimes nonquantifiable objectives, it is generally not possible to use optimizing techniques in this analysis. Simulation and executive judgment are the norms. Although the models may be customized to the specific transaction, the resulting simulations become inputs to the computer-based planning system of the buying company for a macro perspective on the strategic implications of the transaction.

Financial Planning / Finance-America Corporation

Financial planning, as concerned with sources and uses of funds, is a function of most computer-based planning systems. In some organizations, such as FinanceAmerica Corporation, a Bank America financial service company, the orientation of the total system is toward this function. In other organizations, the planning of financial flows is accomplished through using one or a few specialized models. In either case, the computer-based models are used for:

1. Forecasting financial requirements

2. Projecting internal generation of funds

3. Determining borrowing and investment strategy to secure or utilize cash surplus from operations

4. Making financial analyses to compare performance with plan and formulate programs for more effective cash utilization

Uniquely, any action the financial manager takes is translated in full amount to net profits. The marketing manager may increase net profits by X dollars through greater sales of 20 times X, while a change of like amount in interest income or expenses by improved financial planning goes totally into the profit account.

FINANCIAL STRATEGY

Financial planning is sometimes taken as too simple to require the assistance of the computer. Indeed, it can be quite simple if the management visualizes only static inventories of financial resources and is content with merely assuring the solvency of the organization. However, financial planning can also be extremely complex if pursued in an aggressive manner to get the most mileage with available resources. The financial manager in the latter instance uses the computer-based system to simulate the dynamic flow of funds over time.

Consider the decision pattern involved when a substantial, unplanned cash deficit appears within the planning horizon (Figure 9-1). The first choice is whether the unexpected need will be accepted as

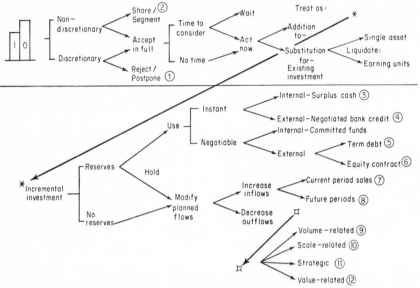

Figure 9-1. The structure of choice for a strategy of financial mobility. *(by permission of the Division of Research, Harvard Business School, for the copyright holder, The President and Fellows of Harvard College, copyright 1969.)*

valid. If the need is accepted, the planner then has the choice between committing reserves or modifying previously planned flows. Reserves may be instantly available or negotiable. Planned flows may be modified by increasing inflows or decreasing outflows. The decision structure becomes more and more complex as specific alternatives are defined.

Specific questions concerning the flow of funds to be simulated on the system may include:

1. Working capital

    a. What if cost inflation continues at *X* percent through the planning period?

    b. What if sales increase *Y* percent over plan?

    c. What if we go to *Z* days on payables, excepting those paying a cash discount?

    d. What if we tighten our trade credit to distributors?

 e. What if we extend the shelf life of our product to *M* months?
 f. What if we increase the down payment for special orders?
 g. How shall we allocate interest charges?

2. Short-term financing

 a. What if we lease instead of buy?
 b. What if we refinance our short-term debt?
 c. What should be the timing of the refinancing?
 d. What if interest rates decline one-half point?
 e. What line of credit will we need at the bank?
 f. What is our exposure to a 10 percent devaluation in pounds sterling?

3. Strategic planning

 a. Equity versus debt financing?
 b. Dividend policies?
 c. Acquisitions and mergers?
 d. Terms of financing?
 e. Inventory policy?

Although the planning system is not used for accounting purposes, it is sharply impacted by accounting policies as represented in the logic of the system. A leasing company, for example, uses the same computer-based system to simulate alternatively the organization as it appears to management, to the shareholders, and to the government. Planning models are frequently used to simulate alternative accounting policies as applied to specific problems or to the public image of the corporation. For example:

Methods of depreciation

Methods of accounting for income

Methods of cost allocation

Term of write-off

Adjustment of reserves

Timing is frequently a critical question in financial simulations. Management is interested not only in what action should take place, but also in when it should occur. Cash flows are very substantially affected by time relationships, such as receivables to sales, sales to promotion, and promotion to seasonality. The computer is vitally important in handling these complex functions.

Capital projects having major impact on short- and/or long-term profit and cash flow are frequently modeled individually and interfaced with the planning system. The timing of these capital expenditures is important. Many organizations are concerned with maintaining a pattern of smooth growth, which may be seriously distorted by a concentration of capital investment in any one period.

THE FINANCE MODEL

The individual finance model (as distinguished from a financial planning system such as is described for FinanceAmerica in the following case) should be an integral part of the computer-based planning system, as shown in Figure 9-2. Most planning systems of any scope have such a model.

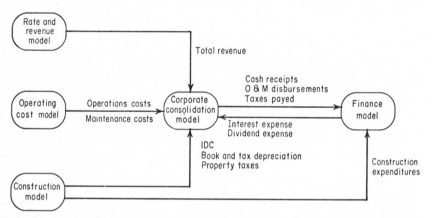

Figure 9-2. Financing model in context. *(From John Ogden, "What Happens If," Public Utilities Fortnightly, 1972.)*

The structure of the financing model may be similar to that shown in Figure 9-3. The purpose of this model is to simulate the effect of various financing programs as they impact projected profits and cash flows. The model also generates bank lines of credit, interest payments and expense schedules, and loan repayment schedules. The time scale is usually monthly for the first year, after which it may be quarterly or annually out to ten years or more.

The inputs for the finance model are the operating cash requirements as generated by the annual planning model, or in some instances, the strategic planning or MACRO model, plus the requirements for the capital budget. Key input variables include anticipated money-market conditions and terms of proposed financing programs. The planning system files contain information on existing financing arrangements as well as policy guidelines and/or constraints imposed by lending agencies or previous financial instruments.

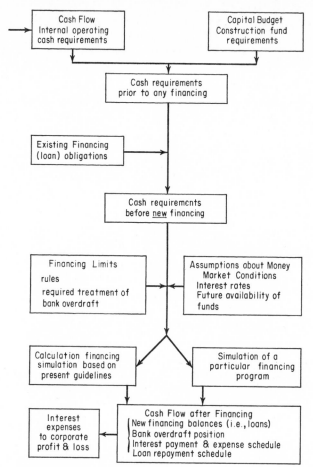

Figure 9-3. Structure of financing model. *(Courtesy of On-Line Decisions, Inc.)*

The cash requirements for internal operations are consolidated with the capital budget requirements and adjusted for any existing financial obligations, such as loan repayments. The resulting calculation represents cash required before new financing. Financing strategy can then be calculated automatically, given the planners' assumptions of money-market conditions and preestablished financing constraints, such as ratios of debt to equity. Alternatively, the planner can input the requirements of a particular financing program, such as a major acquisition, and explore methods of providing the resources for that project.

The output of the system is a new cash flow forecast for the organization as well as detailed schedules for interest expense and loan repayment and the bank overdraft position. Interest expense data become input to the profit-planning system in computing corporate profit and loss and generating the revised balance sheet.

The finance model is normally interactive so as to accommodate a broad range of alternative financial proposals and analyses. The purpose of the model is to remove the busy work from financial planning, thereby releasing planners to do the creative analytical and qualitative work for which they are trained.

FINANCEAMERICA, INC., 1972–1974[1] : A LARGE INTEGRATED FINANCIAL PLANNING SYSTEM

FinanceAmerica Corporation provides a broad range of financial services. The total assets of the company at the end of 1972 were 714 million dollars and net worth was 124 million dollars. The activities of the company, as measured by volume of receivables purchased and loans made, have been rather level at approximately one billion dollars per year over the period of 1968 to 1972. Net income in 1972 exceeded 6 million dollars.

FinanceAmerica Corporation operated as a wholly owned subsidiary of GAC Corporation until the end of 1973, when it was sold to Bank-America Corporation. FinanceAmerica has been selected for discussion because of the difficult problems of money management characteristic of the business in which it is engaged and for which application it has developed a very effective interactive computer-based planning system.

Organization and Operations

The organization structure of FinanceAmerica in 1973 is indicated by Figure 9-4. The line operations in the company are Consumer Credit, Diversified, and Rediscount. Consumer Credit activities are conducted through 440 offices operating in 41 states. This division provides direct loans to consumers, finances retail sales, and furnishes wholesale financing for mobile home, marine, and other large consumer purchases. The average installment loan is approximately $1,000, which amount is continually increasing in accordance with continuing emphasis on larger loans to meet consumer demand and realize the increased profit potential of this type of loan.

The Diversified Division provides financing for product distribution primarily from manufacturer to retailer. This private-brands service

---

[1]Much of the following material is abstracted from a presentation developed by Leo G. Connors, Vice President, Financial Planning, FinanceAmerica Corporation.

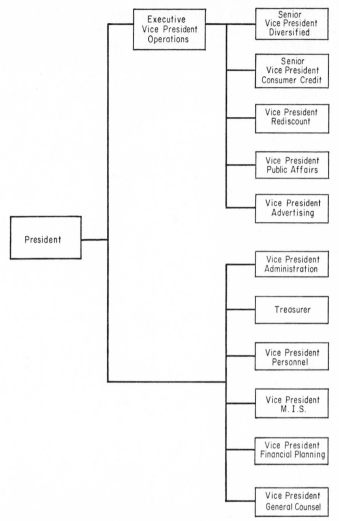

Figure 9-4. FinanceAmerica organization chart. *(Courtesy of Finance-America Corporation.)*

utilizes an in-branch network of computer systems to furnish marketing data, financial records, and other management and business information to clients. Private-brands volume of business has been continually increasing over the past decade, largely through the financing of consumer products in distributor and dealer inventories.

General Rediscount Corporation, the rediscount financing division, provides funds to independent finance companies. This division has experienced the effect of increased competitive activity from commercial banks, but has succeeded in adding new clients to its portfolio by new rediscount financing programs for companies with receivables in related fields.

Operations of the company include extensive facilities for credit evaluation ranging from the level of the small consumer loan to include multi-million-dollar business financing. The company channels sizable premium writings for credit life, accident, and health and property coverages to insurance companies, primarily to a group of companies which were direct subsidiaries until the end of 1973.

An important facet of the company activity is the management of money. Sources of this raw material include bank line borrowings, commercial paper, long-term debt issues placed both privately and publicly, preferred issues, and common stock equity. The debt categories are senior subordinated and junior subordinated debt, and capital notes.

The ability of a finance company to expand is based on the leverage which lenders provide, and this varies with the type and quality of financing activity. A ratio of eighteen debt and preferred over one common equity is possible. Leverage is an important variable for simulation on the computer-based planning system, with particular reference to individual profit centers. A related and very important planning variable is borrowing cost, which constitutes 40 percent of gross income.

As a result of the complex debt structure, there are many borrowing restrictions on the finance company. General restrictions relate to net worth, senior debt, and dividends. Other very specific restrictions apply to certain receivables or categories of lending.

Planning

The management of finance companies has historically been opportunistic in nature as developed in the major periods of expansion during the 1920s, 1930s, and 1940s, when major emphasis was placed on automobile financing. Operating and financial guidelines were developed at that time and used for intuitive planning by often-autocratic management. These policies loosened in some companies over the intervening years, with several spectacular failures as a result. The deterioration of the commercial-paper market resulting from the Penn Central episode in 1970 had a direct effect on the finance industry, since the sale of commercial paper had developed as a substantial source of funds in the late 1950s and in the 1960s. Management executives in many finance companies have undergone reorientation and self-evaluation in recent years to reacquaint themselves with the policy guidelines and safeguards which had been proven during the earlier years of the industry's growth and to develop new guidelines appropriate to the current business environment.

Prior to developing the computer-based planning system, FinanceAmerica Corporation had one-year budgets by profit centers and a two-year rough forecast of money needs, and had attempted long-range planning over a five-year horizon, using a number of different approaches.

The system was basically manual but did utilize a time-sharing feature which was a by-product of a monthly reporting program for comparing actual data with budgeted data and which was essentially income statement-oriented. Underlying detail was often obscure, there was a substantial possibility of undetected errors, and the estimated cost of borrowings was spread to all units proportionately, based on invested funds. The latter ignored the reality that certain types of financing business were related to short-term sources of funds and other types to long-term. Theoretically, planning responsibility had been delegated to profit-centers, but in actuality, decision making continued to be opportunistic and somewhat autocratic.

A first step toward computer-based planning was the development of relatively simple computer models by GAC Corporation (the former parent) for limited applications to nonfinance business, particularly land development sales. The computer model was viewed as a vehicle for mathematical projection of certain activities and not as a means for coordination and consolidation of the multiple planning elements.

As FinanceAmerica Corporation became more planning-oriented, questions arose as to what the profit objectives of the planning units should be. What are the competitors doing? What type of customer is desired? The solution to these questions required the ability to look at the detail components of each aspect of the business.

These components involved assets and asset-evaluation data; relationships of income to external influences; cost factors; and debt and equity components applicable to each aspect of the business. The interrelationship of balance sheet and income statement data had to be recognized. Furthermore, responsibility for establishing line objectives had to be identified with profit-center responsibility, whereas management of FinanceAmerica (and GAC Corporation) would move toward setting basic objectives as to profitability, control, and coordination of the planning function.

Definition Study and Systems Development

At about this time, two significant studies developed independently. The Management Information Systems Department of GAC Corporation began a study in early 1971 to determine the feasibility and desirability of developing computer-based planning systems. This study involved:

1. Determination of areas where planning models could be most effectively used

2. Evaluation of the scope and depth of data available to support planning models

3. Identification of management and staff personnel to develop the system and use the models

At approximately the same time, GAC Corporation management established that a 15 percent return on common equity should be the profitability objective for FinanceAmerica. In order to carry this down to individual profit-center responsibilities, the FinanceAmerica Financial Planning Department developed a so-called pyramid concept which included:

1. Establishment of specific debt/equity configurations for each profit center, based on its type of business. These were based on analysis of appropriate competitor configurations, identification of key factors relating to leverage probability, and resolution of a distinction between need for short- and long-term funds. This included assignment of nonearning assets to profit centers either by specific identification or allocation.

2. Formalization of criteria for charging out the cost of borrowed funds to the profit centers on a somewhat "stand alone" profit-center basis.

3. Definition of equity commitments for each profit center, thereby providing for evaluation under a return-on-equity basis.

4. Provision for developing financing objectives for the company by comparing the sum of profit-center funding needs with the company's debt/equity mix.

The effective utilization of this concept would have required either substantial manual effort or computerization. Fortunately, the study of computer-based planning systems by the parent company had concurrently progressed to a point where the GAC subsidiary, FinanceAmerica, the ideal subject for the first corporate venture of this sort, and a decision was made to invite outside consultants to make an exploratory study of this company.

The first determination of the definition study was that certain data necessary for planning were not readily available. A second determination was that line management was not always in tune with respect to overall planning assumptions of the company. Also, planning under the manual system was a single-shot process which allowed little opportunity to generate alternative plans under different assumptions. The capacity properly to evaluate opportunities and/or problems was limited because of the small staff available.

One important output of this exploratory study was a definition of organizational objectives and of priorities in systems applications. Primary importance was assigned to those planning activities that significantly affected the operating divisions, the capital structure, and the consolidated performance of the company. Data availability and timing were indicated for each potential model in the system. A program of phased development was suggested.

Personnel resources for systems implementation were determined in the course of the definition study. Tasks were defined and schedules established. Performance criteria for the general system were established, including a determination of time dimensions. Top management was actively involved throughout the planning and development of the computer-based system. The chief executive would retain primary responsibility for the long-range planning function in the company and was to utilize outputs from the system. The funding and immediate sponsorship of the system were handled by the vice president of financial planning.

The proposed development of a computer-based planning model for FinanceAmerica Corporation was authorized by management in August 1972. Some factors of the rationale of this action were:

1. Recognition of a need for greater flexibility in planning—for the ability to change the planning assumptions, including the magnitude of business.

2. Belief that the planning process should identify significant data needs rather than accept existing availability of data from the accounting and statistical system.

3. Need for greater reliability in planning documentation.

4. Possibilities of savings through being able to select a "best"course of action from various alternatives.

5. Although not essential to the decision, recognition that that the pyramid concept could be effectively incorporated in the model logic.

The initial systems development took three months of calendar time and about two work years of effort. The task force consisted of the internal management information system (MIS) and finance staffs as well as outside consultants. Additional planning and data deficiencies were brought to light as the development progressed, but they were circumvented somewhat by designing the models to use planning rather than accounting data.

The resulting system provides for structuring each profit center with its designated capital structure and allows operations management to plan in much greater detail than previously possible, with many benefits in improved comprehension of plan by profit-center management and company management. The method of allocation of borrowing costs, an important element of the pyramid concept, forced profit-center managers to recognize the influence of the money market as represented in their costs.

The system was finished on schedule in December 1972, and it immediately validated using the completed budget data for 1971. As it turned out, the budget was verified, not the model. A number of discrepancies were identified, some small and some large. One staff member, for example, believed the long-term debt interest could be scheduled more easily and more accurately by hand than with a computer. It was scheduled manually, and when it was later simulated on the system, it was determined that the manual schedule had thirteen months' interest expense for one issue instead of twelve. The difference was one-half million dollars.

The next six months were spent on internal modification and refinement of the planning system and procedures. The initial design of the model was not necessarily in error, but additional developments were suggested by use of the system. The major weaknesses were not so much in the computer system, but in the operational-planning techniques. It was found, for example, that, although average funds invested for a period in an operation were the key to planning for that activity, a consistent and proper formula for this vital statistic was not being used in either historical statistical reports produced by accounting personnel or in the development of planning data by profit-center planners. This omission was rectified by promulgating the system logic which was verified as a proper formula for all such calculations.

The Computer-based Planning System

This is an interactive planning system on time-share computers operated by an outside vendor. An overview of the computer-based planning system and external interfaces is shown in Figure 9-5. The models in the system may be summarized as follows:

1. *Operations:* Describes the fund-using activities of the company in terms of results before interest and taxes.

2. *Debt:* Describes existing and planned long-term debt and preferred stock issues.

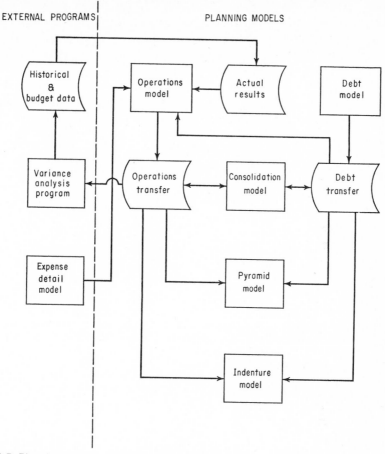

Figure 9-5. Planning system overview and external interfaces. *(Courtesy of Finance-America Corporation and On-Line Decisions, Inc.)*

3. *Consolidation:* Describes the consolidated performance of FinanceAmerica Corporation.

4. *Pyramid:* integrates the fund-providing and fund-using activities as an aid to financing decisions and analyzes performance.

5. *Indenture:* Analyzes latest corporate plan for possible indenture-restrictions violation.

An operations model, for example, may be used to forecast the performance of an operating division. The system operator can evaluate volume, financing mix, and yield plans in formulating a strategy to boost the performance of a product line or the entire division. Having selected a course of action, the user can determine the impact on capital structure with the debt-capacity model or the impact on consolidated company performance with the consolidation model. The effects or changed assumptions in any planning model are accounted for throughout the entire planning system.

The total number of lines of logic in the system is approximately 1,000. Over 10,000 data elements are inputted to the system through an online data loader. Data modes are used extensively. The planning horizon is five years. Primary outputs are the operations plan and the financing plans. There are two levels of consolidation in the system. One output format is generated. The most extensive report has 100 lines.

Operations Model. The operations model describes the fund-using activities of the company by profit center. The objective of the model is to help assess the impact of alternative loan category and profit-center planning assumptions on the category and division profitability. Profit estimates for major loan categories are developed from projections of:

1. Volume

2. Collections (liquidation)

3. Yield

4. Losses

5. Loan mix

6. Cost of money

7. Operating expenses

This model provides management with an increased ability to evaluate such questions as:

1. What is the impact of change in volume, liquidation of a loan category with respect to the category, or profit-center performance?

2. What is the impact of change in yield and cost of money?

3. What is the impact of change in operating and allocated expenses?

4. What is the impact of an increase in insurance earnings rates?

5. What is the impact of a bulk purchase of receivables on funds used?

This model allows simulation of fifteen profit centers with ten business lines per profit center. Ten profit-center direct-expense categories were accommodated, including fixed and variable components and inflation factors. These have been deleted because of difficulty relating to a problem of appropriate modification of accounting records. The model has five profit-center indirect-expense categories, four options for gross receivables, and seven options for finance charges.

A number of options are available for calculations performed within the operations model. It is desirable in the case of some receivables, for example, to calculate gross income based on outstanding receivables, whereas in other cases the criterion is percentage of funds invested. In still other cases, it is necessary to take into consideration the volume of business as well as the outstanding receivables. Outputs of the model are in thousands of dollars and/or percentage of funds invested.

Debt Model. This planning model describes the fund-providing activities of FinanceAmerica Corporation. The model is designed to assist decision makers in evaluating the impact on the debt/equity structure of changes in operations, interest expenses, and debt pyramids of each division. The planning horizon of the model corresponds directly to that of the operations model.

The debt model contains all the existing issues of the company which may include up to 170 long-term issues plus 40 preferred/preference issues. The model can accommodate over 100 treasury purchases. The specifications of each issue are described in the model, which allows for:

1. Any of three types of sinking funds

2. A preferred/preference issue outstanding, but not paying dividends

3. Two methods of applying treasury to a sinking fund payment

4. A varying interest rate

5. Issue dates other than first of a month

Three different types of bank-loan credit situations and one commercial-paper issue situation are accommodated in the model. Both bank lines and commercial paper are ideal possibilities for submodels, which have not yet been developed.

Pyramid Model. The pyramid model integrates the fund-providing and fund-using activities of the company as an aid to financing decisions and analyzing performance. This model takes all the fund requirements and designates appropriate fund sources for each profit center to design a financing structure for each profit center. These financing structures are then totaled for the company to see whether the overall structure is appropriate or should be modified. This has the potential of suggesting the long-range funding strategy for the company.

This model has the capability of determining what is open for issue in each level of debt. For example, given certain levels of common equity and subordinated debt, it can indicate the capability of the company to issue more subordinated debt within present lending restrictions.

The interest costs are analyzed for line management personnel so that they will be informed as to what they are being charged for the funds employed in receivables as well as in other assets. The outputs of the model are cost of money statements by profit center, a funds-provided statement and an open-to-buy statement by major category.

The capabilities of the pyramid model are as follows:

1. Development of support required in each profit-center structure

   a. Funds employed
   b. Compensating balances
   c. Insurance company investment (now negated)
   d. Other allowed assets net of other liabilities
   e. Unamortized debt discount and expense
   f. Other disallowed assets

2. Generation of ideal structure for each profit center and total company

3. Generation of total company open-to-issue according to two options:

   a. Debt capacity based on no addition to existing debt
   b. Debt capacity based on maximum addition to each level of debt

4. Allocation of actual company interest expense to profit centers, based on their ideal structures at company effective rates applied appropriately to each category of debt usage

5. Analysis of profit-center interest charges, including the impact of:

   a. Funds employed
   b. Other allowed assets (type I)
   c. Disallowed assets (type II)
   d. Actual company debt mix

6. Generation of profit-center performance, based upon target goal for return on ideal common equity and preferred dividend load

Consolidation Model. This model describes the aggregate performance of FinanceAmerica Corporation. It is designed to help decision makers at the corporate level project the impact of alternative operations plans and capital structures. The consolidated model brings together the operations and debt data and permits inputting of extraneous information from functions that are not part of the system.

Inputs to the model include the following:

1. Funds used by month from the operations model

2. Funds provided by month from the debt and pyramid models

3. Operating expenses that are not directly associated with the divisions by quarter and year

4. Abbreviated profit and loss of up to five subsidiaries by month and quarter

The consolidation model has the capability to generate all results that are not specific to particular profit centers or long-term debt issues, including:

1. Subsidiary investments

2. Taxes

3. Other payables

4. Marketable securities

5. Funds due the parent company

6. Contributions/dividends

7. Subsidiary borrowings

The model accommodates three types of bank borrowings and one type of commercial paper. The logic of the model computes automatic bank and/or commercial-paper borrowing to meet a specified ending free cash target. The model also checks on commercial-paper coverage, bank-borrowing ratio, and Standard & Poor's interest calculation. The calculations are very important, as management is much interested in knowing exactly what effect any decision will have on these factors.

Outputs of the consolidation model include the balance sheet, profit and loss statement, cash flow statement, and significant ratios. Performance is recorded by months, quarters, or years in thousands of dollars or ratios.

Indenture Model. The purpose of this model is to see that a proposed plan does not violate any borrowing restrictions. Specific checks include the following:

1. Three restrictions pertaining to receivables

2. Adjusted net worth check

3. Four specific debt restrictions

4. Total leverage check

Running the System

Line-operations managers submit basic data for input to the system, which is operated by a representative of the Financial Planning Department. System printouts of balance sheet and income statement are immediately returned to the line manager for analysis and change if desired. Revised outputs are then submitted for review by top management in preparing a final plan for the period.

Once the operating data have had final approval, the Financial Planning Department begins to fill in the financial requirements, based primarily on the cash flow report from the system. This report shows all funding requirements and computes the deficit cash position. Alternative financing strategies are then simulated to eliminate the deficit.

The system accepts both plan and actual data; it is used primarily for testing alternatives in the development of the plan and providing review material for management in the planning process. The system is used quarterly for forecasting probabilities for the remainder of the year. Long-range planning data for up to five years are inputted annually.

The system is fully interactive with user control of inputs and outputs. Sensitivity analysis can be performed to vary automatically a designated input variable and examine the impact of each value on the model's output.

The operating system allows the models to be run both forward and backward. The planner can input assumptions and forecast performance. Alternatively, the planner can present a desired goal and work the model backward to determine the required values of input variables. The latter technique is not currently being used because of deficiencies in the logic of the operations model. Several planners can interrogate the planning system simultaneously. The models are linked in the system so that the impact of changed assumptions in any model can be reflected throughout the entire system.

The user modes in the data loader provide prompting assistance so that the task can be accomplished by clerical labor. A tape cartridge device was added to the user terminal to reduce data-loading line time. The system applies various consistency checks to reduce error and loads the data into the proper computer files. User modes are also available for running the system. They provide prompting for the user in selecting reports and time periods as well as in setting parameters manually or automatically. The result is increased efficiency in human/machine interaction and reduction of errors.

The design for each profit center is such that the system can be expanded easily in modular fashion using the same data structure. More comprehensive modeling is expected to be built in the future within the generalized model for each profit center. Certain operations, for example, suggest the ability to plan by states to which operations are oriented. Other operations are national in nature and would be conducive to planning by customer types. The modularity structure is illustrated in Figure 9-6.

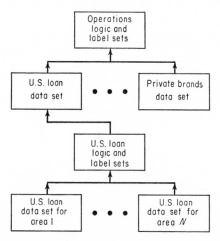

Figure 9-6. Model modularity and flexibility. *(Courtesy of FinanceAmerica Corporation and On-Line Decisions, Inc.)*

Management's Evaluation

The general evaluation of systems performance after two years of operation is that the acceptance was initially slow, but that the benefits from use of the system have more than justified the expenditures. Usage of the system is expected to increase in the future. Specific observations by the vice president of financial planning and his associates are as follows:

The system is used essentially as the focal point of our planning process, into which we input basic data in respect to operational planning and relate this to funding requirements. The system includes detailed information on all long term debt issues of the company and has logic for a number of short term funding sources common to our industry which enables us to select the components of meeting the plan period funding requirements. The system also has what could be described as a transfer pricing method of allocating borrowing cost to profit centers by viewing each operational component as though it were in business for itself but capable of borrowing at the company rates. Model printouts are the basis of management reviews of short and long range planning financial effects.

Simulations have been somewhat limited, primarily because the operations part of the system does not have sufficiently detailed logic. This was recognized at the time the system was developed but was a concession made in the interest of time, cost and lack of some significant historical data. We have done simulations in respect to funding requirements and in one example eliminated a standby coverage arrangement based on evaluation of system output. We do have considerable capability in respect to simulating changes in short term borrowing cost and also as to planning our total financing. We have simulated the effect of eliminating certain lines of business or of altering the business level in certain operations. The latter type is slightly cumbersome for the reason noted above.

Certain problems relate more to the company than to the computer-based planning system. For example, there is some dissimilarity between the accounting view and the operations concept. An operator must have a total view of the lending relationship and may consider making a loan. Consequently he or she will be interested in the nature of the customer, the yield on that loan over time, and the probability of loss. The accounting department, in contrast, has a time-dependent record-keeping perspective. As a further constraint, the accounting system was not automated at the time the model was developed so that the capability for making comparisons between actual data and plan was limited to profit centers and above. These comparisons are generally done outside the financial model system, using an internally developed time-sharing system which compares actual data with objective.

A second organization problem is the natural tendency of the profit-center manager to think in terms of only a single operation rather than the total company. There is also some profit-center apprehension in thinking about the future, but this is attributable to misconceptions about planning and the tendency to view it as a commitment process rather than as a means of exploring alternatives for sound decision making.

The reports have been used extensively in budgeting and reforecasting and, to a limited degree, in long-range planning. Acceptance was slow at first but has improved steadily. There was a tendency to feel that the system was intended to usurp decision-making roles, and pencil jotters often strived to beat the system instead of striving to understand its utility. Invariably, the quickie manual technique ignored interrelating effects which the system considered automatically.

The curing period appears to be in its waning stages and some efforts to eliminate information voids in the historical data have been activated. Attempts are being made to identify and include the data necessary as a basis for plan-period assumptions.

The atmosphere has changed sufficiently to begin further refinements, such as the state and customer subsystems and possibly reactivation of the fixed/variable expense concept. It is probable that these will be phased in gradually as historical information problems are solved and in palatable bites to minimize confusion and normal resistance to change.

Involvement has been stressed as necessary for management and user understanding. Further, the system was designed to use basically the planning techniques that managers were already using. Although the system may have benefited from improving planning techniques and concepts prior to development, there was an advantage to retaining a semblance of similarity to the system to which management was accustomed.

In fact, it is possible that a much more sophisticated system might have had an early demise if management had not been able to recognize substantial compatibility with the previous planning concepts and techniques. The system did include a breakthrough to a finer level of operational planning in certain key elements, facilitated monthly planning in the short range, and produced more informative output for reports. These features were probably responsible for some of the early resistance to the system until their advantages in the planning review process were recognized and accepted.

However, some refinements that were originally incorporated were not utilized, such as the expense feature for fixed and variable data. This provision was not really compatible with the historical accounting system.

The system has been very effective in applications of debt and equity planning. The system's violation checks have been useful in financial strategy planning. The operational applications have been fairly successful in their contribution to time savings and better planning analysis.

The interactive feature of the system is considered invaluable; however, certain problems exist in coordination since multiple vendors are involved for the operating software, time-share computers, terminals, and telephone lines. This difficulty, usually attributable to lack of proper people communication, has been essentially corrected. Response time is occasionally slow, telephone lines are sometimes unavailable, and terminals may break down. Data-base problems have not been difficult.

Initially, the major threats to the system were managerial, rather than technical, in nature. Perhaps they were symptomatic of a more general lack of appreciation of the benefits in planning. Use of the computer-based system assumes an acceptance of planning. There is substantial evidence, after two years of usage, that the system has been instrumental in improving management's understanding of business planning and has been helpful in the establishment and utilization of more effective planning techniques.

10

Marketing / Van Den Berghs & Jurgens, Limited

The marketing manager has historically been one of the greatest skeptics of computer-based planning systems, being all too aware of the uncertainties of the marketplace and the necessity to make highly subjective judgments concerning customer buying behavior. The marketing manager is forced to take a pragmatic viewpoint toward performance and knows from experience that relationships between sales volume, pricing, and promotional expenditures are very difficult to quantify.

Although qualitative judgment and management intuition may remain the prime assets in many industries, marketing management today is also often equipped with extremely sophisticated planning tools. The following case study is an excellent example of an advanced computer-based planning system with a marketing orientation.

INTRODUCTION

Van den Berghs & Jurgens Limited, a subsidiary of Unilever Limited, U.K., is a major producer of white and yellow fats in the United Kingdom. The margarine brands account for 65 percent of the company's total annual sales, which approximate $200 million. This case has been selected for thorough discussion because of:

The highly effective and extremely thorough manner in which the project was organized and executed

The marketing orientation of the models for use at the level of brand management

The inclusion of an optimization subroutine in the total simulation system

The utilization of both batch computers and interactive time-sharing facilities to obtain the unique advantages of each

Unique decision features incorporated into the system and the models, including effective use of a central data file with its own editor

GENERAL DESCRIPTION (23, pp. 14–15)

The company's organization structure, shown in Figure 10-1, is devised to allow the firm to approach three distinct segments of the market in the most appropriate manner. The retail sales of package margarines and white fats are controlled by Van Den Berghs. Yellow and white fats of a similar nature that are required by the bakery and catering industries are supplied in commercial-sized packages by Cragi-Millar, while

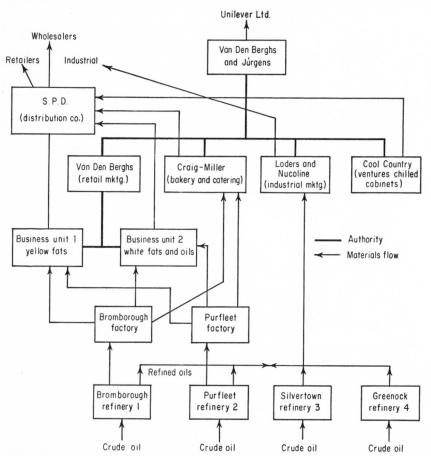

Figure 10-1. Organization structure and materials flow at VdB & J. *(Courtesy of VdB & J Division of Unilever, Ltd., and On-Line Decisions, Inc.)*

the industrial demand for refined and processed oils from manufactured and other food products is handled by the Loders and Nucoline Division. A fourth division has recently been added to handle diversified products other than those falling within the edible oils and fats market.

The process of manufacture of edible oils and fats is, in itself, extremely complex. Figure 10-2 is a schematic diagram showing the

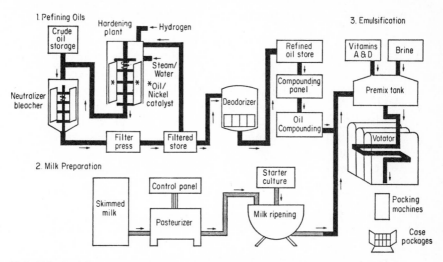

Figure 10-2. Principal flows and basic stages of the process of manufacture of edible oils and fat. *(Courtesy of VdB & J Division of Unilever, Ltd., and On-Line Decisions, Inc.)*

principal material flows and the basic stages in the operation. As many as twenty-five different crude edible oils are used in combinations of up to four or five oils per product for some sixty products manufactured by VdB & J. Any or all of these oils are passed through some or all of the processes indicated in the oil-refining section of the flow diagram. The characteristics of the end product must remain constant, and yet, the qualities of the input oil vary from batch to batch and will certainly vary across a total range of edible oils in use. In consequence, the refining capacity of the company, while fixed in physcial terms, is directly related to the oils that are being processed at a given time and to the end formulation of the individual products.

At a further level of complexity in this problem, variations may be made in individual product formulations to be able to optimize on the use of lower-cost raw materials. In the day-to-day operational sense, formulations are calculated, using a least-cost linear program based on the prices of the individual batches of oils against expected demand. Mandatory changes in formulation are made in the summer and winter months so that the final characteristics of the product remain the same despite significant changes in temperatures.

With no fixed capacity or formulation, but with all factors linked to the raw material price forecast of the crude oils, a more than usually complex model was necessary to provide the ability to determine profit margins and to ensure that the anticipated volume would not exceed the total capacity.

ORGANIZATION AND PLANNING AT VdB & J (23, pp. 15–17)

The annual and the five-year planning activities occur somewhat independently at VdB & J and at different times in the year, although similar procedures are followed in their preparation. The general planning processes are shown in Figure 10-3. The Policy Committee at the board level of VdB & J established general guidelines for the operating divisions. The business units establish basic product-lines strategy and refer their plans to brand managers for their forecasts of tonnages. These tonnage forecasts are then referred to the factories, which use them in estimating costs of manufacture. The same forecasts are also used in establishing marketing cost and the estimation of other expenses.

This information all flows to the management accountants who prepare the forecasts which are submitted to the business units for consolidation and hence for reconsolidation into their division plans and subsequently into the plan for VdB & J for Board approval.

This planning practice has been in existence for a number of years — with significant drawbacks. First, the time devoted to the creation of the plan, from both the revenue and the cost aspects, was enormous. The accountancy staff of the company were occupied full time, for approximately six months of the year in preparing the annual plan alone. Over 7,000 values were computed as input for the annual plan to generate 125 reports in 12 primary formats. Data were manipulated in a number of ways by various classifications, for example, all brands sold to bakeries, all yellow fats, and so on. When an assumption was changed in one area, thousands of recalculations were necessary.

With the tremendous amount of effort necessary to undertake the creation of a plan, it was impossible for the staff to submit several alternatives to the board of directors for consideration; in the event of a plan being disapproved, it was extremely difficult to generate a new one. Further, the ability to update the plan was restricted to annual or biannual exercises because of the time involved. This limitation was clearly unacceptable in an environment where the raw material costs were rapidly fluctuating, some costs having varied more than 100 percent in the past two years.

The ability to maintain the level of profits in the face of changing cost factors is critical. The need to merge the short- and medium-term plans into a continuous planning process was recognized and the search for a

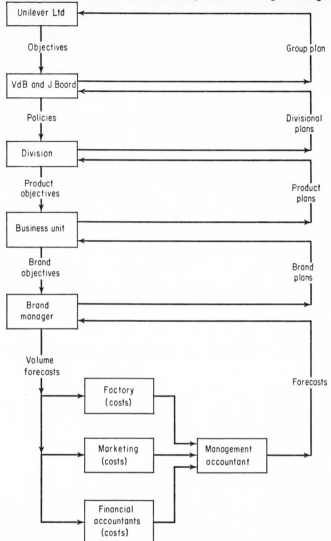

Figure 10-3. VdB & J planning process. *(Courtesy of VdB & J Division of Unilever, Ltd., and On-Line Decisions, Inc.)*

tool capable of providing this process was undertaken by a group of internal and external consultants under the guidance of the head of planning for VdB & J.

THE SYSTEM (26)

The VdB & J planning system is described by its designers in the following paragraphs.

For many years we have heard from the computer experts of the benefits to be derived from using simulation models, models which reflect the complexities of the business and allow management to see the effect of any potential decision before they take that course of action. With management determined to have a real decision tool, a number of attempts were made to achieve this during the late 1950's and the 1960's.

These simulation models did not achieve their objectives because, like the dinosaur, they were not sufficiently flexible to meet the changing needs of the environment, the improved understanding of the management itself and, in consequence, simulation did not succeed in the format of massive batch models, in many cases.

With the advent of time-sharing techniques, a manager's ability to understand and to interface directly with a machine capable of carrying out instructions with accuracy and speed provided an entirely new approach to simulation.

The problem that now confronts senior management is to decide between a number of tools and to select the one most appropriate to their needs. This was the position we found ourselves in, in August 1970.

In order to simplify our decision-making process, we designed a simple guide (Figure 10-4), which categorizes these systems into four principal formats, arranged to show the relative flexibility of logic and input/output.

		Logic	
	Flexibility	High	Low
Input	High	Type 1	Type 2
Output	Low	Type 3	Type 4

Type 1. Full modeling systems   Type 2. Report generators
Type 3. Specialized systems   Type 4. Predefined systems

Figure 10-4. A guide categorizes the systems into four principal formats. *(From John Cooper and Peter Jones, "The Corporate Decision,"* Data Processing, *March–April 1972.)*

Within these classifications the full modeling system is a highly flexible relationship between logic and input/output whilst the pre-defined system, a standard logistics system, for example, has a very much more rigid logic and input/output.

Having completed the classification of the systems available, the following points were considered to evaluate and select the most appropriate system:

1. The detailed function—short- or long-term.

2. Who will:

    a. Use the models?

    b. Create the models?

3. What are the modeling resources of the organization?

4. Is a time-sharing facility necessary to fulfill these means?

5. What data security and data transfer problems may arise by using time-sharing ex-house?

6. What sort of expenditure:

    a. Initially?

    b. In the future is the organization prepared to bear?

7. Does the process to be modeled require complex model interlinking and the use of statistical routine?

8. Is there a tangible cash benefit? If not, why not? Are there intangible benefits or is it a gimmick?

Through this process of evaluation and selection, it became apparent that the facilities being offered by On-Line Decision Systems Incorporated were most suitable to our needs and fulfilled the requirements outlined above.

It was our plan to establish a long-term strategy for our company using five years' historical data, with the facility to project forward for a further five years. We believed that the models should be used by members of Line Management at both a Divisional and a Product Group level and that they would not be required to build the models.

The building of the models was undertaken by members of the Data Processing and Operations Research Department on an architecture specified by the company's management. In this architecture, the primary features of the company were clearly defined: Three divisions competing (Figure 10-5) for a common resource, namely, production capacity; an aggregation of the individual brands to a division; of individual divisions to the total company for the comparison of the demand against production capacity available, or to determine what would be required to meet various aggregations of alternative strategies. (Diversification is a separate operation not considered in this analysis—JBB.)

Time-sharing was essential to allow managers with line responsibility the facility to explore the alternative strategies that they might undertake under varying environmental conditions and to relate these to the profit contribution objectives for their divisions.

Data security and transfer problems were investigated at the start and considerable exploration was made into the security arrangements both of the time-

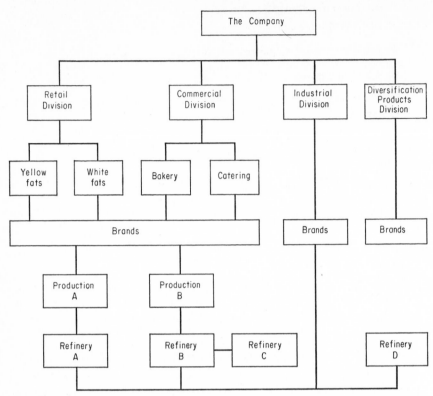

Figure 10-5. The models were built on an architecture specified by the company's management. (*From John Cooper and Peter Jones, "The Corporate Decision,"* Data Processing, *March–April 1972.*)

sharing system and of the simulation system before live company data was lodged. The security of our computer system is now greater than that of written data held within the company's offices.

The initial development costs and the operating costs for the system were estimated and these were found acceptable to the Board of Directors and were calculated to run at a rate of less than 2.5 percent of the total computer budget. It was also very obvious from the proposed architecture that the models would require complex interlinking and a highly developed use of statistical routines in the projection of market volumes.

Finally, we believed that there would be considerable intangible benefit from the better use of management time, a greater understanding of the problems we were likely to face and more clearly defined alternative courses of action that we believed we could take. By being prepared for these eventualities, our ability to respond to rapidly changing conditions effectively and profitably would give a marked advantage over our competitors.

General Description

We commenced the process of modeling the company in February 1971 using the facilities provided by the On-Line Financial Analysis and Planning System, and had completed the first working model by June 1st, 1971. As our knowledge and our understanding of the potential of the facility became greater, it became apparent that the initial specifications could be considerably developed and that the results would receive a greater response from management

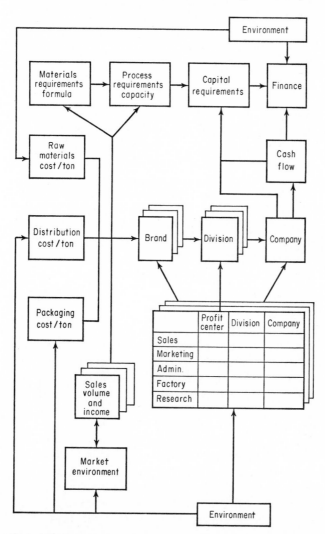

Figure 10-6. The total operational system which is now in daily use. *(From John Cooper and Peter Jones, "The Corporate Decision," Data Processing, March–April 1972.)*

than we had previously anticipated. To this end, further improvements were made and the total operational system now in daily use can be seen in Figure 10-6.

The system is based on VANGUARD,[1] a corporate simulator which allows the user to explore the effect on the company trading position of changes in the whole range of variables applicable to the operation, for example, (a) total market sizes and market shares; (b) brand sales values; (c) raw material prices; (d) product formulations; (e) refinery capacities; (f) personnel costs; (g) taxation rates; (h) working capital requirements, etc.

The system comprises a set of fifteen interrelated programs, or models, each relevant to a separate aspect of the company operation. These models operate within the framework of the Financial Analysis and Planning System (FAPS). The overall system structure is shown in Figure 10-7.

The system is accessed from the teletype terminal, the various models being called by the user, at whose disposal is a range of system commands. Certain commands are used to set up the output format required, others specify lines of output and years. Other commands enter new data, modify existing data as necessary, or examine values of the data.

An appropriate command executes the selected model in one of a variety of modes. The model may simply be executed and the output printed; alternatively, it may be set up to run a number of times, with any given item being incremented by a given amount on each run; this is used to examine the sensitivity of defined lines of output to changes in related inputs.

Finally, by entering a required value of an output line, the model may be commanded to search iteratively for the value of the predetermined variable which generates the output. For example, a desired brand profit may be entered, and the system instructed to seek the variable cost figure needed to generate this profit; as a more complex example, a target budgeted divisional expenses figure may be entered for 1976, and the system instructed to calculate the highest permissable growth rate in personnel costs if this budget figure is to be attained.

The Brand Model may be regarded as the heart of the system. Basically, it is used to examine the margin statement for any brand up to the level of profit before fixed expenses. All necessary data are stored on the Brand Data File, but any element of this may be changed by direct input from the terminal: This change may be either to provide a new value or, alternatively, the current values may be inflated from a given year by a desired percentage.

[1]VANGUARD: Van den Berghs General Utility for the Allocation of Resources and Development.

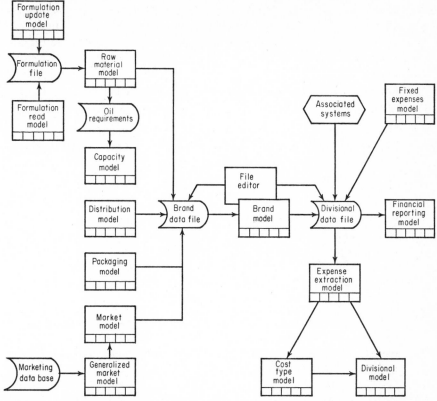

Figure 10-7. The models operate within the framework of the Financial Analysis and Planning System—FAPS. (*From John Cooper and Peter Jones, "The Corporate Decision," Data Processing, March–April 1972.*)

Apart from looking at an individual brand, the model is used to aggregate brand data to the level of the company divisions. Very powerful data handling capabilities are provided within the model to cater for this. The fixed aggregations of brands, corresponding to the company profit reporting hierarchy, are stored within the model but any other desired aggregation may be selected by the user to generate new hierarchies on-line; a new aggregation created in this way may be needed only once, but if desired can be stored for future use. The system allows an unlimited number of hierarchies.

A maximum of five complete sets of data corresponding to alternative possible strategies may be stored for each brand. The aggregation facility allows the user to specify for each brand the strategy selected when aggregating.

Any given aggregation can be passed to the Divisional Data File as the basis for a given divisional strategy. Each division may also have as many as five individually specified strategies.

The Fixed Expenses Model is then used to enter appropriate divisional expenses for each strategy, and to aggregate divisions to sub-totals and finally the company total, with the same degree of flexibility as at the Brand level. Thus the five-year company forward plan may be generated adaptively, with as many changes to values as desired, simulating the effects of combining various strategies for each operating division, and each business unit or product group within the division.

The total company source and use of funds is examined in the Financial Reporting Model, which is based on selected Divisional Strategies projected to the level of trading profit, and leading to the calculation of operational cash flow.

The actual costs and expenses forming any version of the plan may be examined in greater detail using the Cost Type and Divisional Models to break each expense down into categories (personnel, accommodation, etc.); any cost type may be changed with new values or by compound inflation rates (e.g., inflate all personnel expenditure by ten percent compound from 1972). The model then applies the desired change to the expenses, and re-calculates and prints the divisional or company statement.

Referring again to Figure 10-7, the brand date needed by the Brand Model may be input directly using the File Editor. The scope of the system is vastly increased by using the various elemental models (Packaging, Distribution, etc.) to generate brand data.

Environment Considered

In generating Sales Volume forecasts, and setting NSV[2] per ton for each brand, the environment in which the company is operating is taken into account. This is one of the functions of the Market Model. Apart from dealing with individual brands in terms of tonnage, marketing appropriation, NSV and Profitability, this model checks the total estimates for volume market sectors (yellow fats, oils, white fats, etc.) against predetermined estimates of the market size.

Powerful analysis facilities are offered in the Generalized Marketing Model. A marketing data base dealing with total markets, market splits, individual brand prices, volumes, advertising appropriations, etc., is drawn from historical market research and company data. Significant relationships between any of these variables may be sought on-line using single or multiple linear regression analysis. Complex relationships may be developed by appropriate transformation, using analysis of variance to test improvements in fit derived from the introduction of successive terms in the relationship. In this way, interbrand

[2]Normal Sales Value.

sensitivity, price-volume elasticity, advertising appropriation/volume correlations, overall market trends, etc., may be explored. Any relationship found to have a satisfactory degree of significance may be used to generate forecasts which may then be passed forward into the Market Model.

THE BUILDUP OF THE FIVE-YEAR PLAN

To explain the logic of each model, and to indicate how they are linked together to generate a complete plan, more detailed explanation is helpful.

The Market Model accepts, as input, estimates of tonnage, NSV per ton, marketing appropriation and variable costs, and calculates the margin statement and "Guideline Ratios" of marketing appropriation as a proportion of NSV, and as a cost per ton. From desired values of these ratios the required values of the inputs can be generated. The market can also be examined at a total level. When the estimates of tonnage and price are satisfactory, and consistent with the overall market, these figures can be passed forward for use in calculating fluctuating costs and margins, together with the various marketing appropriations, to establish the Brand Model output.

The Distribution Model calculates the total distribution cost per ton for each brand. It accepts as input the projected sales tonnages, and the estimated split between direct delivery from the factories, and indirect delivery via a depot distribution network, with the relevant projected stock cover.

The estimates for storage, delivery and other associated costs, which are a function of tonnage throughput, are stored in the model, and on the basis of the sales volume, the unit distribution cost per ton is calculated.

In addition, this model calculates an estimate of the cost of "out-of-condition" product anticipated. Changing and manipulating data are simple. For example, changes to unit distribution rates, or depot stock cover, or the split between direct and indirect deliveries can easily be effected.

Once again, the output data may be passed forward to the Brand Data File.

The Packaging Model is a simple program which calculates the packaging cost per ton for each brand. The costs are composed of four elements: (1) the primary packaging (bottles, tubs, wrapping, etc.); (2) the secondary packing (cartons, sleeves, etc.); (3) fiberites; and (4) others, including tapes, paste, labels, gum, etc. These are input by the user, and may be changed or inflated as desired.

The packaging cost is then also passed forward to the Brand Data File.

The Raw Materials Model. The raw materials cost of a product is a function of the formulation selected for tne product, and this formulation may be altered as raw material prices change. The solution to a least cost formulation problem lies in the use of a linear program [LP].

However, it is not practical to load a full-size formulation LP within a time-sharing system of this type; nor indeed would it be worthwhile to do so when preparing a long-range plan; the greater resolution in formulation selection provided by a linear program would be masked by the uncertainty associated with the projected raw material prices and tonnages. What is required is a technique to vary input (oil prices, sales volumes, etc.) to study their effect on the net product raw material price and total raw material requirement; this must, however, automatically switch formulations if a raw material cost moves past its economic value. The Raw Materials Model allows this to be done.

The basic inputs and outputs are shown in Figure 10-8. The logic of the model is as follows: each crude oil price is converted to a refined oil price by adding average refining costs per ton and dividing by the yield.

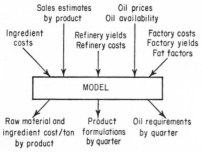

Figure 10-8. The raw materials model enables formulations to be switched if a raw material cost moves past its economic value. *(From John Cooper and Peter Jones, "The Corporate Decision,"* Data Processing, *March–April 1972.)*

A formulation is selected for the product on the basis of the refined oil prices. Up to twelve typical formulations are stored for each product: These are generated by an off-line linear program. The user may override this and force the product into a formulation to be input via the Formulation Model (see Figure 10-7).

The oil blend tonnage requirement is calculated from the selected formulation multiplied by wastage and fat factor. This oil blend tonnage is now exploded to individual oil requirements, and a running total for each is built up.

When all products have been formulated, the oil blend cost is converted to finished product cost by multiplying by the wastage and fat factor and adding fixed factory and other ingredient costs. Oil requirements are stored for use by the Capacity Model, and the raw material costs are passed to the Brand Data File. This file is now complete.

The Capacity Model.   One of the key questions to be answered when endeavoring to maximize company profitability is the level of capacity required for each stage of the process.

The Capacity Model makes the following assumptions:

1. The refining process is divided into steps, where each step is independent of its neighbors. Where this is not the case, the inter-step buffering may be included as a process.

2. Each step in the process contains real alternatives for processing input oils. For example, deodorizing may have three alternative machine groups, a ten-ton batch processor, a twenty-ton batch processor and a five-ton per hour continuous processor.

The refinery may now be represented by running the model independently for each individual step.

The Raw Materials Model provides a list of required oil tonnages, and the user provides a list of machine types, a technology matrix of the unit processing times for each oil on each machine, and the total capacity available each quarter on each machine type.

If we . . . [technical discussion omitted], the model is an LP. The output is the step index X_0 for each step. If a given index is less than unity, then a shortage of capacity is indicated in that time period; obviously the smallest index in each period isolates the critical processing stage.

Full manipulative capability is provided in this model; it may be run backwards from a required index of unity to determine either the maximum tonnages of oil which can be processed under the given formulation range, or alternatively the exact level of capacity needed to process the oil requirement in a quarter.

The power of the simulation, however, is greatly increased by utilizing the Market, Raw Materials and Capacity Models together, as indicated in Figure 10-9. If, under given assumptions, capacity will be insufficient to process projected tonnages of all brands, then apart from increasing capacity, changes could be made to various formulations, or product tonnages adjusted or all three combined: Increased capacity cost, for example, might have to be justified by sales of products with the smallest fluctuating margin.

In this way, as the plans are developed we can begin to build up a range of alternative possible strategies for each brand, for further examination at the consolidation levels within the company.

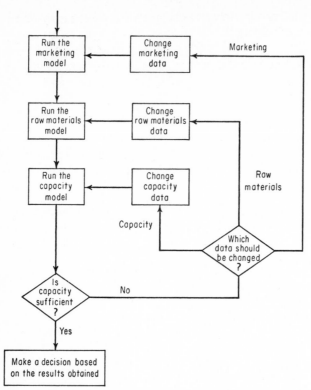

Figure 10-9. Simulating power is greatly increased by utilizing the market, raw materials, and capacity models together. *(From John Cooper and Peter Jones, "The Corporate Decision," Data Processing, March–April 1972.)*

The Brand Model.　　Having generated the possible brand strategies, and checked that they are consistent with capacity, the profitability of the various brands can be examined in the Brand Model. The use of the model was previously described and the output of an aggregation of brands which have been written up to the Divisional Data File then constitutes the basis for a given divisional strategy.

The Fixed Expenses Model.　　This may be used to aggregate various product group, business unit and divisional strategies, for further analysis. This data file may also be directly updated by using the File Editor, and is also written to by other associated systems, e.g., the Diversification Products Division has an entirely independent simulation system, reflecting its particular needs in planning. However, for company consolidation, this system is integrated into the overall system at this level.

The Cost Type Model.   The divisional fixed expenses may be examined and manipulated in greater detail using the Cost Type Model, which also controls the breakdown of factory expenses, and the calculation of depreciation for use in the Financial Reporting Model.

All these expenses are broken down into predetermined types such as personnel, accommodation, computer expense, market research, depreciation, etc. The totals of these cost types are then summarized and printed.

Changes can now be generated either to identified expenses, or expense cost types. These changed expenses may be printed out and may also be passed back to the system to study their impact on profitability.

The Divisional Model.   The output from this model is identical in format to that of the Fixed Expenses Model. It can be used to provide either a divisional statement on the basis of revised expenses as modified by the Cost Type Model or to manipulate a divisional strategy stored on the data file.

A real growth factor, a simple inflator, or a compound inflator may be applied to any item for each year of the model independently to simulate changing inflation rates, or generate costs and expenses as a function of their value in a given base year.

The Financial Reporting Model.   This deals with the total company source and use of funds. The company trading profit is drawn from the Divisional Data File, selecting the preferred strategy for each division. The depreciation figures are similarly drawn from this file.

All other data, which includes other sources of funds, statistical tax, figures for stocks, creditors and debtors on a divisional basis and so on, are stored in the model.

Capital expenditure is treated in two ways. Expenditure may simply be entered on a cost center basis.

After calculating the total source and use of funds and the movement in working capital required, the model generates the company operational cash flow.

CONCLUSION

In conclusion, therefore, to bring together this information, the VANGUARD System has the following principal features:

1. Fifteen interlinked models.

2. A flexible hierarchy.

3. The capacity to establish ten divisional groupings.

4. It consists of sixty products/product groups.

5. It has five alternative strategies held at each level in the hierarchy.

6. A ten-year operating period.

7. It operates within 3.5K^3 of core.

The first operating model was constructed in four months' elapsed time by a team drawn from Operations Research and headed by a Project Manager drawn from the Data Processing Department of the company and taking 2.5 man-years work to complete.

The cost of the System, including a detailed initial validation study and description of the architecture, a one-time charge for initial installation, the use of computer time for development, payment of royalties, storage and computer operations during the course of 1971, has been Twenty-four thousand pounds.

With the models fully developed, it is estimated that a sixty-hour per month usage will be appropriate and that the royalties and computer time charges in 1972 will not exceed fourteen thousand pounds.

Management has been trained in the use of the model; the number of commands are extremely simple and it has been our experience that an accountant or a brand manager, who has a reasoned degree of numerousy, can become familiar with the system within half a day. Access to the system and to the component parts of the system is controlled through access security codes and only those parts relevant to a manager's responsibility are directly available. In the initial operation, the divisional management accountants, because of their familiarity with the mathematical and financial processes that have been modeled, were the first people to accept responsibility for its use. Brand management is now being trained and is accepting this as a reasonable and realistic way in which to evaluate potential courses of action within its own jurisdiction.

"WHAT IF?" CAPABILITY (23, pp. 26–28)

The general capability of the system to answer "What if?" questions is indicated by the following specific questions:

1. If the price of Brand X is reduced by 10 percent, how does this change affect sales, profits, cash flow, and return on capital, and do we have the production capacity available?

---

^{3}In reference to storage capacity, K equals 2^{10}, or 1024.

2. If palm oil ceases to be available for product *Z,* what would be the best substitute and how is profitability affected?

3. What would be the effect on profitability of cutting out Brands A and B and replacing tonnage by Brand C; how much additional refining capacity would be created?

4. If labor costs were to rise by 15 percent per annum over three years, and 20 percent in the following two years, by how much would we have to increase prices to maintain margins?

5. Where brands are highly interactive in one market, what is the most profitable mix of brand strategies?

6. What would be the effect of the closure of a major production unit for a long period because of a natural disaster or strikes?

7. What would be the effect of a totally new diversification project upon company resources and profits? This simulation will include the acquisition of another company versus direct diversification.

8. What is the minimum necessary increase in a brand sale volume to justify a price decrease?

9. When and how should brand selling prices be changed in a competitive market to offset forecasted changes in cost?

10. What utilization of existing production capacity is likely to service alternative marketing strategies from each sales division? Will a particular combination of strategies require additional capacity for processes, and if so, how much?

11. Which particular combination of alternative divisional strategies is preferable for the company in each time period, with particular references to risk?

12. What would be the best response to a competitor's action in lowering prices?

13. If the price of a particular raw material were to increase, which products would be affected and what price adjustments would be necessary?

14. If a particular raw material were to be in short supply, which products would have priority call upon the limited quantities available?

15. What would be the effect upon company resources and profits if the company should acquire a competitor in the same business?

16. If the share of a particular market changes, what would be the effect upon short- and long-term profits?

17. What is the effect of alternative forecasts of market size upon sales volume and production capacity available?

11

Operations / Xerox of Canada Limited

The Xerox Corporation manufactures copying equipment, computers, and computer printers. Net income for all consolidated operations in 1973 was $300 million on sales of $2.4 billion, resulting in an average annual profit increase of 25 percent over the last five years (27, p. 47).

The system described in this chapter consists of a family of time-shared models developed for Xerox of Canada Limited (XCL) by that organization's functional manager (Ronald Seaberg) and consultant (Charlotte Seaberg). The purpose of the system is to link the functional areas for communication, planning, and control purposes by assisting and guiding management all the way from deriving product-demand forecasts to simulating the day-to-day operations of the firm to formulating divisional financial statements to preparing corporate operating and medium-range plans.

The Xerox of Canada system is interesting as being of a significantly different architectural style from those presented in the other cases. Moreover, the system reaches the level of first-line management with detailed "chart of account" budgets for operational planning and for use as a tool in controlling ongoing operations and in the preparation of short-term forecasts. The simplicity and power of the APL computer language are impressive. The success of the system is demonstrated by the fact that it has been adopted, in part, by corporate and regional offices of Xerox in the United States.

SYSTEM DESIGN PROCESS (28, pp. 576–577)

Our modelling effort developed as a direct result of a primary objective to improve the quality of the planning process. We concluded that such improvement could be accomplished by having direct access to more timely, accurate, in-depth, and logically-consistent information plus a flexible system for coping with a dynamic environment.

We felt that the overriding consideration in the design process was to develop models that would *(a)* be used, *(b)* be relevant and responsive to the needs of the user, and *(c)* be implemented with a minimum of time delay. To assist in this endeavor we attempted to design models around the decision maker. We have done this by our approach to modelling, by the scope and type of models we designed, and by the computer system we utilized.

In the model design phase we attempted to replicate either the existing decision process or alternative processes as suggested by the functional manager. Involvement in model-development has led managers, in many instances, to view their operation in differing ways. This new insight frequently resulted in improved business operations, thereby realizing a major goal of the modelling effort.

We utilized a variety of models with varying degrees of scope of operation and complexity so that the manager does not have to wade through a detailed model if he is only interested in aggregate and/or simplistic solutions. We relied primarily on simulation (case study or heuristic) models rather than optimization (algorithmic or linear programming) models which are restricted to single predetermined objectives. We found that simulation models most closely replicate managerial decision making and are most readily understood by managers as well as being easier to design from a modelling viewpoint. We found that as management became more familiar with the power of models we could begin approaching the incorporation of optimization techniques into our models.

It was our opinion that the advantages a timeshared system has for the decision-making process significantly offset any limitations such as reduced core storage and increased execution time. The program-size limitation was, for the most part, overcome by the development of smaller functional models which could either be run on a stand-alone basis or linked together into a corporate model. We decided to utilize the APL programming language (a very macro-oriented language) because it minimizes time and cost of program development and because knowledge of only a few basic commands allows the user considerable "programming" capability.

The advantages of timeshared computer models has been discussed in the literature. Our experience, which bears favorably upon their conclusions, has shown the following to be significant:

1. Reduced Information Data Overload. Planning involves a large number of variables which must be simultaneously considered. Computerized models

aid the decision maker by processing information for him quickly and efficiently.

2. Information Selection. Key variables, identified within the model-building process, assisted in defining information to be included in a data base. Statistical analysis models were used to perform sensitivity analysis to aid in this selection process in addition to simulation models which allowed the user to vary input variables and observe the results against a "base case."

3. Economical Solutions. Models provided answers at low cost and with a minimum of manpower resources by enabling managers to experiment with a variety of alternatives, forecasts, and cases.

4. Fast Turnaround. Generally, managers are unwilling to delay the decision process. The timeshared system, since it provided nearly instantaneous information and solutions, allowed the decision models to be explicitly incorporated into the managerial planning process.

5. Interrelation of Operations and Planning Systems. Computer-based models facilitated the incorporation of operating results explicitly into the planning process. This was achieved by analysis and control models having direct access to operating and financial data thereby promoting detailed plan, actual and forecast comparisons.

6. Communication Aid. A large integrated model, encompassing the functional areas of the business, provided a common language between the areas and enhanced the communication of ideas.

7. Direct Involvement. A modelling capability was placed directly into the hands of the decision maker. This allowed him to bypass intermediary obstacles such as coding sheets, keypunching, and programmers.

IMPLEMENTATION OF INITIAL SYSTEM (28, pp. 577–580)

A manually-performed forecast and control activity (referred to in Xerox as the Outlook) was the impetus for the initial modelling effort. The Outlook, which is essentially a rolling 12-month forward look at the business, was considered a prime target for mechanization because (a) it was a major responsibility which incorporated the activities of several functional areas, (b) it was performed monthly, and (c) it required considerable, high-level manpower resources. It was felt that successful mechanization of the Outlook would pave the way for the development of additional man-machine decision systems for such areas as operational and long-range planning.

A major question that arises during the Outlook cycle is the impact of cumulative performance to date upon the full year Operating Plan. All areas of the business are affected—marketing, finance, service, manufacturing and distribution. An answer to this question requires examination and analysis of cumulative and current performance, forecasted trends, and a provision for management action where "gaps" exist or are projected to exist. Computerized analytical and statistical control models provide answers to the first two points. Forecasting and simulation models are utilized by functional managers to assist in providing solutions to the last point.

The initial model, a deterministic simulation model which produced a rolling 12-month forecast of the major areas of the business, required two man-months to develop. Inputs to the model consisted of assumptions, parameters, and strategies; many of which were manager-controlled. Approximately thirty input variables, such as growth rates, various fixed and variable costs, trade assumptions, and inventory parameters, together with the model equations produce about three hundred output variables such as sales orders, inventory levels, net profit, produce revenue, expenses and manpower requirements. A schematic of this early system is illustrated in Figure 11-1. A sample report is displayed in Table 11-1.

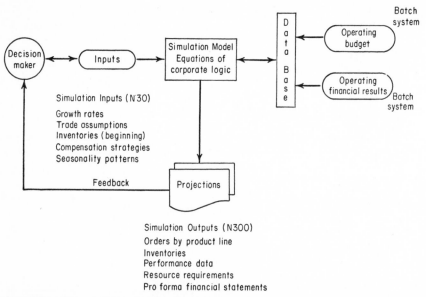

Figure 11-1. Schematic of XCL system. *(From Ronald A. Seaberg and Charlotte Seaberg "Computer Based Decision Systems in Xerox Corporate Planning,"* Management Science, *vol. 20, no. 4, 1973.)*

This sample report could be analyzed in the following way:

● Customer installations for product line 8 is currently ahead of plan on a year-to-date basis and is forecasted to maintain this favorable position for the balance of the operating year.

TABLE 11-1. Xerox of Canada Limited Control Report (28, p. 579) Sample Data

| | Actual performance | | | | Outlook (forecast) | | | | |
| | June year to date | | Current month | | | | | Full year impact | |
	Amount	Percent of plan	Amount	Percent of plan	July	August	September	Amount	Percent of plan
Product line 8:									
Orders	1550	146	130	140	177	146	156	2462	119
Better than plan	473		66		20	7	(24)	397	
Better than PMO*	(4)	97	22	97	0	(20)	(42)	(149)	90
Inventory	273	97	273	97	37	36	36	485	90
Better than plan	9		9		7	8	8	56	
Better than PMO	(31)		(31)		0	1	0	(7)	
Revenue:									
Product 8	1420	101	233	99	200	198	185	2626	96
Better than plan	(11)		2		22	15	36	121	
Better than PMO	164		(3)		21	12	43	42	
Total revenue	2037	105	626	131	572	609	657	3692	112
Better than plan	91		149		152	191	264	387	
Better than PMO	37		(18)		5	53	50	150	
Expenses:									
Salaries	525	96	130	140	104	100	94	1195	102
Better than plan	23		(37)		(14)	(13)	5	(23)	
Better than PMO	130		(3)		3	(4)	1	(73)	

*PMO—Prior Month Outlook (Forecast).

• The revenue resulting from this product is below plan indicating the fact that our customer leased inventory of this product is currently and projected to remain below plan. The negative impact of this product is more than overcome by the favorable position of other product lines on total revenue.

• The management group may execute additional simulations to determine the impact of various decision alternatives (such as increasing the commission rate, adjusting price, or an extensive advertising campaign) on other product lines in terms of functional department effectiveness and efficiency and the total corporate effect in terms of revenues and profits.

Although the above is highly simplistic in terms of how the system is actually put to use by XCL management it, nevertheless, serves to highlight the types of situations which can be investigated by the system.

The "what if" aspect of the model aided management in deriving solutions to such questions as:

• Determine the most likely effect on salesman performance (and productivity) by changes in the compensation plan?

• Given current sales trends, what will profits look like twelve months hence? How will this picture be influenced if *(a)* changes are made to the pricing structure of certain products, and *(b)* sales manpower is increased by 3%?

• How should the manufacturing mix of production be changed to achieve the profit plan given current and projected sales trends?

The above are representative of the types of questions which the model assisted management in solving either at a functional level (finance or marketing) or at the corporate level.

Use of the model resulted in significant time and cost benefits. Each simulation required an average of 8 to 10 CPU seconds with the initial model. Generally, 4 to 6 simulations (performed within an elapse time of two days) were executed to produce each finalized 12-month forecast. Less than 10% of analyst time was required for data manipulation versus 80% in the manual environment.

The manual system had been characterized by:

1. Considerable resource requirements. Approximately 6 man-weeks of analyst-level effort was allocated to this task each month with only one complete forecast being generated.

2. Forecasting logic not rigidly defined. Lack of a universally-accepted logic resulted in non-standardized forecasts.

3. On-the-spot changes. Because of the severe time constraints, adjustments were made to the forecast without consideration of the impact such changes (e.g. increase in sales) might have on other variables (e.g. inventory levels, expenses). As a result forecasts were not always internally consistent.

4. There was insufficient time for analysis. Utilizing worksheets, tab-runs, and calculators, a high proportion of analyst effort and time was spent on number-crunching. Operating plans and budgets (at the time) were outputs of a large batch planning system. This system was operated in a simulation mode; dozens of test plans or simulations were run over a three-to-six month period before the final plan was derived. Extensive input data, manually derived, was a prerequisite for each simulation. Considerable time (several days in some instances) was required to analyze and transform the data into a suitable format for the batch model. With the manual handling of large quantities of data it was also error-prone in addition to being a slow process. The simulation output had to be manually manipulated if any analysis was required that was not already programmed.

The timesharing capability was initially used to develop the required input data for the batch planning system and to perform user-defined analysis on the output. These initial efforts established a foundation for a series of timeshared planning models which were developed the following year and, subsequently, replaced the batch system.

PLANNING AT XCL WITH THE PRESENT COMPUTERIZED SYSTEM (28, pp. 580–584)

On-line models at XCL have become an integral part of the management planning and control process. This approach has greatly reduced time and manpower resources to accomplish the task and has allowed managers to quickly ascertain the effects of various courses of action in developing plans and/or responding to operating variances.

Planning at XCL begins with top management defining corporate objectives and philosophy (Strategic Planning). Strategic Planning anticipates the future and formulates strategies to foster progress towards goals. It includes the long range conceptualization and forecasting of markets, estimating resources, and developing alternative strategies to achieve these broad corporate objectives. Being a highly intuitive and judgmental exercise, it is generally not quantifiable.

The identification of Key Result Areas (KRA) is an important part of strategic planning. Once KRA (profitability objectives, productivity assumptions) have been defined, models can assist the planner in several ways. Sensitivity analysis helps select those critical operational variables having significant effect on the KRA. Simulation models provide a readily accessible analytical tool to assist top management in the design and development of alternatives to achieve the KRA and to evaluate the effects of various alternatives in terms of a "base case" or specified goals. These simulations then provide the basis for our long range plan.

Operational Planning

Operating and financial plans become the basis for the implementation of decisions and the control of the business. Operational Planning, relying on input from the Strategic Plan, is involved with the detailed development of selected strategies and relies extensively on cost benefit analysis to aid in the alternative selection process. Much of our modelling efforts have been in this area.

The long range plan is a 10-year forward look of the business and focuses on timephasing our KRA strategic variables at a summarized level by functional area. Simulation models are utilized to identify alternative approaches to achieve the targeted levels. The two-year Operation Plan, on the other hand, is a highly detailed document which provides the first line manager with a set of specified objectives and a financial budget. Financial budget models are used to quickly and economically calculate detailed "chart of accounts" budgets by directly interfacing the output from corporate operational models and other input assumptions (salary levels, travel rates) and special algorithms (depreciation). In addition to the "line item" budgets a set of pro-forma financial operating plan statements are generated.

Short Term Forecasts

Forecasting is the process of saying "Here I am today and this is where I will be tomorrow if I maintain substantially my present course and speed." Although related to planning, it is a different process. At XCL the computer has made a significant impact when applied to forecasting. We have implemented statistical models to analyze and project our key operational and financial variables. These "analysis-control-forecasting" models were designed to be used primarily for estimating the input variables necessary for the planning and forecasting (12-month rolling outlook) simulation models.

The forecasting system, including three exponential smoothing models and a regression model, analyzes current actual data into demand levels, trends and seasonals, and uses these estimates together with past information to project the most likely future level. All products are forecasted by each of the statistical techniques. In addition, the "best" forecasting method (defined as the one that has the lowest mean-absolute-deviation based on historical forecasting) is determined. A forecastability index, serving as a warning signal, indicates which product lines and/or variables are being poorly forecasted.

The statistical forecasts of all critical variables are available within a few seconds. Management has the option of overriding any forecast. This flexibility is critical as frequently the manager has insight into changing events that invalidate statistical approaches and, also, he can often influence and control a variable to achieve particular objectives. The basis for overrides have been (1) a poor reforecastability index, (2) a manager in possession of special knowledge not controlled by the model, and (3) a "what if" position.

The Overall System

It is important to realize that we do not have a planning model as such, rather, we have a series of models (control, forecasting and simulation) which assist in improving our planning and decision-making capability and which are changing over time as we learn more about our business. The entire forecasting and planning system is referred to as the Computer Assisted Outlook and Planning System (CAO/CAP). The classification scheme developed by Little (1970) will aid in understanding the component parts of this decision system which is illustrated below.

The following points clarify events depicted in Figure 11-2.

1. The data base is updated from two sources.

   a. Actual operating and financial performance is collected by in-house batch systems.

      - Salesman order related activity—MAPS
      - Current and historical financial data—General Ledger
      - Customer information—MIS

      This information is transferred tape-to-disc from the batch systems to the timeshared system where it is highly summarized and stored "on-line."

   b. Data, primarily plans and forecasts, is created as output from the various models and is stored on the on-line data base.

2. Management information is made accessible to the models in the following ways:

   a. Projections of management decision variables are obtained from the statistical/econometric forecasting models and are made available directly to decision tables embedded within the simulation models. The decision maker has the option of over-riding any parameter.

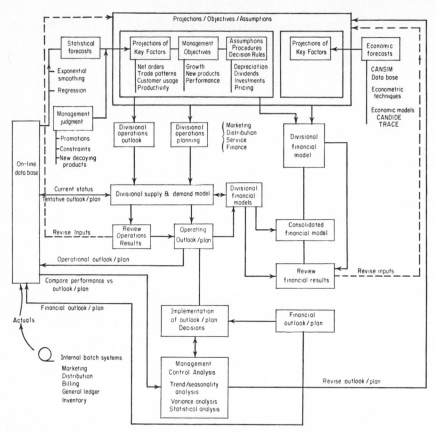

Figure 11-2. Information flow in XCL system. *(From Ronald A. Seaberg and Charlotte Seaberg, "Computer Based Decision Systems in Xerox Corporate Planning,"* Management Science, *vol. 20, no. 4, 1973.)*

    b. Management assumptions and objectives can be set up in decision tables prior to execution of a model or can be entered "conversationally" during execution.

3. Man-machine interaction occurs at multiple points throughout the system.

    a. Each activity (module) shown is a computerized process except those denoted as judgment or review.

    b. Each module contains an interactive model which, in many instances, is comprised of several micro-models. These micro-models, generally possessing a greater amount of detail and complexity, allow the decision maker to examine a problem area independently and in greater depth.

c. A module may describe the activities of several divisions such as ISG, CMD, XRC, XRO, Cheshire and Toner Plant. Each of these divisional models may incorporate the activities of several functional areas such as marketing or finance.

d. Each manager retains control (execution and updating) of models directly related to his functional area. Information generated by one model automatically becomes available to all other models requiring that information.

e. A decision maker is required to execute a series of models sequentially to derive a financial outlook or operating plan. Intermediary information can be retrieved via standard reports or direct data base inquiry with each model.

Information System

The heart of the overall system is the timeshared, on-line data bank. This is a repository of XCL operational and financial data, comprised of actuals, plans and forecasts. The mechanical links (tapes) between XCL operations which reside on in-house batch computers and the information system maintains the timeliness and integrity of the actual/performance data.

The information system can be accessed in two ways. Raw data can be retrieved and manipulated by the analyst or report generators can be used to output information in a variety of standard formats. The keynote is flexibility in accessing and manipulating the data via the terminal. The functional departments control levels of data access for other functional users and, thereby, maintain data integrity and security.

Simulation System

The simulation models developed to date have been primarily the man-machine type although later models were designed to operate with a minimum of human intervention. The initial simulation model has been expanded and refined to describe in additional detail the operations of the functional areas and the financial procedures of XCL. More complex, integrated models have evolved from this effort for use in forecasting, planning, and simulating procedural changes (operations or financial) and for special one-time or infrequent studies such as pricing reviews, promotional campaigns, and facility locations analysis.

The modelling effort, subsequent to the initial simulation model, has been, for the most part, heavily reliant upon the particular functional area for initiation and support. While this approach resulted in uneven development of models (sophistication and depth) it did assure that each manager had models that were responsive to his needs.

Modelling at XCL has been and is a continuous process. We found that solutions to one problem generally resulted in additional questions or demonstrated a lack of understanding of other processes. Model updates and revisions are processed on an on-going basis by changing, discarding and recreating, or at the same time both enlarging some models (to account for added complexities) and adding simplifying models for summary level analysis.

Management Control and Analysis

The planning process should provide a timely feedback mechanism to measure how well objectives are being attained, a methodology to investigate deviations to determine their causes and a means for management to correct unsatisfactory performance that is within control or to adjust plans in light of altered external conditions outside control.

As performance data becomes available to the information system, differences between actual results and plan or previous forecast are monitored for varying historical time periods. Specialized techniques are utilized to perform comparative analysis, determine if the differences are statistically significant and interpret the results in a way that is meaningful to management. Trend analysis and variance analysis are two well-used techniques. Trend analysis assists in identifying changing trend levels and seasonality patterns in critical factors. Variance analysis is used to split revenue and expense deviations into rate and volume components.

These "actual-forecast-plan" relationships are made available through routine or exception reporting or by data base inquiry from a terminal. While these "control" models are passive in the sense that they do not trigger action by themselves to correct perceived deviations, they do convey exception information which, when coupled with the simulation models in an on-line environment, provides the manager with an adaptive mechanism for positive action.

Decision System

The decision system is the most important part of the total system. At the core is the decision maker. Since the other systems have been designed to support the decision maker, it is essential that the right individual be in this position otherwise the most elaborate models will be rendered useless. On the other hand, ineffective computer models, regardless of how sophisticated they are, will impede the decision-making process.

The information and simulation systems are under complete control of the functional areas from the initial design state through routine execution of the system. In no case has decision making been turned over to the computer. With the introduction of the mechanized planning and control systems we have experienced substantially more functional participation in the planning and control activities.

CONCLUSION

In conclusion, timeshared models have proved to be imminently successful in assisting in the planning process at XCL. They have extended the capabilities of the decision maker by providing him with an instantaneous data retriever, analyzer and projector. The simulation models have been adopted in the U.S. company as well as being adapted to our smallest divisions; a fact which demonstrates that computer-based models are economically viable in small as well as large businesses.

This experience has proved to our satisfaction that (1) the basic philosophy is sound, (2) the key element of the process was the application of the scientific method to the business environment, and (3) the decision maker can be intimately involved in the initiation, implementation and execution of on-line models.

12

Budgeting / Wells Fargo Bank

This chapter focuses on the annual planning process as reflected in budgets for revenue and expenses, cash flow, assets and liabilities, and various nonfinancial plans for utilization of time, space, materials, and facilities. The common characteristic of all budgets is that they are expressed in quantitative terms and hence are ideal for computer application. The emphasis today is increasingly on the budget as a tool for planning rather than on control.

CONCEPT

The traditional bottom-up manual approach to budgeting is a time-consuming, frustrating task. As the operating plans are laboriously consolidated at progressively higher levels of the hierarchy, it becomes apparent that (1) certain plans are incompatible, and/or (2) the sum of the plans is not acceptable when compared to the general goals of the total organization. Again and again the plan is sent back to the operating units for rework and resubmittal. Tempers and time grow short until a plan finally materializes, and everyone breathes a sigh of relief until the next planning period.

The management and staff effort consumed in the budgeting process is tremendous and the impact on human relationships is disastrous. Fortunately, this is an area in which the computer can be of great assistance by:

1. Permitting top management to formulate achievable goals by making a reasonably accurate simulation of the total organization.

2. "Exploding" these goals into specific planning guidelines for the major organizational units.

3. Aggregating abbreviated plans from the multitude of operating units into consolidated budgets for the major units.

4. Comparing and analyzing variances between the bottom-up and top-down plans as a basis for productive discussion and reconciliation.

5. "Exploding" the agreed plans into detail for the operating units according to negotiated criteria for allocation.

The relative importance of these computer functions will depend upon the extent to which authority is centralized in the organization. A top-down system will have a very sophisticated modeling network with functional relationships quantitatively defined among the various operations. A system used primarily for bottom-up budgeting, on the other hand, will emphasize the simple arithmetic of consolidation and report generation.

Either way the computer-based planning system is used, the result is a great reduction in the management time consumed in the budgeting process. Because of more specific planning guidelines developed with the computer-based planning system, it is frequently necessary to make only one pass through the budgeting process. Managers and staff can devote themselves to developing better goals rather than to performing the time-consuming mechanics of report generation. Consistency among plans is assured by internal linkages of the system.

Surprisingly, the computer-based planning system actually simplifies the planning process by reducing, rather than increasing, the number of input variables. Many budget cost elements, for example, are very straight functions of other variables and need not be specified by managers.

Using a computer-based system, the line manager need only submit an abbreviated budget proposal consisting of a few critical elements, such as staffing, sales, and capital requirements. The computer simply applies agreed percentages or other adjustments to key input variables and proceeds to "explode" these into a multitude of line items in the budget.

Another unexpected payoff of a computer-based budgeting system is the improvement in accuracy. Consider the number of calculations in a manually prepared budget. It is apparent that human error in the arithmetic is inevitable, especially in the chaotic last-minute periods of revision when the staff is exhausted from long midnight hours. The magnitude of this error becomes evident when the new computer-based system is first run in parallel with the old manual system. One example comes to mind which involved a multi-million-dollar positive cash flow simulated by the computer and a large deficit computed by manual methods. The policy impact of this error was tremendous.

Let us also consider the matter of flexibility, which is a major problem encountered by manual budgeting systems. A normal time for preparing a budget is in the order of four months, which means that conditions have often changed considerably between the time that goals were initially set and the time that the budget is finalized. The manually prepared budget cannot be revised, because of the time involved in its mechanical preparation. The result is that the firm goes into the planning period with an obsolete budget. In contrast, the computer-based planning system allows budget revision at any time with very little effort. In fact, many firms today have not one, but several, approved budgets, depending upon major environmental developments during the planning periods.

BUDGETING REVIEW AND UPDATE

The primary value of planning models in the budget area is the capability of providing a rolling, twelve-month forecast capable of being updated on a monthly basis with actual information and reprojected for twelve months. This is a new, conceptual approach toward budgeting which is being implemented by many firms. A metals company, for example, was able to accomplish only quarterly reviews and very limited analysis prior to development of the computer. Now the controller produces a review and an update by the tenth of each month. Perhaps more important, the staff members now spend their time in analyzing variances from plan rather than in mechanically generating reports.

Normally, the operating budgets are not revised during the year, while the management budgets are updated as the occasion demands. An illustrative system for monthly review and update was shown in Figure 1-7. The system handles both current and cumulative time periods, with comparisons with previous performance. It can operate in terms of percentages as well as absolute amounts, or it can provide data per unit of output.

One of the more important applications of the computer is to project the results for the current year, given performance to date and present trends. The manager can see what the year will look like if present trends continue and what must be accomplished in each remaining month if performance is to be brought back up to plan. This capability is particularly important in the instance of marketing units, for example, which may expend their total promotional resources in accomplishing sales targets to date without consideration of what the rest of the year may look like. In other words, they are in trouble and do not know it.

BREAK-EVEN ANALYSIS

This concept is seldom of practical value without the computer because of the complex cost functions encountered in real life. Costs are not *fixed* or *variable,* but are often some combination of the two. Expenses may increase by discrete jumps, as in the instance of going to overtime rates or cutting in a new facility. Most usually, the cost functions are curvilinear with time and volume. The solution of such complexity is beyond manual methods.

The computer-based system, utilizing search routines, can quickly determine the volume necessary to achieve not only break-even, but any other level of profit. This is the backward search facility, discussed earlier, whereby the planners can specify a value for any line item in any time period, and the system will search to determine what specified performance or condition is necessary for its achievement, other variables remaining constant.

TRANSFER PRICING AND OVERHEAD ALLOCATION

The performance of an organizational unit is often highly dependent upon charges which it must pay for services received from other parts of the organization and upon revenue with which it is credited for services provided internally. It is little wonder that this subject is so sensitive, possibly being exceeded only by the controversies which rage in regard to the methods of overhead allocation. No manager wishes to be charged for services he or she does not control.

The computer-based system allows senior management to examine the sensitivity of performance to pricing or overhead allocation policy. Further, management can simulate alternative policies and obtain specific information for use in negotiations between the managers affected. The computer does not solve the management problem of allocation, but it does make it explicit and does provide a vehicle for mediation.

WELLS FARGO BANK, NATIONAL ASSOCIATION

The Wells Fargo Bank is a full-service banking institution headquartered in San Francisco. Total income of the bank has increased at an annual rate in excess of 14 percent over the past five years and currently exceeds one-half billion dollars. Growth in earnings per share, which is the prime management objective, has averaged approximately 6 percent annually over the same period. Total deposits are now in excess of 8 billion dollars, placing the bank in eleventh place in the United States by this criterion.

The Wells Fargo Bank has been selected as a case for four very good reasons: (1) The computer-based planning system is well conceived and successfully implemented as a budgeting tool; (2) the bank has experimented extensively with both top-down and bottom-up planning; (3) both batch and time-share computers are used for their complementary capabilities; and (4) the bank management is extraordinary in willingness to share information on both its successes and its failures.[1]

Orientation

The senior line management of the retail bank consists of a chief executive officer, an executive vice president (EVP) to whom the branch system reports, and additional EVPs who handle staff functions such as loan administration, marketing, and operations. The chief executive is young, sophisticated, and quantitatively oriented. The 300 bank branches are organized into 5 geographic divisions (Figure 12-1).

Policy, as established by senior management, is implemented by the divisional staff with adjustments to regional needs. The divisional staff departments roughly parallel the staff functions at the senior management level, to which they have dual reporting relationships in addition to divisional accountability. The divisional staff has contact with the daily problems of the operating units as well as frequent access to senior managers who provide a bankwide perspective.

Budgeting, called profit planning at Wells Fargo Bank, has been practiced with some form of computer assistance since 1964. At that time the process began with the collection of separate plans from the individual units of the bank; these plans were subsequently aggregated into a bankwide total for comparison with the goals of senior management. This practice was in accord with management theory, which stresses that short-term planning must involve line personnel whose performance is to be measured. Emphasis was placed on communication among managers to assure consistency and commitment to goals.

The negative reality of this practice of bottom-up management was that the process required many months for execution and consumed extensive time of the managers. This time factor created an inflexibility in the plan which caused it to fall gradually into disuse as the year proceeded. Revision was not feasible. Unit managers were unhappy when their best efforts at planning were overridden by senior management, thus creating strains in the organization.

As a consequence, the senior management determined that the 1971

[1]Appreciation is due Ronald Lanstein of Wells Fargo, who coordinated this study and from whose publications certain of the material was abstracted.

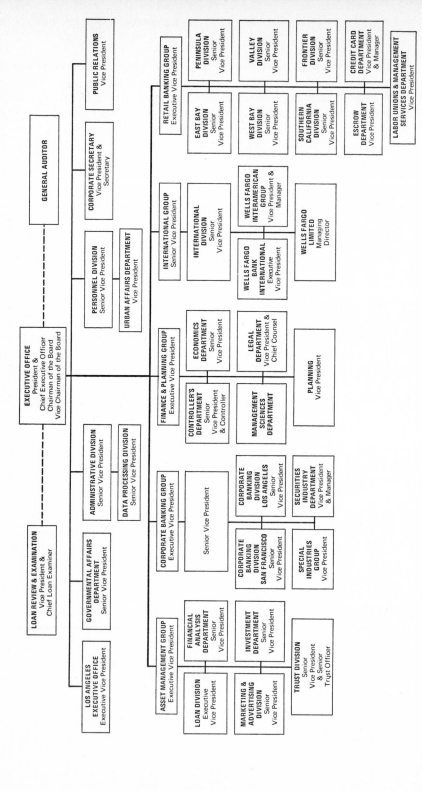

Figure 12-1. Organization chart for Wells Fargo Bank, N.A., and international subsidiary companies. *(Courtesy of Wells Fargo Bank, N.A.)*

profit plan would be generated to agree with the total bank plan and distributed top down to the units. Discussions would be held among managers to determine the viability of the plan and the strategies needed to achieve it. This trend to centralization of the planning function has continued to the 1974 planning cycle.

The Planning Process

The general flow of planning as practiced at Wells Fargo Bank in 1974 is charted in Figure 12-2. Note particularly the parallel but indepen-

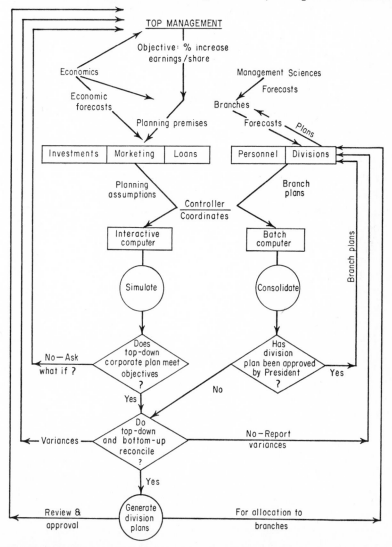

Figure 12-2. Wells Fargo Bank planning process (simplified). *(Courtesy of Wells Fargo Bank, N.A.)*

dent planning efforts from the top down and from the bottom up, with the latter being reconciled with the former through review and discussion. The various steps in the process are as follows:

Economic Contest (July). The annual planning cycle begins with a meeting at which the economists give a briefing to top management concerning their predictions for the following year. These economic assumptions are then inputted to an econometric model of the national economy to obtain forecasts of the key variables for the bank, including interest rates, loan demand, and growth in money supply. A second meeting is then held to discuss these key-variable forecasts and provisionally determine the operative assumptions for the profit plan.

Total Bank Portfolio Forecast. Bank officers chiefly responsible for the overall levels of loans, deposits, and investments proceed to generate the most likely outcome for the bank under the provisional policies and within the assumed economic context. Meetings are held to refine the forecasts and develop initial predictions for the next stage. A computer model is used to relate the short-term economic forecasts to bankwide performance.

Setting Bank Performance Goals (August). The financial statement simulator, which is stored on an outside time-sharing service, is next used by the controller to prepare a complete balance sheet and income statement for the bank, consistent with the total bank portfolio forecast. Input assumptions are either solicited from responsible officers or forecasted to complete the pro forma statement. Key variables and economic assumptions as well as strategies are kept fixed through the first run-out.

The first pro forma income statement is then presented to the chief executive officer, who uses it in discussions with other senior managers relative to developing alternative strategies to improve the outcome. The interactive planning system is used to simulate the sensitivity on outcome of possible variations in key assumptions toward development of the best plan. Performance goals are set toward motivating superior performance.

Bottom-up Planning (August). Concurrently and independently of this top-down planning activity, the operating units have been building abbreviated plans based on the published economic assumptions. The Management Sciences Department provides a service to the branches by utilizing a large computer model to mechanically generate forecasts for each individual planning unit based totally on historical performance.

The extent of involvement of the branch managers varies with the leadership style of each division manager. At a minimum, the manager is required to provide information concerning staffing levels and requirements. Beyond this, branch managers may be asked to generate forecasts of key planning volumes and noninterest income and expenses. These plans are consolidated for the division manager by the Controllers Department, utilizing a batch-run model. The division plan is then compared to the top-down plan and an analysis is provided by the controller for the division manager if it is desired (September).

The group heads review the bottom-up plans in light of the comparative analysis and resubmit the adjusted plans to the controller, who then uses the computer to make a complete comparative-plans analysis with reference to the top-down plan.

The Annual Plan (October). A dialog now begins between corporate management and the division managers, with the objective of preparation of the final plan. The management committee reviews and adjusts the group plans to conform to corporate objectives and strategies. The economics department inputs revised forecasts if required, and the final plan is submitted to the president for review and approval.

Final plan negotiations begin between the group heads and the individual planning units. Unique problems and opportunities in each geographic area are considered and detailed plans prepared for each branch and department. The approved plans are distributed in January to each unit.

Evaluation and Motivation. The final profit-center profit plan contains a variety of goals for each manager. Although profit is the most important single goal, it conveys little information to the profit-center manager as to how to allocate resources if a conflict occurs among the many other goals. Therefore, over half the total weighted standard of performance concerns goals derived from the various special strategies developed in the planning cycle. Weighting of goals is determined by both relative difficulty and importance. This weighting allows management to maintain the central control of policy variables, such as portfolio mix and pricing, while still conveying meaningful goals to the profit centers.

The progress of the profit centers is made explicit by three types of reports. The Goal Performance Report (GPR) is received monthly and records the achievement of the weighted measure. Only the goals which are assigned weights are reported upon, and the percentage of goal achievement is translated into a point score. The second document is the Monthly Operating Report, a fully detailed backup to the Goal Performance Report which shows the manager what has been condensed into a few lines of the GPR. Finally, a Quarterly Profit Plan Report is received four times a year and records in exactly the same detail as the Profit-Center Profit Plan the achievements of the profit center.

Salary review is the primary formal device used in the bank for motivating management performance. The review process is tied directly to the achievement of the profit-plan goals, although including other subjective measures. Thus, the incentive plan provides the real engine driving the implementation of the budget and assures that the budget is explicitly meaningful to all involved.

Progress Measurement and Plan Revision. The profit plan is prepared under an explicit set of economic assumptions with the full realization that many of these expectations will not materialize and that readjustment will be necessary. The economics staff continually monitor changes in the environment which may indicate revision in the plan. The posture of management is to prepare for, rather than react to, new contingencies.

Since one of the major goals of the bank is to outperform its competitors, accomplishment of the plan while the competition does still better may indicate that the goals have been too modest. Therefore, the bank has modeled its competitors in order to estimate the contribution of various factors to profits. The bank closely monitors key policies as compared with these modeled comparisons and reviews the implications of unexpected deviations to determine whether corrective action is advised.

Mathematical models have also been prepared in two additional areas involving repetitive decisions within a highly complex structure. The first concerns decisions on when and to what extent to purchase long-term funds. For this area, a linear programming model has been built which allows for uncertainty under varying assumptions. The second application involves decisions relating to the tax position of the bank, for which a detailed simulation model is used.

Management Commentary

Now that we have examined the theory of the system, let us take a rare opportunity to review how the system functions in practice as related by the various managers and staff who utilize the system. The following comments are very representative of the reactions in many companies.

Executive Vice President of Finance

"I originated the effort to computerize the bank planning process, but am now out of touch with the day-to-day details of that project. The computer is just a slave to get the mechanical work done. It is useful in allocating, recording, and tracking. The development of our system has been evolutionary, and the major difficulty has been vacillation between the top-down and bottom-up approaches to the planning process.

"Bottom-up planning utilizes the computer simply as an accumulator to get bank totals; it continually sums up unit plans until the total is satisfactory. In contrast, top-down planning would be impossible without the computer to break corporate goals down into meaningful operating groups. The problem is to slice up the planning components logically, and that is a very large task.

"Bottom-up planning depends on the autonomy of the operating units as to whether they have the critical variables under their control. Since bank branches do not have control over either market factors or their resources, and since many important decisions are centralized, our planning comes increasingly from the top down. The present planning process results in considerable gaming with respect to operating expenses, and this is an irritation to top management. In the future, our planning will be more top down.

"The key variables in planning are deposits, loans, investments, and interest rates. The computer is used to play with volumes and rates at the corporate level. Senior managers ask such 'what if?' questions as the impact on profits if we cut the volume of deposits, or if interest rates are different, or if we cannot get the planned loan volume, or if we change the mix of bank services. Several variables are often changed at once. The computer-based planning system is used to test the reasonableness of the general objectives of the bank.

"We do not have a formal contingency plan, but do give considerable thought to alternatives and always update the corporate plan with the computer when significant changes occur in the environment."

Controller

"The computer contributes a great deal to budgeting. In fact, certain aspects of the planning process, as it is currently practiced, would be impossible without the computer. Our biggest problem with the computer is systems inflexibility. Since we are working with 900 profit centers, it is quite difficult to change specific numbers or categories. The interactive mode of operation for the corporate modeling system is indispensable, since the turnaround on in-house batch runs is very poor. Budgeting is given a low priority by the computer group.

"The interactive system is used to ask such 'what if?' questions as, 'What will be the effect on total bank earnings if a specific division increases the loan mix?' Most of the 'what if?' questions look at the overall bank performance. The batch system operates on an IBM 360-65 and an IBM 360-67 in-house, and is used to explode the corporate plan into detail for the operating units.

"Maintaining a balance of management involvement is a problem. Top management sets the goals while the controller's role is to coordinate and give suggestions, especially with respect to expenses. Unfortunately, operating management does not get adequately involved and fails to do adequate screening of the plan before it reaches the top. The result is that top management in this bank becomes too involved in detail and the president has to play the bad guy. Managers play games and do not set tough goals for themselves.

"Our next step in the evolution of a complete computer-based planning system is to expand the capabilities of comparing actual to plan and computation of variances. We need to access income and expenses bankwide by categories."

Vice President of Marketing

"My principle involvement in the planning process is to provide input assumptions concerning fees, deposits, and loan yields. Marketing research uses its own computer models in generating these forecasts. Our key planning figure is earnings per share. Forecasting is very difficult for the branches to do, but it does give them an opportunity for participation in the planning process. The bank is really very centralized in planning.

"We know that the first run on the plan will be low, as the operating managers do that on purpose. Then we really go to work on how to meet the corporate goals. We are especially concerned with policies relating to allocation of effort among various areas of income producing activity. We know from experience how much a change in any variable will affect earnings, so we do not need to use math or the computer. We do not run options or ask 'what if?' questions, since the turnaround from the controller's office is too long. It is our understanding that the controller usually has to do computations by hand to answer our inquiries. We do not have computer terminals in marketing.

"Marketing takes the annual plan and turns it into the branch managers' incentive system. This is what really makes the plan meaningful. Various performance measures are weighed to reflect relative difficulty of achievement and relative profit contribution."

Management Sciences

"The computer-based planning system was originated by the executive vice president of finance, built by management science and operated by the controller. There is no user, and very little technical, documentation because the system changes so frequently. None of the bank staff or managers has a theoretical knowledge of the system.

"The computer-based system has had the effect of forcing planners to put something on each line of the plan and to consider all important variables. Previously there were often unpleasant surprises because significant considerations had been overlooked as the planning procedure was not well documented. A secondary benefit is that both management and staff have learned much about the bank operations in the course of building the system.

"The system has shortened the time for the controller physically to generate a budget from three weeks to thirty minutes. We are now able to do thirteen iterations on the budget compared to one previously. The top-down and bottom-up forecasts are getting much closer because everyone is using the same set of assumptions. The discussions between general management and operations are now much more sophisticated as the system evolves into its third full year of operation.

"The objectives of the computer-based planning system have changed since its inception, so that it is no longer used so much as a corporate forecasting tool as in the total planning process. Further, the system has not proven useful in analyzing variances from plan, since greater detail is necessary than is available and analysis is very subjective.

"A problem remains that many managers still think only in terms of their area of specialization; for example, the loan officer thinks the total purpose of the bank is to make loans. Managers do not maintain the total systems viewpoint, but hopefully the computer-based planning system will help improve this perspective."

Executive Vice President, Branch Divisions

"The bank is evolving to top-down planning. We have tried participatory bottom-up planning, but the base units did not understand the overall picture and the sum of the parts was not acceptable for the total corporate performance. We also had the problem that there were discontinuities between the plans, for example, total loans exceeded the deposit base. When the individual branches were asked to forecast salary expense, a little extra from many units made the total get out of hand.

"I am recommending that we go exclusively to top down with volumes given to the divisions. When we asked the branches to prepare the plans, they had to rework them many times, and this led to confusion and a problem of morale. Through sheer exhaustion we would finally arrive at a plan.

"This centralization would have been very difficult without the computer. We do not have terminals in the division, but hope to in the future. I do not ask many 'what if?' questions, as I am more interested in day-to-day operations. Our major objective is return on equity and earnings per share. The main problem is to keep up with economic changes, especially changes in the prime rate. Internally, our major problem is to inform people as to the planning procedure and settle matters of semantics. Many disagreements or misunderstandings arise because of lack of precise definition on what variables mean. People work from different perspectives, but each assumes that others will understand his verbal plans."

Division Operations Officer

"It is my responsibility to prepare the divisional plan covering some seventy branches. As the focal point in the divisional planning process, I am concerned with input from the branches as well as from economics, marketing, and the controller's office. We provide volumes to the controller, who uses the computer to sum the branch plans and apply yields (interest rate on loans).

"We try to prepare a plan that is acceptable to the corporate staff, who then take it to the president, who always says it is not enough, and then comes the top-down pressure. The division is told to revise the plan so that it is acceptable to the president. The head of the branch divisions tells each division its allocation of the sales objective and cost. We usually think the corporation has set the goals too high, but we always make them, so we do not know anymore.

"We are involved in allocating the division quota between branches. This is done by hand according to percentages toward the end of the planning cycle when we have much better information. The computer is used for the massive task of generating the individual branch profit plans."

Branch Manager

"The planning forms start arriving in early August with a request for key cost estimates. I always give a high figure because we know we will get less than requested. We use percentages in making income and cost estimates with adjustments for major factors, such as losing a big account. We were not informed of final approval for the 1973 plan until April of that year. There is a long lag on report of actuals as compared to plan.

"The staff seems to forecast well for the established branches, but not for the new ones. We know they pay very little attention to our forecasts, so spend very little time on it—just put down a figure the night before. The first year I was a manager, I spent a lot of time planning, but no more.

"I am not concerned with 'what if?' questions, but 'how come' costs exceeded forecast. I have never heard of the incentive system. (It has not been formally announced yet.) My plan is not revised, even when major changes occur."

Application Summary

The computer is used at Wells Fargo Bank in the interactive mode to develop the bankwide profit plan. The Controllers Department operates the system to answer "what if?" questions by policy-level managers in developing the general corporate strategy. A batch-run computer-based system is used to sum abbreviated branch plans into division consolidations. The online system prepares extensive comparisons of the top-down and bottom-up plans with analysis of variances. This system is also used to explode the final corporate plan into plans for the operating divisions.

The computer is used to produce input assumptions for the system. The economists use a national model to generate assumptions concerning the economy. Marketing research uses computer models to simulate pricing strategies and to determine which bank services to stress. Bank competitors and the tax position of the bank have been modeled. The Management Sciences Department operates a large model, tied to the general ledger through file editors, which is used to produce mechanistic forecasts for some 500 line items for each of the 300 branches.

The computer generates the annual plan, accomplishes revisions, compares performance with plan, and generates follow-up reports. Computer models are used for simulating the long-term financial commitments of the bank as well as for various special-purpose decisions.

Since introduction of computer-based planning, the bank has moved up substantially against its major competitors in both earnings and volume growth. Plans for the past few years have been achieved to within a percentage point or so. Policy innovations based on use of the system have proven successful, so that greater reliance among bank management has developed toward planning. A recent survey of management determined that 100 percent of the division managers considered the profit plan a useful tool and 82 percent of the branch managers agreed.

CONCLUSION

This case presents an unusual opportunity to study the major problems of computer-based planning. Although these problems are universal, the case is unusual because Wells Fargo has been willing to provide information which other firms normally suppress from all publicity. This unique cooperation is testimony that the firm is secure in the performance of the system.

This case provides an extremely useful illustration of the problem of fragmented perspective as discussed in Chapters 2 and 4. Certain sources of friction are characteristic of computer-based planning systems. The following excerpts from the previous quotations show each speaker's valid viewpoint.

Executive Vice President of Finance: "The computer is just a slave to get the mechanical work done of allocating, recording, and tracking. The present planning process results in considerable gaming with respect to operating expenses, and this is an irritation to top management."

Controller: "Maintaining a balance of management involvement is a problem. The controller's role is to coordinate and give suggestions, especially with respect to expenses."

Vice President of Marketing: "We know from experience how much a change in any variable will affect earnings, so we do not need to use math or the computer. The branch managers' incentive system is what really makes the plan meaningful."

Management Sciences: "There is no user and very little technical documentation because the system changes so frequently. The problem remains that many managers still think only in terms of their area of specialization."

Executive Vice President, Branch Divisions: "I do not ask many 'what if?' questions, as I am more interested in day-to-day operations. Internally, our major problem is to inform people as to the planning procedure and settle matters of semantics."

Division Operations Officer: "The computer is used for the massive task of generating the individual branch profit plans. We are involved in allocating the division quota between branches. This is done by hands."

Branch Manager: "I always give a high figure because we know we will get less than requested. The first year I was a manager, I spent a lot of time planning, but no more. I am not concerned with 'what if?' questions, but 'how come?' costs exceed forecast."

Again, these problems and comments are in no manner unique to this firm. Political gamesmanship, fragmented functional perspectives, continual change, motivation through involvement, and communication malfunction are commonplace in most planning systems. The threats to the computer-based planning system are primarily human, not technical, as will be extensively discussed in Part Three.

13

Multinational Planning Systems (29)

Multinational planning requires advanced tools for handling the complex variety of currencies, languages, and diverse operating conditions characteristic of that environment. The planning process is further complicated by the high degree of uncertainty surrounding political and labor conditions in a number of countries. Computer-based planning systems have particular value in this complex environment because of their capability of providing output reports in any format or language and automatically converting currencies to the planner's specification. This means that information from a number of countries in various languages and currencies can be inputted and the results outputted according to the language and currency specified by the user.

This chapter will describe the manner in which multinational firms are using the computer as an aid to multinational planning, first as a report generator to perform extensive data manipulations to save time and clerical labor; and secondly, at a higher level, as a means of simulating strategies under a wide variety of conditions and under extreme conditions of uncertainty.

BUDGETING

Figure 13-1 illustrates the capability of a multinational corporate simulation system to produce budgets in diverse languages and currencies, with selective report consolidation for various organizational units. In the budgeting applications, the system is capable of producing reports in percentage terms, per unit volume, by ratios, or in any other form in aggregation of reports from various countries, all combined in a consolidated statement.

ENGLISH

Line item	QTR1	QTR2	QTR3	QTR4	TOT
1 Profit & loss					
2 Sales std	1280·00	1282·00	1544·00	1366·00	5471·98
3 Sales midget	728·00	782·40	729·60	740·80	2980·80
4 Sales maxi	688·00	848·00	748·00	848·00	3132·00
5 Total sales					
6 Bad debts					
7 Commissions					
8 Net sales					
9 Material std					
10 Material mid					
11 Material max					
12 Tot material					
13 Labour std					
14 Labour mid					
15 Labour maxi					
16 Total labour					
17 Quality std					
18 Quality mid					
19 Quality maxi					
20 Tot quality					
21 Mfg overhead					
22 Tot mfg cost					
23 Gross profit					
24 Admin exp					
25 R & D expense					
26 Selling exp					
27 Depreciation					
28 Tot gen exp					
29 Pre tax pft					
30 Corp tax					
31 Net profit					
32 Pft/sales					
33 Mfg cost/sls					

FRENCH

Wondr Widget

Line item	TR1 71	TR2 71	TR3 71	TR4 71	ANN71
Exploitation					
2 C.A. std	1280·00	1280·00	1544·00	1366·00	5472·00
3 C.A. midget	728·00	782·40	729·60	740·80	2980·80
4 C.A. maxi	688·00	848·00	748·00	848·00	3132·00
5 C.A. total	2696·00	2912·40	3021·60	2954·80	11584·80
6 Impayes	26·96	29·12	30·22	29·55	115·85
7 Commission	53·92	58·25	60·43	59·10	231·70
8 C.A. net	2615·12	2825·03	2930·95	2866·16	11237·26
9 Mat pr std	666·67	667·71	804·17	711·46	2850·00
10 Mat pr mid	284·37	305·62	285·00	289·37	1164·37
11 Mat pr st					
12 Mat pr mi					
13 Mat pr to					
14 M.O. std					
15 M.O. mid					
16 M.O. maxi					
17 M.O. tot					
18 Cont std					
19 Cont midg					
20 Cont maxi					
21 Tot contr					
22 Aut cts D					
23 Tot cts D					
24 Marge br					
25 Frs admin					
26 Frs R & D					
27 Fsr vente					
28 Amortisst					
29 Couts tot					
30 Ben A.I.					
31 Impots so					
32 Ben net					
33 Ben/ca					
33 Cst dir/c					

NORWEGIAN

Line item	KV1	KV2	KV3	KV4	ART
1 Salg A	540·00	600·00	660·00	600·00	2400·00
2 Salg B	337·00	232·00	256·00	375·00	1200·00
3 Sum salg					
4 Kommisjon A					
5 Kommisjon B					
6 Sum komm					
7 Netto salg					
8 Arb lonn A					
9 Arb lonn B					
10 Material A					
11 Material B					
12 Pr adm kost					
13 Sum dir kost					
14 Brutto fortj					
15 Salgskostn					
16 Adm kost					
17 Renter					
18 Avskrivn					
19 Sum ind kost					
20 Netto fortj					

GERMAN

Lignes	VJ1	VJ2	VJ3	VJ4	JHR
Umsatz A	14666·67	12650·00	11641·67	16041·67	55000·00
Umsatz B	17391·00	20632·33	19946·67	16830·00	74800·00
Ges umsatz	32057·67	33282·33	31588·33	32871·67	129800·00
Material A	4038·11	3535·72	3301·29	4616·74	15491·85
Material B	4789·28	5764·51	5654·87	4842·99	21051·65
Lohn A	7358·38	6558·84	6202·75	8471·83	28591·79
Lohn B	6233·13	7493·83	7393·53	6399·93	27520·42
Gemeink	1323·83	1397·83	1330·00	1348·33	5400·00
Herstellk	23742·73	24750·73	23882·43	25679·82	98055·71
Rohertrag	8314·94	8531·60	7705·90	7191·85	31744·29
Vertrbk	4504·32	4596·17	4469·12	4565·37	18135·00
For & entw	350·00	550·00	350·00	550·00	2200·00
Sons fixk	550·00	350·00	550·00	350·00	1400·00
Gesamtk	29147·05	30246·91	29251·55	31145·19	119790·71
Br gewinn	2910·61	3035·43	2336·78	1726·47	10009·29

In diverse languages and currencies with selective report consolidation and printout on user command.

Figure 13-1. Multinational budget simulation. *(From James B. Boulden, "Multinational Planning Systems," Journal of Long Range Planning, September–October 1972.)*

The budgeting models are further capable of allocating charges, sales, production, and other information among multinational operations. These systems can analyze the variance between actual performance and budget (or between actual and historical data) and can list special ledgers and accounts, such as trade deals outstanding in various countries. The systems are capable of producing widely varying formats where reports are not standardized between multinational operations. Since central computer facilities are used in Europe and in North America, it is possible for various divisions or subsidiaries to input their data to a computer which is easily accessed by the parent corporation without the normal delays in communication.

OPERATIONAL PLANNING

Figure 13-2 demonstrates the capability of a company to solve a complex intercompany sales network. Multinational companies frequently manufacture or purchase subcomponents in one country for assembly in another country into final products sold in still other countries. These complex networks must be solved simultaneously to determine how

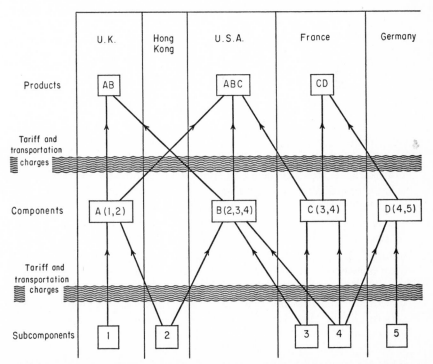

Figure 13-2. Simulation of complex sales network. *(From James B. Boulden, "Multinational Planning Systems,"* Journal of Long Range Planning, *September–October 1972.)*

many subcomponents and components must be produced, and where, to meet the demand forecast for the final products in various countries.

The problem is complicated by the fact that the various companies must continually revaluate their distribution and production strategies. The computer simulation takes into consideration the different labor and materials costs in the various countries as well as transportation expenses and tariffs, and allows the planner to use the computer to search for the lowest-cost production and distribution plan.

Examples of the sorts of question which need to be examined are:

1. Which plants should ship to various markets?

2. How much inventory should we carry in each market?

3. Should we contract out production in the various countries, or should we produce the components ourselves?

4. What will be the impact of a strike in a particular country if it lasts three more months?

5. What is the profit impact of differing product-formulation requirements in the various national markets?

MARKETING TACTICS

Figure 13-3 illustrates the results of a simulation by a French manufacturer whereby one command allows the manager to simulate the profitability of any product group (there are thirty-two) in any of six marketing channels by national markets. The planners in this company may selectively specify the time period and the cost or income items in which they are interested, and instruct the system to analyze either a given product line by individual markets or a given market by products. For example, the company can specify a product line and the computer will automatically simulate the profitability of that line in each market to which it is sold.

The multinational sales manager is faced with the complex problem of pricing in diverse markets and investigating trade-offs between volume and price for individual products. The computer-based planning system allows the sales manager to look at an individual product or even at the packaging of a specific product in a particular market or a particular distribution channel. The effect of varying commission schedules on the profitability of the various product lines can be simulated.

The manager can ask such questions as:

1. What share of the market will we have to realize in Germany to justify establishing an operation at Düsseldorf?

```
PAR  #    3=              .000

LINE ITEMS            DEPARTEMENT:  FON
                      FAMILLE:  FON
                      CANAL:  TOTAL


                      '71
1    CHIFFRE AF       151.00
2    VOLUME            85.60
3    MARGE             65.40
5    CONTRIBUT         36.84
7    RESULTAT


PAR  #    3=             1.000

LINE ITEMS            DEPARTEMENT:  FON
                      FAMILLE:  FON
                      CANAL:  METRPOLE


                      '71
1    CHIFFRE AF       101.00
2    VOLUME            60.60
3    MARGE             40.40
5    CONTRIBUT
7    RESULTAT


PAR  #    3=             2.000

LINE ITEMS            DEPARTEMENT:  FON
                      FAMILLE:  FON
                      CANAL:  EXPORTATION


                      '71
1    CHIFFRE AF        50.00
2    VOLUME            25.00
3    MARGE             25.00
5    CONTRIBUT
7    RESULTAT
```

Figure 13-3. Selective sales and profit analysis by diverse markets. French manufacturer uses one computer command to simulate profitability of any product group in any marketing channel with selective printout. *(From James B. Boulden, "Multinational Planning Systems," Journal of Long Range Planning, September–October 1972.)*

2. How must the international pricing structure be adjusted to maintain profit margins in the face of recent raw material price increases?

3. How should prices be adjusted to reflect changing tariffs and transportation costs as well as the realignment of currencies?

4. What deal can we quote to the Paris distributor for product *D* and quantity *Z* in July?

The sales manager may also wish to simulate the introduction of new products into the various national markets, especially with respect to timing. Through the use of the total simulation system, it is possible to reflect these new-product strategies as they impact inventory policies and manufacturing capacities.

PROFIT PLANNING

The end objective of all strategy simulations is, of course, to investigate their impact on profits. By using a computer-based multinational planning system, the manager is able to explore the interdependencies between production, sales, and cash flows. Further, it is possible to look at any level of detail in the organization, that is, at individual profit centers, countries, divisions, or company total.

The manager of international operations is faced with the problem of allocating resources among countries. Using the simulation system, it is possible to relate this resource allocation to market potentials and cash flow requirements to determine how much profit should be taken and in which country.

The planner is able to simulate alternative pricing policies for intercompany sales of products and services or for transactions between production and distribution, and so to arrive at transfer pricing policies which minimize the tax consequences.

It is important that the computer has the capability to work backward from objectives to determine what strategies will give the manager the profits that are sought. Rather than input various alternative pricing and production strategies, the manager can specify profit objectives and the constraints within which he or she is operating and can instruct the computer to search backward to compute the share of market, pricing, and so on, which will allow the achievement of those objectives.

Many problems become more complex at the multinational level because of varying political, economic, currency, and marketing risks among different countries. For example:

1. What combination of high-risk and low-risk strategies will give the best overall combination of risk and return?

2. What terms are necessary for a proposed joint venture to produce a satisfactory profit?

3. Should we set up a separate operation in country X?

4. Should we combine the operations in the adjoining countries Y and Z?

It is becoming increasingly important that international managers develop more than one corporate strategy so that they can switch plans rapidly as market conditions change within and between the various countries.

CASH PLANNING AND FINANCE

Profit planning is not, by itself, sufficient. The fuel of a business is its cash. Owing to widely varying conditions in different countries, cash management can be one of the most difficult aspects of multinational planning.

Figure 13-4 illustrates the problem of cash planning in a rapidly

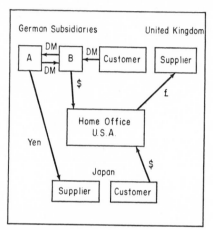

Figure 13-4. Multinational cash planning. *(From James B. Boulden, "Multinational Planning Systems,"* Journal of Long Range Planning, *September–October 1972.)*

changing multinational network. Frequently a company both buys and sells in the same country. Adequate financial planning requires solving the immediate and projected receivables and payables network simultaneously by time periods. The multinational manager of finance uses the computer-based planning system to simulate the flow of cash within and between countries. It is then possible to net out the various intercompany receivables and payables, explore the impact of alternative inventory strategies on cash flow, simulate alternative credit and payment policies, and determine the net position in various currencies for future time periods.

The multinational manager then simulates various alternative hedging strategies to reduce possible exposure to loss from currency fluctuations. Apart from helping to determine the amount and type of financing that should be raised in the various national markets, the computer can help to provide answers to questions such as:

1. What is the impact of the recent exchange controls imposed in Country Y as they affect our cash flow?

2. How much should the Belgian subsidiary lend to the new German operation, and on what terms?

3. Of total finance, how much should be debt, and where should we raise it and on what terms?

4. Which combination of projects with different lives will give the most satisfactory overall long-term cash flow pattern?

The use of the computer in multinational planning is a natural extension of its application to domestic operations, and is rapidly being accepted as a necessary tool to handle the complexities of international operations.

Part Three

IMPLEMENTATION

Implementation

The material in this section is the result of (1) extensive field experience in developing computer-based planning systems, and (2) a detailed statistical analysis of 125 variables in 25 systems over their lifetime to date of publication. The structure and application of computer-based planning systems are evolving very rapidly in an environment relatively free from technical restraints. Very specific data, such as size of models, data storage, languages, and data processing equipment, have been deleted from the text in recognition that they would be obsolete almost at the time of writing.

Even a cursory review of computer-based planning systems leads to the conclusion that there are many failures or marginal successes. System design and construction, as discussed in Chapter 14, is very much an art rather than a science. Inadequate attention is often given to the problems of system implementation and control, as reviewed in Chapter 15. Once the system is built, the technical staff frequently departs for a new assignment with the assumption that the work is complete when, in fact, the problems are just beginning.

The reasons for systems failure, as summarized in Chapter 16, would probably find general agreement among experienced field personnel; however, the relative weighting of these problems would be debated at some length. The best we can say is that the most difficult problems are human rather than technical, which is probably true of all management systems. It is reassuring to review the rich rewards which accrue when the system is even partially successful.

A management philosophy appropriate to improving the likelihood of success is presented in the final chapter. This structure will be meaningful only insofar as it is read in the context of the preceding discussions, of which the philosophy is a summary.

14

System Design and Construction

It is disheartening to watch company after company discard recently completed computer-based planning systems because the original design was accomplished without adequate research into the managerial requirements, both present and future, which the system was to serve. The purpose of this chapter and the one that follows is to present basic concepts as well as step-by-step procedures for the successful design and implementation of computer-based planning systems.

THE DEFINITION STUDY

The first step in the evolution of a computer-based planning system must be the accomplishment of a *definition study* to answer such questions as the following:

1. What are the legitimate areas of application?

2. What are the relative priorities for development?

3. Who will use the system? For what purposes? Define specific "what if" interrogation requirements.

4. What will be the economic costs and benefits of the system?

5. Who will build, maintain and modify the system?

6. How will the new system integrate with existing systems and models?

7. What environmental and internal constraints must be considered?

8. What are the availability and quality of data?

9. How receptive is management?

10. How much detail is required in the models?

11. What will be the technological structure of the system?

This definition study is highly beneficial in itself as a discipline on management. Not infrequently, managers report that the requirement to adopt a systems perspective of the organization and to precisely define decision structure and priorities is much more valuable than the traditional organization study performed by management consultants. Definition studies should be repeated at phased intervals in the evolution of the planning system as it is expanded in scope and depth.

Organization of the Study

The study should be directed by a steering committee composed of the senior executives who will be the ultimate customers for the system. This participation is necessary as a motivational device both to assure later acceptance and to provide the multidisciplinary representation required for a true systems perspective. The function of the steering committee is to resolve conflicts between functional areas, establish priorities, and generally ascertain that the proposed system will meet the requirements of management.

The steering committee will meet weekly during the initial phases of the project to review work done by the task force during that period and answer the many questions which inevitably arise. The chairmanship of the committee should go to the primary customer for the system. The committee will normally consist of the controller, the director of planning, the vice president of marketing, the vice president of operations, and the vice president of finance. The authority implied by this committee is important in later acceptance of the system, so substitution of lower staff must be approached with caution.

The key man in the project is the director of the task force, who reports to the steering committee and is responsible to see that its directions are implemented in the final design. Normally, the task force director will carry through supervision of the project from design to implementation. This supervision will include presenting periodic written progress reports to the steering committee and ensuring compliance to time and cost schedules.

The task force director is distinguished by a systems perspective concerning the particular organization to be simulated. Often the director is not a particularly senior person in authority and may not have a very strong quantitative background. However, this executive is an old-timer who has been around a good while and who knows key people as well as "where the bodies are buried." The task force director is familiar enough with company data to know what is reliable and what is not, knows personalities sufficiently to direct the project into areas where it will be favorably received and understands how functions interrelate. It is important that this individual be free from normal operations for a period of at least six months to carry the first phase of systems design through to implementation.

The project director must be sufficiently tough to keep the very individualistic members of the task force to a preestablished schedule of time and costs. This person cannot be conveniently imported from a consulting firm, although outside assistance may be invaluable in supporting the performance and covering the personal weaknesses of the individual. A company should not enter into the project unless it is willing to commit such a person to the operation. Intimate knowledge of the specific organization is indispensable.

The task force is normally composed initially of the project director, a technical specialist, an accountant, and the systems architect. The architect may be an outside consultant, the project manager, or a very senior operations research person. This individual is critical to the success of the system because of the responsibility to interview managers and translate their general comments into a conceptual design of the overall system. This task is obviously very difficult and requires extensive experience in working with these systems. Often such a person is a specialist in high-level conceptualization and goes from one organization to another performing this function but not becoming involved in the detailed design of the systems elements.

The architect is responsible for the *structure* of the system and development of design specifications to guide the model builders and programmers. Much as in the field of building architecture, computer-assisted planning systems can later be broadly modified if the basic architecture is sound; if it is not, the system will fail despite the best patchwork. The designer must have a personality suitable for top-management exposure.

The accountant on the team will check for data quality and availability as a possible constraint on the system. The technical specialist will prepare some preliminary specifications for systems modules, give thought to the file-handling structure, and investigate integration with existing systems and models in the organization. Other specialists will be called in as the occasion requires to provide inputs in the various functional areas.

Obviously, the definition study represents a significant investment in the time of key personnel; it is a serious organizational commitment. For this reason, the study should not be prolonged. Two to three calendar months should be adequate to complete the first phase, for which the tangible output should be a formal document. This information will provide a basis for management decision as to implementation of the project as well as serve as specifications for the technical team in implementing the design. Assuming the definition study is performed satisfactorily, the project should proceed immediately to implementation to preserve the momentum developed in the form of know-how and management interest.

Performing the Study

The project team will first assemble all formal documentation pertaining to:

1. The planning process

2. Organization chart with staffing

3. Samples of report outputs

4. Documentation on existing models and systems

5. Previous studies or consultant reports

6. Policy statements as may appear in the annual report, speeches by the president, or internal memoranda

7. Environmental information from marketing research or economics

An early question concerns the primary focus of the system. At any given time, management will be particularly concerned with some major problem. Perhaps there is a cash shortage, or maybe a major division is losing money. The task force will search for the "hot button."

The best starting point for systems implementation is an application that will treat a problem of great interest at the policy level. Successful application to this problem will achieve executive visibility and support for subsequent extensions of the system. This is much better than sneaking in the back door on an unimportant application in the hope of expanding the system later. Such strategy is known as "the camel's head in the Arab's tent" and normally is used by technicians when they have not been able to get management support for the initial study.

The best way to identify the "hot button" is obviously to ask management. The level of exposure is critical, since a junior manager will often have quite a different perspective than will a senior executive. The best insurance is to ask both. Therefore, an early task in the project is to scan the organization chart for key contacts and set up formal interviews for the systems architect. It is difficult to arrange meetings at the executive level, and advanced scheduling is indispensable.

How to conduct the interview? This is a matter of personal style and relates to the experience of the architect. Normally the discussion follows whatever managers wish to talk about, with particular emphasis on what they do and what the problems are. The discussion should be held in confidence, with the agreement that the managers will have the opportunity later to review any comments which may be released in the report. The most useful information, of course, is often presented in confidence.

The architect, realizing that all managers operate from intuitive models of the organization, is continually attentive for clues that will help make these models explicit. In other words, the problem of the architect is not so much to come up with a new design as to pick the minds of experienced managers and to translate their concepts into a formally defined framework for simulation. The architect will be particularly interested in those decisions which are (1) repetitive, (2) quantitative in nature, and (3) important enough to justify exploring numerous alternatives. Computer models reflect management needs *both* perceived *and* actual.

The task force will chart the planning process and determine in what manner the interfaces between the various systems are accomplished. Not infrequently, it is found that the strategic planning process is incompatible with the annual planning process. Inconsistencies which may be overlooked in the manual systems become very important in the design of the computer-assisted system. A European food company, for example, reduced the cost of the system by 30 percent after restructuring the various planning processes to assure compatibility.

A frequent practice is to use the existing manual planning system, no matter how defective, as a base for bringing up a computer-assisted system quickly. The result may be similar to building castles in the sand. A very legitimate output of the definition study may be a recommendation that the computer system be deferred until certain deficiencies in the supporting and using systems are corrected, and/or a suggestion that the planning processes and reporting structure be restructured for compatibility. At least a certain minimum level of data organization is certainly necessary, although conditions will never be perfect. Frequently, the approval of such changes are at the board level, since the basic planning and control structure of the organization may be affected.

ARCHITECTURAL DESIGN

Should systems development begin at a general corporate level or with a major division, and if the latter, which division? Managers are often surprised to learn that it is much easier to simulate the behavior of a large organizational unit than one of its small operating components.

The steel-making division of a metals company may be simulated, for example, with rather simple models considering only inputs and outputs to major processing units. A model of a specific blast furnace, in contrast, requires a somewhat detailed knowledge of the metallurgical processes involved. Modeling becomes progressively more difficult as the system approaches the level and detail of operations.

The task force will wish to briefly examine all major alternatives before zeroing in on the most likely applications. The primary consideration is receptiveness of management, with secondary importance given to availability of data, legitimacy of the application, quality of the planning system, and other matters.

Procedure

The design can proceed without an intimate knowledge of the internal systems. "Resemblance in behavior of systems without identity of the inner systems is particularly feasible if the aspects in which we are interested arise out of the *organization* of the parts, independently of all but a few properties of the individual components" (30, p. 17).

We can understand human behavior without a detailed understanding of psychology or physiology, for example, through a study of the environment to which the individual organism is adapting. The hierarchical structure of the organization is a major facilitating factor in permitting the simulation of complexity using simple models. The most simple model of all is normally at the level of the corporate consolidation.

The design begins with an examination of the organizational environment. What are the major problems that the organization faces in the next five years? What questions must be answered by management to permit adaptation to anticipated changes in the environment? Customers, sources of supply, financial markets, personnel, and competitors are all of interest at a conceptual, not detailed, level of observation. The objective of this phase of investigation is to identify the requirements imposed on the system by its environment.

The study is then directed toward the organization within which the planning system functions. The design criteria as well as constraints to be incorporated into the system are defined. What input premises will be made to the system concerning the environment? What is the area of permissible solutions? At this point we are concerned with both inputs and the specific outputs of the system as to number and purpose as well as specific formats. Will the system be used for analysis? For "what if?" interrogation? What power is required of the report generator? What loads will be imposed on the system? What are the requirements for flexibility, for accuracy, and for detail? Is the system driven primarily by marketing or production? What is the base planning period?

This phase of the investigation will define the characteristics of present systems with particular attention to limiting factors. What are the constraints, human and technical? Perhaps data are available only in certain forms of aggregation. What are the redundancies in the present system which can be eliminated? What are the quality and characteristics of the supporting and using systems with which the computer-based system will interface? Are special-purpose computer models presently available? What is the basic unit which remains constant through reorganization and upon which all planning is focused? The identification of the proper building block is critical for flexibility, as discussed in Chapter 5.

In total systems design, certain inputs are converted to outputs by various processes known as the transfer function. These inputs and outputs and their functional interrelationships must be precisely defined. The procedure of investigation is first to specify the objectives which serve as the measure of performance of the system. Precisely what is this computer-based planning system to accomplish? This is perhaps the most difficult question of all, and its answer is quite critical to all that follows. Who will use the system and for what purpose?

The architect will then proceed to examine the conversion of inputs to outputs in the planning system. What are the important functions to be considered as they affect scanning requirements for information transfer between time periods? Time dimensions and flows must be made explicit. Levels of consolidation should correspond to the reporting structure of the organization. Alternative criteria for aggregation may be specified. Flexibility may be necessary to accommodate alternative accounting procedures.

Inclusion and Structuring

It may be seen that the design process consists of both inclusion and structuring. The inclusion study is concerned with identifying those entities, out of all possible ones, which will be included in the system. Structuring involves the determination of how the attributes of these entities are to be related (31). Both the inclusion and structuring aspects of the design problem are guided by the criteria established in connection with the goal definition.

Since system design is only partially science, the personal artistry of the architect is very important. In fact, it is often possible to identify the architect simply by looking at the design. Designers place differing values on the elements and hence vary both in their decisions for inclusion of entities and in the structuring of attributes. The design process is creative and involves highly subjective "feelings" or "intuition" on the part of the architect. Inexperienced designers often focus their attention on the more mechanical problems of structuring without recognizing that the more frustrating and intangible matter of determining variables to be included in the system is of more critical importance.

The various subsystems must be designed so that their measurements of performance match the criteria set for major organizational units, that is, there must be goal congruence. Suboptimization results from the noncongruency of goals. The transplantation of previous experience by the system designer will greatly shorten the time required in this process. Advantage may be taken of previously developed "canned" systems.

The Economy of Design

The architect recognizes that it is a diseconomy to develop one part of the system disproportionately to the capacities of other sectors. Only the most simple structure may be justified if marketing inputs are unreliable or if the data input is faulty. The logic of the models can be no more sophisticated than is justified by available costing relationships.

The architect will focus attention on those organizational units and relationships that are really significant. One operation may account for 60 percent of profits and hence justify great study. Similarly, functions relating labor or materials to volume may be critical while certain administrative expenses are of only minor importance. It is not unusual for some models in the system to consist of no more than a few lines of aggregation. Priorities must be established.

The architect will evolve a proposed program of evolution for the system that will consist of a sequence of defined phases. Once approved by the steering committee, this program defines priorities in the future evolution of the system and hence the basic structural requirements. In designing a home, the architect is very much interested in whether the owners later intend to add another bedroom or even a second story. It will affect the foundation design and the selection of the main structural members. Similarly, the architect of the planning system can anticipate file-handling requirements and important linkages if given some initial conceptualization of the ultimate system.

An important principle of interior systems design is that the provision for all possible occurrences leads to overwhelming costs in the system. The computer-based planning system cannot be everything to every one for now and all time in the future. For this reason, the efficiencies of the design increase with the precision with which its purpose is defined.

SYSTEM DEVELOPMENT

The time required for systems development depends more on the quality than on the quantity of staff assigned to the project. Normally, the design will break naturally into about three major sectors which can be assigned to specialists in the respective functional areas. Additional staff will just get in the way, create undue confusion, and generally prolong the project. Training can be accomplished later after the system has been developed.

Scheduling

A key to expedient development is preparing the initial work schedule, using PERT (Program Evaluation and Review Technique) or some other programming technique to permit parallel development effort. Once the interfaces between the models have been defined with respect to inputs and outputs, the modelers can proceed independently with their construction. Data requirements can be rather well defined at this early stage, so that an accountant can start collecting and refining data for the system. The programming of the data loader and file-handling system can begin at an early point. An illustrative schedule is shown in Figure 14-1.

Normally, a team may consist of the project manager (who may also handle the general systems work), three technical specialists, an accountant, and a programmer. Progress meetings should be held weekly to assure that compatibility is being achieved and to establish matters of technical policy. Technical documentation should be accomplished as the project progresses. It is only too often ignored, and later found to be lacking after the team has disbanded at the conclusion of the project.

Management participation is important throughout the development of the system. The only way the technician can understand how the brand model will work, for example, is to sit down with the brand manager and review step by step how to compute specific items in the plan. If the manager asks certain "what if?" questions concerning pricing, the modeler will provide logic which contains symbols for those decision variables. The decision process must be understood in detail. As discussed previously, the data will be derivative from the logic and must be in a form defined by the accounting system.

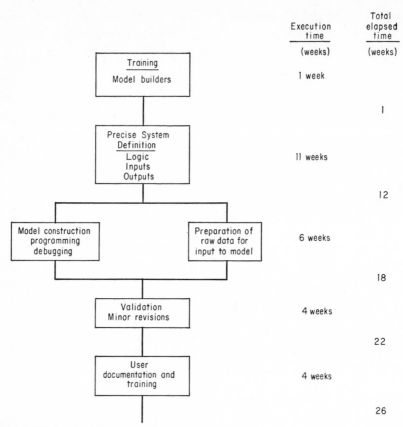

	Execution time	Total elapsed time
	(weeks)	(weeks)
Training — Model builders	1 week	
		1
Precise System Definition — Logic Inputs Outputs	11 weeks	
		12
Model construction programming debugging / Preparation of raw data for input to model	6 weeks	
		18
Validation Minor revisions	4 weeks	
		22
User documentation and training	4 weeks	
		26

Figure 14-1. Work schedule.

Model Building

Just as even the largest and most complex computer is constructed of many simple building blocks, so are models built. Model building is a time-consuming, tedious process of examining each input and output and determining their functional relationships. This is primarily a mechanical process to the point that a high-level technical person may become bored before the conclusion of the project and attempt to insert unwarranted sophistication. *It is very difficult to keep a design simple.* Technical elaboration is the signature of a novice.

Problems in accomplishing the integration of the system may develop at this point. Frequently the model builders have previous experience in constructing isolated models for special-purpose applications, but have no previous exposure to the demands of a large, integrated system. Such modelers may tend to go into a corner and do their own thing rather than cooperate with other modelers working on the project. Strong leadership is required to coordinate these efforts and assure that the models are compatible and properly interfaced.

Models are often judged on their visible output, which must be intelligible to management. Technical jargon and computerese should be avoided. The report generator must contain sufficient flexibility to accommodate frequent changes in format as well as provide differing reports to various users as desired. Printout must be clear and uncluttered. Online systems in particular require, on the part of the modeler, a good understanding of the requirements of the user.

Modularity in the system is very important for both flexibility and simplicity. A restructuring of the models may be easily accomplished to conform to changes in the structure of the organization, if the basic modules are sound. Frequently, new consolidation logic is all that is required. Similarly, we know from experience that a manager interacting with a model cannot handle more than perhaps twenty variables which are *actively* manipulated, although there may be a large number of relatively static variables. This means that complexity must be achieved through modularity if simplicity of individual models is to be preserved. This problem is similar to that of span of control as encountered in organizational designs.

Note that, in many instances, this modeling process (*not* the validation) may be accomplished with "dummy data" while the accountant is working independently and in parallel on the data base. The focus of attention is initially on the symbolic logic of the model, which is later tested and validated against real data.

The models pass from design to coding to integration to validation. Management participation is again very important in this latter stage. Models almost never work properly the first time! Here the value of simple deterministic logic is apparent. The modeler will review the logic, line by line, with an experienced manager, and the errors will immediately become apparent. The model will be revised and run again, and the manager will be most useful in spotting further omissions or errors. This process continues until the ultimate user is convinced that (1) it is operating correctly and (2) the model will be useful,

The procedure for validation is shown in Figure 14-2. Normally, the previous year's data will be omitted in developing the logic of the

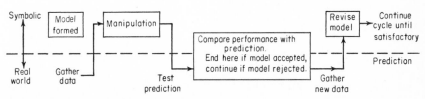

Figure 14-2. Evolution of a model.

models, and then the system will be run against accounting reports for that period. Once the computer-based system is operational, it may be run in parallel to the manual system for the first planning period to assure that it is functioning properly before the latter system is discontinued and total reliance placed upon the computer. Note that there may be arithmetic errors in the manual run which give rise to inconsistency.

User documentation must be prepared which is sufficiently detailed to be useful but not so voluminous as to frighten the users. One compromise is to prepare a very short systems overview to be supplemented by specialized presentations for each functional user. It is helpful if this documentation is physically prepared by a nontechnical person who will eliminate jargon and assure intelligibility to those unfamiliar with such systems.

The total time for system development, excluding the definition study and assuming systems software is purchased outside, should not exceed six months. Specifically, the system must be up and operational within this time for practical application, such as use in the next budgeting cycle.

If the development for any phase of the system takes longer than six months, either (1) the initial design was too ambitious, or (2) the technical staff is busy rediscovering the wheel. The proper philosophy is to accomplish a phased development with utility demonstrated at each step in the evolution. The "ultimate" total system cannot be built in one giant stride, since the precise definition of some sectors of the system will depend upon knowledge gained by operating relating sectors. Inputs, marketing assumptions for example, may be initially manual and later replaced by outputs of a market-forecasting system built in subsequent stages.

A computer-based planning system offers many interesting opportunities for technical excursions if the project is not kept under close control. Many excellent systems have been built, and very useful libraries of modeling routines, statistical packages, programming environment, report generators, and other components of the technical system are already in existence. The programming problems and mathematical structure should be straight forward. If they are not, the system may never become operational.

OPERATING HARDWARE

It has been previously suggested that both batch and time-share capabilities are desirable for a computer-based planning system. Normally, a firm of sufficient size to justify such a system will have an adequate in-house computer system to provide the batch requirements for generating detailed budgets and similar aspects of the planning function. The interactive computer facilities will often be purchased from an outside source because of the software deficiencies of the computer manufacturers, the economics of shared time, and the extensive communication networks and technical support facilities of the time-share vendors (although a strong trend to in-house facilities is predictable.)

The choice of vendor is difficult because the published rates and performance characteristics are not directly comparable. Central processing time, for example, is defined differently by each of the major systems. Some systems charge little for connect time and more for the central processing unit (CPU). Storage charges vary broadly. The computer-based planning system will have a high use of CPU seconds per terminal connect hour, often much greater than that required even for engineering.

Unfortunately, the *only* way to determine the relative cost of running a computer-based system on different computer configurations is to bring the planning system up and run it. That is a very expensive process. Bench marks are interesting, but of little value in forecasting actual costs. Small modeling systems can be used for demonstration, but with very misleading results. Seemingly minor deficiencies in a time-share system can become critical when subjected to the very exacting demands of a computer-based planning system.

The best approach is simply to contact other organizations or independent consultants who have had experience in running a full online planning system on diverse systems and who can advise as to their relative merits. The difference in cost can be a factor of 3 or more; the variations in service are great.

SUMMARY

A comprehensive, definitive study is a must prior to any technical effort directed toward model building and implementation. What are the present and potential managerial requirements which the system is to serve, and what are the constraints under which it must function?

Involvement is a key word at all phases of development and implementation. The potential customer for the system must be represented on the committee guiding its development. The evolution of the system should be by well-defined phases, with performance demonstrated each step along the way.

The guiding principle in systems design is simplicity. It is almost unheard of for a system to fail because it is too simple in terms of number of variables and the intricacies of their relationships. Complexity is easy to add if the system is flexible and modular. Utility rather than technical sophistication is the measure of design excellence.

15

System Implementation and Control

Implementation is that phase of the project wherein the technically sound computer-based planning system is made to operate effectively in the real world. An immediate problem appears with the introduction of a highly structured computer system which requires humans to transmit accurate information in a prestructured format and procedure, in contrast with the poorly defined, redundant, unstructured, inaccurate manner to which they are accustomed.

This problem is compounded by the organizational transfer of responsibility that occurs during the implementation period. The technical staff may be eager to be off to new assignments, and the functional staff, which is assuming responsibility for operating the system, may not be adequately trained and may even be highly suspicious of its value. The result is that the system may become a stepchild and fall into this void of accountability. "Implementation . . . tends to be treated as an afterthought. It is, however, the biggest single item that can be responsible for turning a potential system into a shambles. It is responsible, in fact, for more failures in computer systems than all other aspects combined" (33).

It is a mistake to assume that managers will automatically respond in a positive manner to this new and more powerful system. They do not intuitively know what questions to ask of the system or how to interact with the greatly enhanced information environment. An online system with instant access to a large data base will create a new decision environment. Some managers are threatened by the inability to evaluate more alternatives. Fear of personal exposure is great, since decisions can readily be simulated in retrospect to evaluate managerial performance.

Implementation will take place by phases in an evolutionary manner according to the program established by the definition study. The computer system will necessarily be modified to accommodate the human organization, just as managers are expected to adjust to the new planning system and structure. The system should have a tolerance for human error, with appropriate safety features to avoid loss of data and to tutor the operator in the use of the system. Any system features which increase the need for accuracy in the data or for the user's technical sophistication should be questioned carefully.

Managers and staff are often conditioned to use present manual systems. Retraining is then necessary to assure acceptance and use of the new computer-based system, which are usually quite difficult to obtain. Time is required to get acceptance even when such forceful approaches are used as that of increasing reporting requirements so that manual methods are impossible.

THE INTERFACING OF HUMAN AND TECHNICAL SYSTEMS

Formal systems endorsement by the chief executive is of considerable value at this time to counteract the many vested interests which often accompany implementation of the system. An experienced consulting firm uses a formal logic sign-off as an important phase of systems implementation. A full management presentation is scheduled during which the English language logic of the models is reviewed step by step. This conference eliminates controversy as to the amount of detail that should be built into the system, establishes the standard of acceptable logic, and provides a more complete involvement of the management from the president on down.

CONTROL

The development phase of the project should terminate on schedule and one "keeper of the system" should be appointed to perform necessary maintenance as well as to teach users. In a medium-sized organization, this function will probably be reduced to a half-time responsibility by the end of the first year.

One problem in controlling the system after implementation involves the cost of data storage. Time-share vendors charge by both the volume and the time of online data storage. If an outside service is used, the employing firm should determine how that particular vendor computes storage charges and should assure that only necessary information is kept in the systems files. As noted in the previous cases, there is a tendency for the data base to expand rapidly. Much of this information can be kept offline and loaded as required on a few hours' notice.

An accountant should be appointed to supervise the loading of the data to assure that the files are kept current with accurate information. Normally, the act of loading data will be accomplished by a clerk or secretary using a data loader. This program is important in detecting error and making certain that the right data get in the right files. Fortunately, component routines are available which permit the construction of an online data loader within a few days.

The keeper of the system and the accountant responsible for the files (who may be the same person) should have security codes to prevent anyone else from changing the logic of the models or altering the data in the system. A more elaborate system of security may be justified in certain instances to provide selective user access to specified levels of aggregation and data according to the "need to know." The keeper of the system is responsible for the scrambling routines and the frequent revision of security codes to protect the integrity of the system.

Certainly this must all seem obvious. However, many operating systems have no one person accountable for their maintenance and performance. Data files become obsolete and models are not revised to reflect the continually changing organization. It is little wonder that these systems fall into disuse. The initial steering committee should continue to meet quarterly to review the systems performance and evaluate extension into subsequent phases of the design.

A converse problem involves the continued technical evolution of the system ahead of the capacity of managers to use it. A manager accesses a model in which he or she has just been trained only to find that it does not quite work because of some minor change made in the intervening period. Once a system is in use, the temptation to make changes is great as many technical opportunities become apparent. The best practice is to accumulate these changes and accommodate them in one major revision of the system, which should not occur more than once a year.

Online computing differs from batch computing in that when an interactive system does not work, the failure becomes apparent to all users immediately. There is no opportunity for the systems staff to make repairs in the privacy of the computer room. A miscalculation may destroy forever the confidence of a user. For this reason, the new system version should be thoroughly tested on an experimental account before it is released to the organization. The new version will contain all improvements as of that date and will be well documented.

Systems which are continually modified become difficult to document. The only reason that many systems work today is because the technicians who built them continue to run them. Documentation is neglected on the theory that is will soon be obsolete anyway and because it is an unpleasant task unworthy to occupy the time of the technicians who built the system. The system may work for a time without documentation, and then suddenly, after the specialist leaves, strange things begin to happen. It is extremely difficult for the successor to follow through the coding with all the blind alleys that have developed through time. In some instances, it may be easier just to start over with a new system.

A user survey at the end of the first year may be useful to determine precisely who is using the system for what purposes. Meters may be installed on various parts of the system to log usage times. An inquiry may then follow to identify specific weaknesses in the system and to suggest ways of expanding the usage. A recent study of a well-established system revealed that several major divisions of the organization were not even aware that the system was available and that, in fact, two new and incompatible systems were in the process of construction. Training and retraining are important. The system is very vulnerable in the early years of operation.

ECONOMICS

It is risky to make a written commitment on the subject of economics; however, the need to do so is rather apparent. The figures in Table 15-1 are 1975 dollars and assume that a medium-sized firm has purchased the software package and time-share services from outside vendors. These costs are derived solely from personal experience plus a very limited survey, and should be used with caution. ·

A good guess is that a quarter-million-dollar investment is required before the system is operational. This cost of development does not vary proportionately with the size of the organization, since certain basic tasks must be performed in any event. A manufacturing firm of $20-million sales, for example, might encounter a cost of half the estimate, and a firm with $1 billion in sales might spend twice the estimate. The time for development will increase by a factor of 2 or 3, and the costs of technical labor by 100 percent if the software is developed internally. Labor costs for operations, in such event, will also be doubled during the first few years, since continual reprogramming will be necessary to expand and maintain the software.

The primary cost of systems development and implementation is technical labor, which accounts for almost 70 percent of the total. Indirect labor costs for management supervision and training bring this cost up to 80 percent, thus clearly indicating the point where control is required. Any lower estimates are either (1) not including all costs, (2) referring to some lower-order system, such as a report generator or stand-alone corporate model, or (3) inexperienced.

The operating costs of the system will vary greatly month to month and over time. A good guess is $100,000 a year, comprising rather

TABLE 15-1. Expenditures (In thousands of dollars)

Time	Definition study Two months	System development Six months	Implementation Six months	Total $	Total %	Running One year	Percent
Management supervision and training	$ 6	$ 6	$12	$ 24	10	$18	19
Technical staff (including project director)	22	111	30	16	67	30	31
Software rental	0	15	6	21	8	12	12
Computer time	0	15	12	27	11	18	19
Storage	0	4	6	10	4	18	19
Total	$28	$151	$66	$245	100	$96	100

equally technical support, computer costs, and other expenses, including primarily management supervision and training. Storage costs will increase and training costs may decline over time. Computer time will remain rather constant.

Periodic inflation of these running figures may be anticipated during periods when the system undergoes substantial modification and/or extension according to the program of planned evolution. Attempts to reduce the proposed operation costs should be made with caution if they involve cutting down on training time or reducing technical support for the maintenance and update of the system and data base. This may be penny-wise and pound-foolish.

16

Rewards and Penalties

As is evident from previous discussions, computer-based planning alters the power structure, changes patterns of communication, revolutionizes decision making, and makes new demands on the data base and other supporting systems. Also, it changes management roles and in general disturbs human relationships by threatening security and imposing new demands for cooperation. Moreover, these systems require an initial investment in the order of one-quarter-million dollars and an annual operating budget of $100,000. Prudent management practice requires that the risks must be balanced against possible return.

THE EVOLUTION

Computer-based planning systems have undergone a major evolution since the corporate models of the 1950s. Criticisms directed toward the early systems are to a large extent no longer valid, and new problems have arisen. One framework for distinguishing between major periods of corporate modeling is illustrated in Table 16-1.

The bottom-up era of modeling corresponded to the clerically oriented period of computer applications, as discussed in Chapter 1. Modeling emphasis was placed on problems at the operations level because of their ease in quantification and frequency of repetition. Manufacturing engineers were attracted to the computer and communicated rather well with the operations research staff.

The logical extension of the operations modeling effort was to group these models into representations of larger units of the organization. The result was disaster as the detail and data requirements compounded until the system became incomprehensible and inoperable. The lessons learned from the bottom-up period were:

TABLE 16-1. The Characteristics of the Major Periods of Corporate Modeling (32, p. 106)

Design approach	Period	Prevailing computer technology	Feasible applications	Modelers	Major focus of attention	Major fallacy	Lessons learned
Bottom-up	1956–1963	Second generation: batch processing high-level programming languages	Corporate models designed and implemented by technically oriented personnel	Operations researchers	The model	Models of operating processes can be utilized as planning tools	1 Planning models are different from operating models 2 Operations researchers ("outsiders") do not understand the management decision-making process well enough to build general models
Top-down	1964–1969	Third generation: disk storage time sharing model programming languages	Large models (both in size and in data required) easier to build with special languages	Management scientists and systems analysts	The model	Large, "realistic" models are required for planning, and can be responsive to decision making	1 Large models are relatively inflexible 2 Large models overwhelm the manager's ability to understand the assumptions of the model and to integrate its output into the decision-making process

Inside-out	1970–present	Third-plus generation: mass low-cost storage data bases teleprocessing minicomputers	More efficient use of corporate data Sharing data and programs among geographical areas	Ad hoc project team: managers, systems analysts, management scientists	The process	Undetected, but doubtless there	1 The manager must be intimately involved in the model-building process
							2 Simple models are usually the way to start
							3 The model should evolve in complexity or size as required by the decision-maker, and at *his* or *her* pace

1. Operating models are not planning models. The kind of information required is different, procedures are different, and the output required is different.

2. Planning models cannot be built by specialists who are not familiar with the company and its planning process. Knowledge of why and how planning is actually accomplished is necessary [32, p. 106].

The second wave of organizational modeling occurred in the middle 1960s when sophisticated operations research groups were recruited to develop the corporate model. The result was a highly sophisticated, top-down approach to modeling. The technical staff built the models in isolation from the managers who were to use the results, and in some instances even attempted to usurp the latter's decision-making authority.

The result was a total lack of realism, and managers became thoroughly disillusioned with the whole concept. Corporate modeling became a dirty word, subject to endless stories of almost-fraudulent conduct on the part of technical specialists.

The problems of planning in a rapidly changing environment did not disappear, however, and managers were forced in the 1970s to turn again to the computer for assistance. Scars healed with time and the new technological innovations prompted a reevaluation of developing a computer-based planning system. Emphasis changed from the model to the planning process. This time, management determined to maintain control of the development and to assure involvement of personnel who understood the problems. Development of a useful system was recognized as primarily a management, rather than a technical, problem. This has been termed the inside-out era on the matrix of Figure 16-1. Unfortunately, the problems, although of a different nature, continue to be significant, and many systems are failing in the mid 1970s.

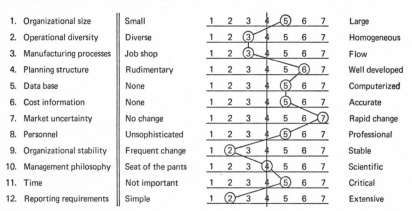

		1	2	3	4	5	6	7	
1. Organizational size	Small	1	2	3	4	(5)	6	7	Large
2. Operational diversity	Diverse	1	2	(3)	4	5	6	7	Homogeneous
3. Manufacturing processes	Job shop	1	2	(3)	4	5	6	7	Flow
4. Planning structure	Rudimentary	1	2	3	4	5	(6)	7	Well developed
5. Data base	None	1	2	3	4	(5)	6	7	Computerized
6. Cost information	None	1	2	3	4	(5)	6	7	Accurate
7. Market uncertainty	No change	1	2	3	4	5	6	(7)	Rapid change
8. Personnel	Unsophisticated	1	2	3	4	(5)	6	7	Professional
9. Organizational stability	Frequent change	1	(2)	3	4	5	6	7	Stable
10. Management philosophy	Seat of the pants	1	2	3	(4)	5	6	7	Scientific
11. Time	Not important	1	2	3	4	(5)	6	7	Critical
12. Reporting requirements	Simple	1	(2)	3	4	5	6	7	Extensive

Figure 16-1. Suitability profile.

WHY SYSTEMS FAIL TODAY

No one really knows precisely why so many computer-based planning systems continue to fail in the sense that they are discarded within the first few years of operation and never used again. The author's experience indicates that approximately one-third of the systems fail in the first two years after implementation and another third provide indifferent performance. Since each system represents a large investment of dollars and human effort, these failures are a serious waste to the society and to the individuals involved.

Certainly, many of the reasons for systems failure relate to the problems encountered by the planning function in general. Professor George Steiner and the Planning Executives Institute conducted a study in 1972 to identify the most important pitfalls in comprehensive long-range planning. The survey included responses from 188 firms (33).

The number one planning pitfall, according to this sampling, was "top management's assumption that it can delegate the planning function to a planner." Comprehensive corporate planning is the responsibility of the chief executive officer, who can delegate parts of the job, but not the responsibility. This executive's strong commitment is absolutely essential.

The second problem in order of priority is the tendency of top management to become so engrossed in current problems that insufficient time is spent on long-range planning; the planning process then becomes discredited among other managers and staff. This problem was identified as *most* important in firms with sales of 50 to 100 million dollars.

The third problem found in Steiner's study was failure to develop company goals for use as a basis for the formulation of long-range plans. The goals were either too vague to be useful or excessively optimistic and not based on realism. The fourth ranking pitfall was failure to obtain the necessary involvement of major line personnel in the planning process. Planning is ultimately a line, not a staff, function, as is necessary for both realism and acceptance by personnel.

Gary Neale has had a broad exposure to the specific problems of computer-based planning systems through his responsibility for managing a leading consulting firm in this field. He comments as follows concerning the reasons for systems failure in order of priority:

1. No planning alternatives are being considered in the company. Day-to-day operations are so pressing that no one thinks in terms of planning. The model keeper is sitting there begging for someone to ask a "what if?" question. [Note Steiner's pitfall number 2.]

2. Poor training of managers on how to ask questions of the system.

3. Planning models have a tendency to cut across internal political boundaries no matter what department is running them. Accounting and finance have to keep the numbers, and this tends to bring to the surface long standing challenges and political feuds which can destroy the models.

4. The company has no in-house technical support for changing and updating the models.

5. The models are too detailed. The data required to keep them up to date is too voluminous and the logic is too complicated to understand.

6. There is no real management involvement in building or subsequent running of the system such that it does not represent the reality of the organization. [See Steiner's pitfall number 4.]

7. The models are not tied to proven manual systems in the accounting and finance area, which means that data is not available.

8. Key users leave the company or are transferred internally and the new people are reluctant to try someone else's system.

9. The manual supporting systems are changed after the models are built so that the computer-based system is no longer compatible.

10. Major organizational changes resulting from mergers and acquisitions, spin offs and so on obsolete the system.

The numerous reasons for failure are understandable when we consider the complex nature of the computer-based planning system itself and the necessity for interfacing with the many supporting and using systems within the organization. Some perspective on the relative seriousness of these problems by major category is indicated by the author's in-depth study of twenty-five successful systems:

Major system threat	Percent reporting
Political conflicts	40
Reorganization	20
Training	12
Data problems	12
Systems complexity	8
Cost	4
Other	4
	100%

Perhaps technical considerations are a relatively minor constraint because the capabilities of computer-based planning systems are generally exercised to only a fraction of their potential. Human constraints are critical in most systems, as discussed in Chapter 4, and they will be overcome only as the potential benefits of these systems are clearly demonstrated.

ORGANIZATIONAL BENEFITS

Why are so many firms braving extreme hazards to pioneer in computer-based planning? These costs and risks can surely not be justified by cost savings resulting from reduction in the clerical staff necessary to prepare reports. In fact, the financial staff frequently expands rather than contracts after introduction of computer-based planning, as required by the greatly increased scope and sophistication of investigation requested by management. Faster and more accurate report generation is nice, but will not justify the effort and expense necessary to develop a computer-based planning system.

The following are a few responses from the organizational viewpoint as to why the use of computer-based planning is expanding so rapidly.

1. A food company accomplished major economies in the use of management resources by shortening the time required to develop the annual plan from five months to two months after installing the system.

2. An animal foods producer estimates that the increased profits in one year, resulting from faster and more accurate price adjustments to changes in commodity prices, more than paid for the complete design and installation of the computer-based planning system plus its projected cost of usage for the next ten years.

3. A forest products company states that it recovered the total costs of developing its computer-based planning system through one application to bidding on a proposed land acquisition.

4. The entire financial analysis section of one European manufacturer threatened to resign rather than go through the personal pressures of one more manual preparation of the annual plan.

5. A government bureau assures most efficient utilization of its field staff by using its conversational system to schedule personnel allocation by projects throughout the United States.

6. A large number of public utilities now use computer-based planning systems to simulate financing for much-needed facilities expansion programs and for negotiating rate adjustments with government agencies.

7. A steel producer achieved the highest profit margin in the industry one year by using its system to develop alternative inventory strategies relating to union negotiations.

The advantages of computer-based planning systems to the organization may be summarized as:

1. Shorter time required to prepare plans

2. Fast, accurate calculations

3. Instant answers to "what if?" questions

4. Ability to evaluate more alternatives and develop contingency plans

5. Broader organization perspective

6. Improved communications

7. Integration of planning and control

8. Better plans based on more current assumptions

MEETING INDIVIDUAL NEEDS

The computer-assisted planning system will be used to the extent it meets the needs of individual managers and staff. The following comments relate to the personal benefits reported by major systems users.

Line Management

The system permits the manager to look at more alternatives in a shorter time. It broadens the manager's perspective, thus facilitating determination of how a decision will impact many areas of the organization. Complex relationships between costs and profits can be simulated. The system will help identify the critical factor in a decision by computing sensitivity of outputs to inputs.

Controller

The controller is interested in the application of the system to the annual planning process, with emphasis on budgeting. The controller needs the computer to expedite the preparation and updating of the annual plan. With the computer, mechanical preparation time may be cut from a matter of weeks to that of a few hours and arithmetic errors are eliminated.

Corporate Planning

This application includes strategic planning, diversification, new-product development, market development, acquisitions, and mergers. The corporate planner uses the system to generate alternative plans and to ask "what if?" questions. The computer-based planning system permits the planner greatly to increase the scope and sophistication of service to senior management.

Vice President of Finance

The financial vice president is the intermediary between top management and the staff specialists who use the system. Inquiries are received at a policy level, and must be translated into specific questions for the analysts to explore on the computer-based system. The financial manager is very much interested in simulating cash flows and developing alternative plans for financing the operations and growth of the organization.

Financial Analysts

This is by far the largest group of users. They are academically trained to use sophisticated tools of analysis, but find themselves doing busy-work in the mechanical preparation of the plans. The computer-based system frees analysts to utilize their full talents in improving the allocation and control of organizational resources. Powerful tools are readily available through the system for exploring functional relationships and simulating alternatives.

Accountants

Accountants are evolving from record keepers to planners. At the present time they are interested in the computer-based planning system primarily as a means of simplifying the data base; however, they are expanding their participation in the total system, with emphasis on its forecasting capabilities.

From the perspective of individual users or customers in the organization, these systems are advantageous in that, in summary, they:

1. *Save time and/or work*: They greatly reduce the manual effort required to generate the long-range plan, the annual plan, and the detailed budgets. They simplify the data base.

2. *Aid decision making*: They permit more alternatives and broader perspective; identification of critical factors; and "what if?" questions.

3. *Improve relationships with superiors, subordinates, and associates*: They improve communications by standardizing and defining planning assumptions and developing a broader organizational perspective.

4. *Result in better job performance*: They eliminate routine activities and facilitate analysis. They permit increased output and shorter response time to inquiries.

5. *Stimulate new ideas*: The user can explore more combinations and permutations. Important interrelationships among variables can be identified and simulated.

6. *Help meet competition*: They permit alternative marketing, production, and financial strategies to be developed in advance—to be implemented quickly when the action of competitors becomes apparent.

7. *Help in meeting sales and profit goals*: They tie all decisions through directly to organizational profits. A change in market forecast is quickly reflected in the plans of all other functional areas. Alternative promotional strategies are simulated under "what if?" conditions.

8. *Avoid costly risk or errors*: Perhaps the biggest payoff of all, they permit management to avoid making bad decisions by simulating them first on the computer before committing the organization. Arithmetic errors are eliminated.

EVALUATING THE POTENTIAL

Experience indicates that the probability of successful implementation of computer-based systems can often be predicted in advance by examining certain organizational and environmental factors. The following factors should be considered by management in evaluating the appropriateness and timing of installing a computer-based planning system.

Size. The cost of a computer-based system does not increase in proportion to the size of the organizational unit. A manufacturing operation with less than 10-million-dollar annual sales should sharply question the desirability of the investment. With more than 50 million dollars, there is usually no problem of justification.

Diversity. A widely diversified company, with many unrelated activities, must evaluate the economics of such systems based on the size of the individual units—for example, a homogeneous company of 20 million dollars in sales may be more favorable than a conglomerate of ten times that size. Of course, consolidation systems are often useful for the corporate staff.

Processes. Computer-based planning systems are normally highly useful in a flow type of operation, such as foods, forest products, or metals. Systems design is much more difficult in job shops with one-of-a-kind activities.

Planning Structure. It is highly desirable that the planning processes be formalized prior to computerization. The company which does not have a history of planning cannot expect the computer to solve its problems immediately.

Data Base. The lack of a computerized management information system (MIS) is a poor excuse for not developing a computerized planning system. However, the lack of even manual data collection systems for basic information is a serious constraint.

Cost Information. Direct costing, or other forms of accurately relating costs to volume, is highly desirable prior to establishing a computer-based planning system. Such information is necessary to assigning realistic values to the variables in the system.

Environmental Uncertainty. Surprisingly, new ventures and highly uncertain markets are very favorable applications of computerized planning. The computer allows the flexibility to ask the many "what if?" types of question which are so numerous in industries, such as consumer products, where the environment is subject to great uncertainty.

Personnel. The system will not operate itself. Technical talent is necessary to develop and maintain the system. How receptive is the staff to innovation? Perhaps the firm can contract part of the initial development to outside professionals.

Organizational Stability. Constant reorganization is a threat to every system, and especially to computer-based planning systems.

Management Philosophy. The system will not be used unless planning is strongly stressed by top management. Such management must also be willing to accept the discipline for increased precision which the system requires in definition of objectives and specification of assumptions.

Geographic Dispersion. This is usually not a problem because of intercontinental communication networks which allow accessing a central computer from widely diverse locations via local telephone calls.

Time. Companies utilizing a fairly straightforward annual plan which does not require frequent update and revision may find it hard to justify a computerized system.

Reporting Requirements. A computerized system is helpful as "slave labor" in producing error-free reports. The more extensive the reports and the more frequent their submittal, the stronger the argument for computerization.

Suitability Profile

A form similar to Figure 16-1 may be useful in evaluating the advisability of installing a computer-based planning system in a given organization at this time. Responses can be graphically connected to form a suitability profile, as in the example.

It is difficult to quantify the scales used in this exercise, and the results should be taken as a general indicator rather than as precise measurements. Unfortunately, a single highly unfavorable factor can, over a period of time, lead to the destruction of the system.

17

Management Guidelines

"A philosophy is a system of thought based on some logical relationships between concepts and principles that explains certain phenomena and supplies a basis for rational solutions of related problems" (34, p. 6). A management philosophy as applied to computer-based planning systems will be concerned first with principles as applied to systems generally. Such a philosophy will then focus on the management systems, subset with emphasis on planning and the guidelines attendant thereto. Further attention will be given to those principles of human behavior which determine the success of the system as measured by acceptance and use. Finally, the philosophy will encompass those general truths or guidelines applicable to the technical aspects of computer-based planning.

A conceptual framework of principles, illustrated in Figure 17-1, may prove a useful checklist to those involved in the design, construction, and implementation of computer-based planning systems. The following sections will first examine the truths applicable to all systems, then discuss management principles, including those related specifically to the function of planning as well as others involved in the implementation and operation of the system. Finally, previous material will be summarized in the form of principles relating to both the human and the technical aspects of computer-based planning systems. The chapter will conclude with a look into the future evolution of these systems.

It is apparent that the development, use, and management of a computer-based planning system depend upon correlating and structuring diverse information and concepts into a coherent philosophy. The development of such a conceptual framework provides a useful opportunity to review and extend previously discussed theory and applications.

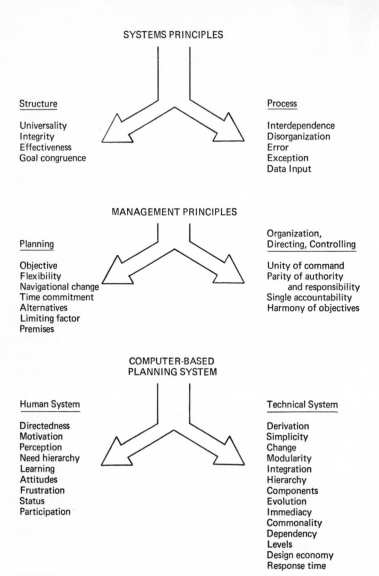

SYSTEMS PRINCIPLES

Structure

Universality
Integrity
Effectiveness
Goal congruence

Process

Interdependence
Disorganization
Error
Exception
Data Input

MANAGEMENT PRINCIPLES

Planning

Objective
Flexibility
Navigational change
Time commitment
Alternatives
Limiting factor
Premises

Organization,
Directing, Controlling

Unity of command
Parity of authority
      and responsibility
Single accountability
Harmony of objectives

COMPUTER-BASED
PLANNING SYSTEM

Human System

Directedness
Motivation
Perception
Need hierarchy
Learning
Attitudes
Frustration
Status
Participation

Technical System

Derivation
Simplicity
Change
Modularity
Integration
Hierarchy
Components
Evolution
Immediacy
Commonality
Dependency
Levels
Design economy
Response time

Figure 17-1. A conceptual framework.

Certain of the following "principles," especially those relating to general systems and to human behavior, are experimentally well documented. However, theorists over the past decades have heatedly debated the existence of general truths applicable to the field of management. Perhaps such observations cannot be labeled "principles" within the rigor of a physical science definition; however, they have predictive value in that problems normally ensue when they are violated.

Many of the following statements sacrifice accuracy for simplicity and can ultimately be defended only on the ground that they appear to be very useful for managers and technical staff in finding rational solutions to problems relating to computer-based planning systems. Principles provide the basis for policies and practice.

PRINCIPLES OF THE SYSTEMS

Organizations are systems of consciously coordinated activities or forces. A system was defined previously as "a regularly interacting or interdependent group of elements forming a unified whole." This definition suggests the systems principle:

Principle of Interdependence: A change in any element of a system will be reflected in many other elements of the system.

The manager must adopt a holistic, rather than a fragmented, perspective of the organization. A pricing decision cannot be made, for example, without regarding the effect on inventories and hence on cash flows. This first principle is reinforced by a principle of universality (the titles are the author's).

Principle of Universality: All systems are parts of still larger systems.

The dividing line between systems is not clear in most instances. The computer-based planning system must be integrated with all supporting and using systems. The design of the planning system will begin with the external environment within which it functions. The identity and uniqueness of each system are established by its goals.

Principle of Integrity: Each system is characterized by a certain integrity to which all parts of the system contribute either directly or indirectly.

The computer-assisted planning system is established to accomplish certain objectives which must be clearly defined, as indicated by the principle of effectiveness.

Principle of Effectiveness: The effectiveness of the systems design increases with the precision with which the objectives can be defined.

Highest priority must be assigned to define the purposes and structure of the system. Since the many organizational elements are interdependent, it is important that goals or measures of performance be mutually reinforcing toward the higher-level purposes of the total system.

Principle of Goal Congruence: The measures of performance for subsystems must match the criteria set for the total system.

The nature of the systems is further illuminated by the thesis that all closed systems in the universe tend toward disorganization. Energy runs downhill. Perhaps we can paraphrase the second law of thermodynamics into a principle of disorganization.

Principle of Disorganization: All systems tend naturally toward disorganization.

Continual maintenance effort is required to preserve the viability of the computer-based planning system. Organization control is customarily achieved through information feedback and comparison of performance with plan. The manager will keep in mind the principle of error when applying the computer-based system to organization control.

Principle of Error: Error is inevitable in a feedback control system subjected to input disturbances.

The magnitude of organizational error is a function of time delay in the control system. The manager may reduce time delay and hence error by taking the information "feedforward" from input disturbances in addition to "feedback" from performance. Corrective action will be taken only on significant deviations from plan, recognizing that the requirements of systems stability are incompatible with the requirements for accuracy.

Principle of the Exception: Management attention should be directed toward those activities or conditions which represent a significant deviation from plan.

These principles suggest that data input can be a major constraint on systems performance.

Principle of Data Input: The quality of systems performance cannot exceed that of the data with which it is provided.

Obsolete, inadequate, or erroneous information can invalidate even the most powerful systems. In fact, the more sophisticated the system, normally the more vulnerable it is to data error.

PRINCIPLES OF MANAGEMENT

Despite the lack of experimental verification, most managers would accept the proposition that there are certain practices which are conducive to organizational success, and that when these principles are violated, trouble often ensues. Management principles seem so simple as to be self-evident, and yet, in practice they are often ignored. It is appropriate to review those general guidelines which are especially pertinent to the design and operation of computer-based planning systems.

The first principles are a reminder that planning should precede performance and that the position of the objective is preeminent. Construction of the computer-based planning system should not begin until the objectives are precisely defined through a definition study.

Principle of the Objective: Objectives should be clearly defined before taking action.

Principle of Management by Objectives: Every individual and unit in the organization should have clearly stated objectives concerning their specific performance responsibilities in the system and against which such performance will be measured and incentives applied.

It has been noted previously that flexibility is a key measure of survival potential for a computer-based planning system which must continually adapt to changes in supporting and using systems as well as in the structure of the organization it simulates. Two additional principles are thereby suggested:

Principle of Flexibility: Flexibility is a major consideration in the selection of plans, although its costs and dangers must be weighed against its advantages [6, p. 202].

Principle of Navigational Change: Effective planning requires continual checking on events and expectations and redrawing of plans to maintain a course toward a desired goal [6, p. 202].

The question of time horizon in planning is addressed by the commitment principle:

The Commitment Principle: Planning should cover a period of time in the future necessary to foresee, through a series of actions, the fulfillment of commitments involved in a decision [6, p. 202]. [That is, the planning horizon should be a minimum of twenty-five years if a capital commitment is to be made for that period.]

At the heart of planning lies the decision-making process involving the selection from among alternative courses of action. Decisions are based on assumptions concerning the future environment and operations of the organization.

Principle of the Limiting Factor: In choosing from among alternative solutions to a problem, primary attention must be given those factors which are limiting or strategic to the solution of the problem [6, p. 201].

Principle of Planning Premises: The understanding of and agreement to utilize consistent planning premises is a prerequisite to coordinated planning [6, p. 200].

Certain other management principles have particular importance relative to computer-based planning. Traditional organizational principles, for example, state that the computer-based planning system must have a "home" to which it reports and that the authority of the manager who administers the system must be commensurate with the responsibility for its performance. Single accountability for the system must be clearly defined and a keeper of the system appointed.

Principle of Unity of Command: Each subordinate should have only one superior.

Principle of Parity of Authority and Responsibility: The responsibility for performance cannot exceed the authority delegated, nor should it be less.

Principle of Single Accountability: Control should be exercised only by the one individual responsible for performance.

We may conclude the review of management principles with recognition that the computer-based planning system will never become operational unless the users of the system perceive that the objectives of the system are in harmony with, and complementary to, their own personal needs.

Principle of Harmony of Objectives: The objective of the organization must be in harmony with the needs of the employees.

PRINCIPLES OF HUMAN BEHAVIOR

Online systems involve the interfacing of a highly structured computer system utilizing precise inputs with a less logical human system that is accustomed to the imprecision of oral communication. Computer-based planning systems are built by people for human use and fail primarily for human reasons. The leadership problems are not new, and in many instances, the principles are well established. A model of human behavior may be built on the following principles:

Principle of Directedness: All human behavior is directed to some goal.

Principle of Motivation: Underlying all human behavior is a want, a need, or a drive.

It is apparent from these principles that a community of interest must be established between the users of the system and the purposes for which the system was designed. Not only must the computer-based planning system have the capacity for assisting managers and staff in achieving their goals; it is important that these individuals *perceive* the value of the system to do this.

Principle of Perception: People behave in accordance with the way they perceive reality, not as it actually is.

The needs of the individual exist in a rather definite order of importance. Once the basic physiological needs have been satisfied, safety and security become important. The security of various members of the organization may be threatened by the computer-based planning system with which they are unfamiliar and to which they must adopt their accustomed patterns of behavior and decision making. This adaptation is accomplished through a learning process.

Principle of Need Hierarchy: Human needs exist in a hierarchy with the higher-level social needs increasing in importance as the primary or physiological needs are satisfied.

Principle of Learning: The individual is continually receiving information, acting on the environment, and modifying personal behavior.

The way in which the individual responds to pressures is greatly influenced by previous experiences as reflected in attitudes. These attitudes are strongly resistant to change.

Principle of Attitudes: The individual has a predisposition to react in a specific manner toward a person or situation according to previous experience. Attitudes are often shared by a group and result in a strong resistance to change.

Managers and staff may resist use of the computer-based planning system because they have had previous unfortunate experiences with the use of computers. The introduction of any new system may then lead to frustration and resulting nonlogical behavior.

Principle of Frustration: Frustration is an inherent characteristic of human interaction and may be aggravated by any change in customary modes of living.

Managers may further resist the introduction of the computer-based planning system because it is initiated by a young operations research team whose members as technical staff, are perceived to be of lower status.

Principle of Status: Human conflict often results when those of lower status originate action for those of higher status in the organization.

It is apparent that even the best-designed and -introduced computer-based planning system will encounter great resistance to change and increased staff frustration within the organization. Perhaps the most powerful technique or practice for reducing the force of these barriers is to obtain involvement of all concerned and assure that relevant information is made available.

Principle of Participation: Individuals are more inclined to accept new developments which they understand and have been personally involved with.

TECHNICAL SYSTEM PRINCIPLES

Each conceptual level in this philosophy has stressed the primacy of objectives. This truth must be stated once more with respect to the technical system for computer-based planning.

Principle of Derivation: Systems structure, computational logic, and data requirements are all derivatives of the systems objective.

The limitations of computer-based planning are human, not technical. Therefore, the system should be simple both in the numbers of variables with which the user must interact and in the functional relationships between these variables. Simplicity in large installations is achieved through small modules using straightforward logic. This modularity also achieves a second systems objective: flexibility. The basic building blocks of the system can be conveniently rearranged to reflect changes in the structure or planning process of the organization being simulated.

Principle of Simplicity: Start simply and add complexity only as required.

Principle of Change: A first requirement of the system is to have the flexibility to accommodate extensive change.

Principle of Modularity: Simplicity and flexibility are best achieved through modularity in the systems structure.

Principle of Integration: All organizational elements are interdependent and hence must be simulated in the planning system by linked models using common data files from which they receive input and to which they output.

The simulation of complex organizations using simple models is made possible by the fact that systems with greatly differing inner systems can have similar external behavior.

Principle of System Components: Certain characteristics of systems behavior arise out of the organization of the parts and are independent of all but a few properties of the individual components.

A closely related principle which allows us to achieve simplicity from complexity relates to the consolidation and elimination that occur at each level in the organizational hierarchy.

Principle of Hierarchy: The systems design should normally proceed from the top down in the organization, since the complexity of functional relationships increases as the simulation approaches the level of operations.

It appears true that systems acceptance is gained best by proved performance and that users are most impressed by their first exposure to the system. It further appears valid that the total computer-based system cannot initially be conceptualized in the ultimate sense, since user requirements will expand and change through experience in application. Policies relating to systems development should be based on the following principles:

Principle of Evolution: The system should evolve in planned phases according to management priority, with utility demonstrated prior to each expansion.

Principle of Immediacy: The initial phase of systems development should be implemented as quickly and inexpensively as possible so as to provide immediate tangible benefits.

This immediacy in development is achievable because of the commonality encountered in these systems. All planning systems utilize similar concepts, processes, and tools. A limited number of readily available statistical, accounting, and formating routines can serve the needs of a broad diversity of systems. Economies in time and cost can be accomplished by customizing these existing resources to the unique requirements of the individual organization.

Principle of Commonality: The concept, process, and tools of planning are universal among all organizations.

The full potential of the computer-based planning system will not be realized unless continuous effort is expended to maintain and improve all supporting and using systems upon which it is dependent.

Principle of Dependency: The computer-based planning system will fail if any of the supporting or user systems with which it interfaces begins to malfunction.

A very important principle, which is difficult to formalize, reflects the sharply different conceptual and technical characteristics of systems used for strategic planning, management control, and operational control. Attempts to satisfy all these requirements in one system may lead to serious compromises.

Principle of Levels: The concept and structure of systems used for strategic planning and management control are incompatible with the requirements for precision and detail at the level of operating control.

Principle of Design Economy: The provision for all possible occurrences and applications leads to overwhelming costs in the system.

As a final principle of the technical system, we may note that the symbiotic relationship of human and computer is a function of response time. The individual is limited in the capacity for short-term information, and even this capacity is sharply reduced by any interruption. Conversational capability is dependent upon fast, error-free transmittal of information.

Principle of Response Time: The planning effectiveness of the technical system is inversely related to the response time between person and computer.

TOWARD THE FUTURE

It is interesting to reflect on the future implications and developments of computer-based planning systems. The field is moving so rapidly that we need not adopt a long-time perspective as measured by years. The year 1985 seems a good target for the following events to occur.

The use of online computer-based planning systems will spread rapidly into all advanced countries where reliable communication networks are available. Most manufacturing firms with sales in excess of 20 million dollars will incorporate the computer into the planning process.

Smaller firms will be using canned programs on a broad scale for routine applications, such as report generation.

This movement to computer-based planning will be accompanied by increased centralization of financial controls. Already, many multinational companies are consolidating their corporate staffs in a central location to which diverse operating units are linked by a worldwide telecommunication network. The predictive accuracy of organizational models is improving rapidly through continued use.

The accounting profession is facing an instant revolution. Society will demand more than certification that financial reporting meets accepted standards of accounting practice. What are the profit forecasts and are they reasonable? What are the planning premises? Is management competent? What are the social costs of the operation?

Computer-based planning is increasing the transparency of internal organizational affairs. Labor unions, government agencies, and investment houses are building their own models for simulating the behavior of organizations in the private sector. Managers in the future will become increasingly subject to second guessing, and former standards of decision excellence will no longer be adequate.

Social purpose and ethical standards have previously been of only academic or public relations interest. The values of the society, however, are becoming increasingly real to management as they are translated into demands for environmental protection, equal opportunity of employment, guaranteed annual wages, conservation of resources, and integrity in political affairs. Such considerations greatly increase the complexity of the organization planning function.

Can society continue to afford the inefficiencies of competition based on only partial knowledge of supply and demand? It is already obvious that the great weakness in many computer-based planning systems consists of the in-put assumptions. Planning systems for related industries in various contries should be linked in much the same manner as are the functional modules in one organization.

Each company ponders production levels and capital-expansion plans without knowledge of what competitors are doing. Bad guesses result in extravagant waste and unnecessary economic disturbances. Central planning in key areas on a multinational and multi-industrial scale is indispensable. Organizational planning systems will be linked to supracomputer-based planning systems operated by the government.

This trend will be accelerated on an international scale by a continuing trend to localization of resources. The natural resources as well as the consumer markets of the world are not equally distributed. The questions of central resource planning is not socialism versus capitalism, but the reality of human survival on planet earth. Competition must give way to cooperation; ignorance must be replaced with knowledge.

The time horizon considered by managers must be extended. Better strategic planning should reduce the urgencies of day-to-day problems so that managers can address new markets, products, and processes. The objective of more and more consumption must give way to improved quality and service over extended time periods. Spiritual values will increase in importance. The multitudinous constraints facing tomorrow's organization will require long periods of research and analysis.

And what of the computer-based planning systems? At the present time, the technology is so far advanced over the state of the art in management that there is no urgency for new technical developments. It is evident that these systems are getting larger, not smaller. Even today it is almost impossible for the user of a large computer-based planning system to maintain perspective and comprehend what is happening while proceeding through an interrogation sequence utilizing various elements of the modeling network. Perhaps the next step in systems evolution will involve linkage of an automatic indexing microfilm unit into the computer-based planning system. This hybrid system will track the user and provide continual visual displays for purposes of orientation and instruction.

The potential for human/computer synergy as applied to management will not be realized unless research is initiated into the nature of these systems as they are used in the planning process. Hundreds of systems have been built, encompassing thousands of models. Hundreds of thousands of human-machine hours have been logged on large systems. Many important decisions have been made, utilizing these systems. Yet out of all this massive activity can be found very little hard data to guide further developments in the field. What is the precise impact of a computer-based planning system on the organization structure? On the communication network? On data requirements? On human relationships?

A massive effort at management reeducation is in order. The quantitative literature of the past two decades has largely passed management by as inappropriate to policy-level decisions. Moreover, classic management theory is too poorly defined and structured for a computer-based environment. Theory must be recast in the context of a management environment where time and information availability are no longer constraints. Present-day managers frequently do not know what questions to ask the system or what to do with the system's output when received.

It is apparent that computer-based planning systems will never achieve their full potential under present management theory and practices. Yet this potential must be realized if the world's depleting resources are to be effectively organized to meet the ever-increasing needs of society. The exponential growth and convergence of computer and communications technology as combined with ever-expanding human knowledge and rising consciousness are essential keys to the continued evolution of the human race.

Appendix:
An Executive Exercise

It would be difficult to improve your golf swing without taking a club in hand. Similarly, the best way to obtain a feeling for the fundamentals of the computer-based planning systems is to pick up a pencil, turn to Table A-1, and become personally involved. Although this sample problem can be "solved on the back of an envelope," it will illustrate most of the principles and applications involved in full-scale planning systems.

This exercise was first introduced at the International Management Symposium at Davos, Switzerland, in 1972, and has since been presented to hundreds of managers, including the professional staffs of several large consulting firms. The time limit on this exercise is 6 minutes, and the record to date is 40 seconds (held by a Frenchman). Please try your hand using Table A-1, and then turn to Table A-3 to check your answers.

MANNER OF APPLICATION

This problem illustrates the three basic ways in which computer-based planning systems are used. The simplest and most straightforward application is *report generation,* as in Question 1. This report is quite easy in the example, but how long does it take your staff people to revise your budget? How many arithmetic errors do they make when pushing through those last-minute changes?

The second question in the exercise illustrates the use of the system to answer the "what if?" type of inquiry. The uncertainty of the future requires management to make assumptions concerning prices, costs, and volumes. The computer is useful as a calculator to tell you quickly the profit performance that will result *if* your assumptions are

TABLE A-1. Vest Pocket Executive Exercise

Objective

Complete the form below in the shortest possible time.

Problem

Your company has a fixed overhead cost and produces only one product.

1. *What* is the budgeted profit *if* the price is $2.00 per unit and the variable cost is $1.50 per unit?
2. *What* will be the annual profits *if* variable costs increase $0.10 per unit?
3. *Assuming* the variable cost increase of $0.10 per unit, *how many* units must be sold during the first half-year to achieve profit break-even for that period?

The problem is straightforward. There are no hidden meanings.

1. *What* is the budgeted profit *if* the price is $2.00 per unit and the variable cost is $1.50 per unit?

LINE	DESCRIPTION	FIRST HALF	SECOND HALF	YEAR
1	UNIT VOLUME	200,000	300,000	500,000
2	SALES	$	$	$
3	VARIABLE COST	$	$	$
4	GROSS MARGIN	$	$	$
5	FIXED COST	$100,000	$100,000	$200,000
6	PROFITS	$	$	$

2. *What* will the annual profits be *if* variable costs increase $0.10 per unit?

$_____

3. *Assuming* the variable cost increase of $0.10 per unit, *how many* units must be sold during the first half year to achieve break-even for that period?

_____UNITS.

correct. Using a manual system, you may be able to look at only two or three alternatives. However, use of the computer allows you to evaluate as many strategies as you wish under a broad range of assumptions. Further, you can determine the sensitivity of results to various critical variables. Note that the system in no way makes the decision for you—it only indicates the consequences of alternative actions.

The third and most interesting application of the system is to search backward from your objectives to the necessary input conditions for their achievement, as in Question 3 of the exercise. Perhaps you were able to solve the simple linear cost relationship in the example, but what of the complex cost functions that occur in the real world? A backward search through such relationships is not feasible without the computer. This activity is called *iteration to objectives*.

Now let us see how we could solve the problem by building a model and running it on the computer.

A COMPUTER MODEL

A computer-based planning system consists of the planner, the computer, the software programs, communication links, the modeling network, and the data base. The model is an algebraic description of operating relationships.

Table A-2 illustrates the construction of a model to solve the exercise. Please note that this is approximately the same procedure you followed in your mind when you worked the problem. In fact, all managers use intuitive, if not formal, models, and the builder of a computer-based planning system simply converts these informal models to mathematical equations.

The output lines of the reports are assigned numbers for ease in specifying selective printout. (Perhaps you only wish to look at third-quarter gross profit, not a stack of reports with all the details.) The lines on your reports are given descriptive names and their method of computation is identified. In certain instances it may not be possible to precisely quantify specific relationships, such as elasticity of sales volume to price. If this is so, the model will be built so that the user may input his or her own assumptions regarding these relationships.

Variables

The variables which enter into the calculations are defined precisely (a major advantage of such systems) and assigned symbols. Parameters such as "P1 = price/unit" are values which stay fixed through certain time periods. Variable arrays such as "V1 = volume" are values which vary through time. The logic of the model is built up with parameters and variable arrays in the form of algebraic equations (normally very simple ones like "profit = sales − costs").

Unlike manual computations, there are no fixed numbers in the logic of a computer model (such as "interest rate = 9 percent"), since you may later wish to change the values. Remember the last time your staff had to alter the financial plan to reflect fluctuating interest rates? A complete set of revised plans can be generated in minutes through use of the computer.

The importance of management involvement in systems development is immediately apparent at this point. Prior to designing the system and developing the model logic, the modeler must understand

TABLE A-2. Computer Model

A model is an algebraic description of organizational relationships.
Computerized models are manipulated by managers to analyze or predict performance under real or assumed operating conditions.

Budget Example

OUTPUT LINE	OUTPUT DESCRIPTION	RELATIONSHIP	MODEL LOGIC	DEFINITIONS	INPUT DATA
1	VOLUME	VOLUME	V1	V1 = VOLUME/6 MONTHS	200,000/300,000
2	SALES	PRICE × VOLUME	P1 × V1	P1 = PRICE/UNIT	$2.00
3	VARIABLE COST	VARIABLE COST × VOLUME	P2 × V1	P2 = VARIABLE COST/UNIT	$1.50
4	GROSS MARGIN	SALES – VARIABLE COSTS	D2 – D3	D2 = LINE 2 D3 = LINE 3	
5	FIXED COST	FIXED COST	P3	P3 = FIXED COST	$100,000
6	PROFITS	GROSS MARGIN – FIXED COSTS	D4 – D5	D4 = GROSS MARGIN D5 = FIXED COST	

the questions which management will later wish to ask. For example, if you wish to inquire concerning district profitability, then the model builder must assign symbols to each district and also must input data by that classification.

Data

The term *data* is used to refer to all numeric values assigned to the symbols in the model logic. Standard costs, for example, would be data input for a manufacturing model to establish the value of the relationship between cost and volume. Sales forecasts are another example of input data. Data are necessary to tailor the model to your unique operations.

It is very important that the data be kept separate from the logic, so that either can be changed without disturbing the other and the two can be used in various combinations. In our exercise, for example, we wish to determine the impact on profits of changing variable costs. This computation can be done simply by changing the data value assigned to the symbol P2 (variable costs) without alternating the logic of the model itself. In real life, you may wish to simulate several similar operations using the same logic but alternative sets of data values, such as costs. We will shortly see (in the paper company example) how this is done.

RUNNING THE SYSTEM

The user accesses the computer-based planning system through a remote terminal, such as a teletype operating over normal voice-telephone lines. The models and data are stored on a computer containing the extensive house-keeping software necessary to permit conversation between human and machine and to accomplish the manipulation of both data and logic.

The following paragraphs will examine the computer/planner conversation as necessary to solve this exercise. This exploration should reassure newcomers to the field that the use of such systems is normally very simple and in no way dependent upon quantitative skills or computer experience. The user can obtain tutoring on request, and there is no manner in which one can damage or become lost in the system. Further, security is at all times protected by scrambling routines.

By typing in preset symbols, the user identifies himself or herself to the computer, gives security codes, and indicates which operations to simulate. The computer calls up the proper logic and data (just as we developed in the example), and the total configuration takes on the behavior characteristics of the specific operation.

COMMAND # (8/)

ENTER LINES
(1/-6//)

COMMAND # (9/)

MODEL   JC   *** MAJOR 72 ***

                                1 HALF 72   2 HALF 72   TOTAL 72

1   VOLUME   200,000   300,000   500,000
2   SALES   400,000   600,000   1,000,000
3   VBLE COST   300,000   450,000   750,000
4   GROSS MARGIN   100,000   150,000   250,000
5   FIXED COST   100,000   100,000   200,000
6   PROFITS   -0   50,000   50,000

COMMAND # (8/)

ENTER LINES
(6//)

COMMAND # (11/)

SENSITIVITY
ENTER ARRAY # / TERM # /
(0/2/)
ENTER MIN/MAX/INCREMENT/
(1.50/1.70/.10/)

PARAMETER # 2   IS NOW 1.5000
                                1 HALF 72   2 HALF 72   TOTAL 72
    6 PROFITS   -0   50,000   50,000

PARAMETER #2   IS NOW 1.6000
    6 PROFITS   -20,000   20,000   0

PARAMETER # 2   IS NOW 1.7000
    6 PROFITS   -40,000   -10,000   -50,000

COMMAND # (12/)

ITERATION
ENTER COLUMN/LINE/DESIRED VALUE/
(1/6/0/)
ENTER ARRAY # / TERM # /
(1/1/)
    TERM # 1   IN V 1   LINE # 6   IN 1 HALF 72

    200,000.0000   -20,000
          0.0000   -100,000
    250,000.4000   0
    250,000.

Figure A-1. Computer interaction (circles indicate user input).

A numeric, as opposed to an English language, command structure is illustrated in Figure A-1 as applied to the subject exercise. Note that the system continually returns to "command," requesting further instructions from the planner. The user refers to a small card containing generalized command codes. In this particular example, the user enters an "8" to specify the line of output to be printed. (Managers' inputs are circled in the sample printout.)

The computer instructs the user to ENTER LINES, which is done by typing "1/-6//," indicating that lines 1 to 6 on the budget statement are to be printed. The user then types a "9" in response to the next command request, thus telling the computer to run and print the budget. The nature of the specific conversation varies, of course, from system to system, but is normally very straightforward.

The planner working on our executive exercise next investigates the effect on profits of changing variable costs by running a sensitivity analysis (technically a single parametric analysis). The computer is first instructed to print only one 6. In response to prompting, the planner indicates that variable costs (array 0, parameter 2) are to be varied from $1.50 to $1.70 by increments of 10 cents. The computer then calculates the full profit and loss for each increment value for variable cost and prints out the resulting profits as previously requested.

The planner in the exercise now wishes to search backward to determine what volume will be necessary in the first half-year to break even for that period, given the increase in variable costs. The command "12" is given for iteration and the computer is told to set column 1, line 6, to zero by varying array 1, term 1. The computer reports that at the planner's forecasted volume of 200,000 units, there will be a loss of $20,000 with the cost increase and that the planner must increase sales to 200,000 units in order to break even. The complete solution to the exercise is presented in Table A-3.

Although the details of this exercise are unimportant, the terminology and concepts are most useful. If management is to converse meaningfully with the technical staff, some education is necessary on both sides to provide a common area of knowledge.

A BASIC SYSTEM

Computer-based planning seemed simple enough in the preceding exercise—*and it is*. This is not a mystical process reserved for mathematicians. In fact, if line managers are not involved in conceiving and validating the system, failure is guaranteed.

Let us now progress to a very straightforward installation, as developed by a medium-sized paper company. This system provides man-

TABLE A-3. Solution: Vest Pocket Executive Exercise

1. *What* is the budgeted profit *if* the price is $2.00 per unit and the variable cost is $1.50 per unit?

LINE	DESCRIPTION	FIRST HALF	SECOND HALF	YEAR
1	UNIT VOLUME	200,000	300,000	500,000
2	SALES	$400,000	$600,000	$1,000,000
3	VARIABLE COST	$300,000	$450,000	$ 750,000
4	GROSS MARGIN	$100,000	$150,000	$ 250,000
5	FIXED COST	$100,000	$100,000	$ 200,000
6	PROFITS	$ 0	$ 50,000	$ 50,000

2. *What* will the annual profits be *if* variable costs increase $0.10 per unit?

$0.00

3. *Assuming* the variable cost increase of $0.10 per unit, *how many* units must be sold during the first half-year to achieve break even for that period?

250,000 UNITS

agement with the capability of quickly and accurately developing quarterly budgets for:

- 300 product groups
- 40 market-plan groups
- 3 product lines
- 30 paper machines
- 6 mills
- 1 division

Design

The layout of the system is shown in Figure A-2, which is reasonably self-explanatory. The planner enters the proposed production schedule into the matrix. The computer checks to see that the paper machines are not overloaded and that products are not scheduled on equipment which is unsuitable. Tonnages and hours are generated by the matrix for analyzing operations by machines, mills, market-plan groups, product lines, or the division consolidation. The computer simply multiplies

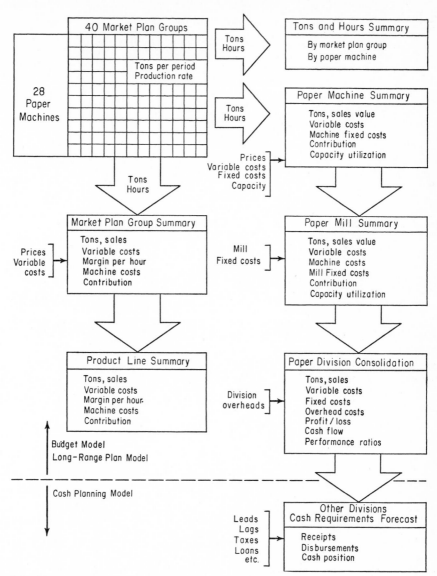

Figure A-2. A basic system. *(Courtesy of Booz, Allen & Hamilton.)*

the quantity of time scheduled on each machine by the production rate for that machine, and sums the output either by machine or by product. The system is completely conversational, so that the user can indicate precisely the areas of interest.

The role of the computer in the planning process is shown in Figure A-3. The marketing plan generates the volumes required by the various

TABLE A-4. Logic for Paper Model

Line no.	Description	Logic
2	Volume	Input
3	Sales	Volume × price
4	Discounts	Sales × % discount
5	Commissions	Sales × % commission
6	Freight	Volume × freight/ton
7	Net sales	Line 3 − 4 − 5 − 6
8	Raw material cost	Raw material cost/ton × volume × % on machine
9	Supplies cost	Supplies cost/ton × volume × % on machine
10	Energy cost	Energy costs/hour × volume × % on machine × hours/ton
11	Total variable cost	Line 8 + 9 + 10
12	Product group contribution	Line 7 − Line 11
13	Capacity used for Product Group 1	Volume P.G. 1 × % on machine × hours/ton

Courtesy of Booz, Allen & Hamilton, Inc.

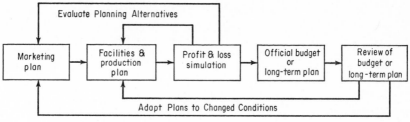

Figure A-3. Role of models in the planning process. *(Courtesy of Booz, Allen & Hamilton.)*

product groups. The facilities and production plans are then developed to meet these market forecasts, and subsequently simulated on the computer. Profitability is evaluated and revisions made either in the marketing plan or the production plan.

Application

The system is designed to answer such questions as the following:

- What if sales tonnage of a product group increases?
- What if the prices change?
- What if operating costs vary?
- What if a paper machine is switched off for a few days?
- Or a whole mill closed for a quarter?
- What if a new product is introduced?
- Or an old product discontinued?

Keeping in mind our earlier experience in building models, let us take a short look at the relationships of the models which permit the solution of the preceding questions (see Table A-4). This logic is converted to symbolic terms and entered into the computer just as in the executive exercise.

Sales volume, line 2, are direct inputs. Sales are computed as volume times price. Does it sound familiar? Using such simple logic, the system is capable of generating over 400 different profit and loss statements expressed either in absolute figures, in percentage of sales, or in per ton estimates. The planner is able to specify any line item and time period which it may be desirable to examine on any of these reports. The same system handles both the budgets and the long-range plan.

Reference List

1. "Energy and Power," *Scientific American*. Earl Cook: "The Flow of Energy in an Industrial Society," W. H. Freeman and Company, San Francisco, 1971, p. 88.

2. Fabun, Don: *The Dynamics of Change*, Prentice-Hall, Inc., Englewood Cliffs, N.J., 1967.

3. Toffler, Alvin: *Future Shock*, The Bodley Head, Ltd., London, 1970.

4. By permission from *Webster's New Collegiate Dictionary*, © 1974, G. & C. Merriam Company, Springfield, Mass. Publishers of the Merriam Webster Dictionaries.

5. Ackoff, Russell L.: *A Concept of Corporate Planning*, Wiley Interscience Publishers, New York, 1970.

6. Koontz, Harold, and Cyril O'Donnell: *Principles of Management*, 3d ed., McGraw-Hill Book Company, New York, 1955.

7. Boulden, James B., and Ephraim R. McLean: "On-Line Executive Support Systems," unpublished manuscript, 1974.

8. Diebold, John: *Business Decisions & Technological Change*, Frederick A. Praeger, Inc., New York, 1970.

9. Beer, Stafford: *Decision and Control*, John Wiley & Sons, Ltd., London, 1966.

10. Churchman, C. West: *The Systems Approach*, Dell Publishing Co., Inc., New York, 1968.

11. Boulding, Kenneth E.: "General Systems Theory: The Skeleton of a Science," *Management Science*, April 1956.

12 Barnard, Chester I. *The Functions of the Executive*, Harvard University Press, Cambridge, Mass., 1938.

13. Graicunas, V. A.: "Relationship in Organization," *Bulletin of the International Management Institute*, International Labor Office, Geneva, 1933.

14. Koontz, Harold, and Robert W. Bradspies: "Managing Through Feed-Forward Control," *Business Horizons*, June 1972.

15. Walton, Clarence C.: *Corporate Social Responsibilities*, Wadsworth Publishing Company, Inc., Belmont, Calif.

16. Drucker, Peter F.: *The Practice of Management*, Harper & Row, Publishers, Incorporated, New York, 1954.

17. Maslow, A. H.: "A Theory of Human Motivation," *Psychological Review*, vol. 50, 1943.

18. Hormann, Aiko N.: "Planning by Man-Machine Synergism," in Harold Sackman and Ronald L. Citrenbaum (eds.), *Online Planning Towards Creative Problem-Solving*, Prentice-Hall, Inc., Englewood Cliffs, N.J., 1972.

19. Emshoff, James: *Design and Use of Computer Simulation Models*, The MacMillan Company, New York, 1970.

20. Morton, Michael S. Scott: *Management Decision Systems*, Harvard University Graduate School of Business Administration, Boston, 1965.

21. Steiner, George A.: *Top Management Planning*, The MacMillan Company, New York, 1969.

22. A comprehensive discussion of this subject may be found in Anthony, Robert N.: *Planning and Control Systems: A Framework for Analysis*, Harvard University Graduate School of Business Administration, Division of Research, 1965.

23. Boulden, James B., and Elwood S. Buffa: "New Developments in On-line Corporate Models," On-Line Decisions, Inc., New York, 1972.

24. Boulden, James B., and Elwood S. Buffa: "Corporate Models: On-line, Real-Time Systems," *Harvard Business Review*, July–August 1970.

25. Boulden, James B.: "Merger Negotiations: A Decision Model," *Business Horizons*, February 1969.

26. Cooper, John, and Peter Jones: "The Corporate Decision," *Data Processing*, March–April 1972.

27. Xerox Corporation, *1973 Annual Report*.

28. Seaberg, Ronald A., and Charlotte Seaberg: "Computer Based Decision Systems in Xerox Corporate Planning," *Management Science*, vol. 20, no. 4, Part II, December 1973.

29. Boulden, James B.: "Multinational Planning Systems," *Journal of Long Range Planning*, September–October 1972.

30. Simon, Herbert A.: *The Sciences of the Artificial*, The M.I.T. Press, Cambridge, Mass., 1969.

31. Nugent, Christopher, and Thomas Vollman: "A Framework for the System Design Process," *Decision Sciences*, vol. 3, 1972. For an expanded discussion of inclusion and structuring.

32. Hayes, Robert H., and Richard L. Nolan: "What Kind of Corporate Modeling Functions Best?" *Harvard Business Review*, May–June 1974.

33. Steiner, George A.: "Pitfalls in Comprehensive Long Range Planning," Planning Executives Institute, Research Series, 1972.

34. Davis, Ralph Currier: *Fundamentals of Top Management*, Harper & Brothers, New York, 1951.

Index